Is Morality Real?

In this book, Spencer Case and Matt Lutz debate whether objective moral facts exist. We often say that actions like murder and institutions like slavery are morally wrong. And sometimes people strenuously disagree about the moral status of actions, as with abortion. But what, if anything, makes statements about morality true? Should we be realists about morality, or anti-realists?

After the authors jointly outline the major contemporary positions in the moral realism debate, each author argues for his own preferred views and responds to the other's constructive arguments and criticisms. Case contends that there are moral truths that don't depend on human beliefs or attitudes. Lutz maintains that there are no moral truths, and even if there were, we wouldn't be in a position to know about them. Along the way, they explore topics like the nature of common sense, the meaning of moral language, and why the realism/anti-realism debate matters. The authors develop their own arguments and responses, but assume no prior knowledge of metaethics. The result is a highly accessible exchange, providing new students with an opinionated gateway to this important area of moral philosophy. But the authors' originality gives food for thought to seasoned philosophers as well.

Key Features

- Gives a comprehensive overview of all the main positions on moral realism, without assuming any prior knowledge on the subject
- Features both traditional and original arguments for each position
- Offers highly accessible language without sacrificing intellectual rigor

- Draws upon, and builds on, recent literature on the realism/anti-realism debate
- Uses only a limited number of technical terms and defines all of them in the glossary

Matt Lutz is Associate Professor of Philosophy at Wuhan University, where he has worked since receiving his PhD in philosophy from the University of Southern California in 2015. He works on metaethics and epistemology, with a particular focus on moral epistemology and moral skepticism.

Spencer Case received his PhD in philosophy from the University of Colorado Boulder in 2018, and teaches online classes there. He is also a freelance writer and podcaster.

Little Debates About Big Questions

About the series:

Philosophy asks questions about the fundamental nature of reality, our place in the world, and what we should do. Some of these questions are perennial: for example, *Do we have free will? What is morality?* Some are much newer: for example, *How far should free speech on campus extend? Are race, sex and gender social constructs?* But all of these are among the big questions in philosophy and they remain controversial.

Each book in the *Little Debates About Big Questions* series features two professors on opposite sides of a big question. Each author presents their own side, and the authors then exchange objections and replies. Short, lively, and accessible, these debates showcase diverse and deep answers. Pedagogical features include standard form arguments, section summaries, bolded key terms and principles, glossaries, and annotated reading lists.

The debate format is an ideal way to learn about controversial topics. Whereas the usual essay or book risks overlooking objections against its own proposition or misrepresenting the opposite side, in a debate each side can make their case at equal length, and then present objections the other side must consider. Debates have a more conversational and fun style too, and we selected particularly talented philosophers—in substance and style—for these kinds of encounters.

Debates can be combative—sometimes even descending into anger and animosity. But debates can also be cooperative. While our authors disagree strongly, they work together to help each other and the reader get clearer on the ideas, arguments, and objections. This is intellectual progress, and a much-needed model for civil and constructive disagreement.

The substance and style of the debates will captivate interested readers new to the questions. But there's enough to interest experts too. The debates will be especially useful for courses in philosophy and related subjects—whether as primary or secondary readings—and a few debates can be combined to make up the reading for an entire course.

We thank the authors for their help in constructing this series. We are honored to showcase their work. They are all preeminent scholars or rising-stars in their fields, and through these debates they share what's been discovered with a wider audience. This is a paradigm for public philosophy, and will impress upon students, scholars, and other interested readers the enduring importance of debating the big questions.

Tyron Goldschmidt, Fellow of the Rutgers Center for Philosophy of Religion, USA
Dustin Crummett, Ludwig Maximilian University of Munich, Germany

Selected Published Titles:

Is There a God?: A Debate
Kenneth L. Pearce and Graham Oppy

Is Political Authority an Illusion?: A Debate
Michael Huemer and Daniel Layman

Selected Forthcoming Titles:

Should We Want to Live Forever?: A Debate
Stephen Cave and John Martin Fischer

Do Numbers Exist?: A Debate
William Lane Craig and Peter van Inwagen

What Do We Owe Other Animals?: A Debate
Bob Fischer and Anja Jauernig

Consequentialism or Virtue Ethics?: A Debate
Jorge L.A. Garcia and Alastair Norcross

For more information about this series, please visit:
www.routledge.com/Little-Debates-about-Big-Questions/
book-series/LDABQ

Is Morality Real?

A Debate

Matt Lutz and
Spencer Case

Routledge
Taylor & Francis Group

NEW YORK AND LONDON

Designed cover image: © Getty Images

First published 2024
by Routledge
605 Third Avenue, New York, NY 10158

and by Routledge
4 Park Square, Milton Park, Abingdon, Oxon, OX14 4RN

Routledge is an imprint of the Taylor & Francis Group, an informa business

© 2024 Taylor & Francis

Library of Congress Cataloging-in-Publication Data
A catalog record for this book has been requested

ISBN: 978-1-032-02388-5 (hbk)
ISBN: 978-1-032-02387-8 (pbk)
ISBN: 978-1-003-18317-4 (ebk)

DOI: 10.4324/9781003183174

Typeset in Sabon
by Apex CoVantage, LLC

To William James (Bill) McCurdy
(October 4, 1947–October 4, 2021)
—Spencer

For Auron
—Matt

Contents

Acknowledgements

For annoying bureaucratic reasons, Lutz had to be listed as a coauthor before Case. Nonetheless, this book was a joint effort, with equal work from each. We'd like to thank all those who have given us helpful comments on this manuscript, whether in whole or in part: Tim Perrine, Peter Finocchiaro, Terence Cuneo, Steven Finlay, Mike Huemer, J. P. Andrews, Jim Skidmore, Justin Kalef, Graham Oddie, Eric Sampson, Tyler Paytas, Tyron Goldschmidt, Stephen Herrod, Stephanie Wong, Laurie Lutz (thanks, Mom!), and an anonymous referee. We'd also like to thank the staff at Devils' Brewery in Wuhan, China, where we hashed out many issues with the manuscript over "work beers." Thanks to Xingzhu Chen and Qingyuan Gu for compiling the index. Last, but certainly not least, we'd like to thank our wives, May (Spencer's wife) and Taddy (Matt's wife), for their patience and support throughout this project. We give our apologies to anyone we've omitted. All of the flaws remaining in this book are the fault of the authors. Each of us prefers that you blame the other.

Foreword

Neil Sinhababu

This book showcases two of the best-developed views in contemporary metaethics, advocated by two of the field's rising stars. Spencer Case defends non-naturalism, according to which many of our ordinary moral judgments are true because they correspond with moral facts existing beyond natural reality. Matt Lutz defends error theory, according to which moral judgments as uncontroversial as "lying is wrong" and "pleasure is good" are false because there are no moral facts to make our judgments true.

Today's most popular metaethical theories are non-naturalist theories like Spencer's, and naturalistic anti-realist views supported by arguments like those Matt presents for error theory. Spencer's non-naturalism and Matt's error theory may be the best contemporary versions of these views. The debates between them take place at the cutting edge of contemporary metaethics.

Despite their stark differences, non-naturalism and error theory share important presuppositions regarding the psychological states constituting moral judgment. Both theories agree that moral judgments are beliefs about objective moral facts. If these beliefs correspond with objective facts, they're true. If they fail to correspond, perhaps because there are no objective moral facts, they're false and should be given up like other false beliefs.

Because Spencer and Matt agree about the nature of moral judgment, their disagreements regarding moral facts stand out more starkly. They disagree about the ontological questions of whether and how moral facts fit into reality. Spencer believes that there are objective moral facts that science can't discover, while Matt denies the existence of moral facts on grounds that there is no good evidence for them. This disagreement has significant consequences for normative ethics. Spencer regards lying as having the non-natural property of wrongness, which makes it wrong. Matt doesn't believe that lying is wrong, because he thinks beliefs in wrongness take us beyond the scientific evidence.

Metaethics is concerned with a number of theoretical issues regarding morality. These issues include whether moral facts exist and what they're like if they do, whether and how we can get evidence about them, and what sort of psychological state constitutes a moral judgment. To explain why these issues matter, I'll describe how metaethical questions relate to the normative ethical questions that our ordinary moral judgments aim to answer—which actions are right and which are wrong? Which character traits are virtues and which are vices? Which events are good and which are bad? Judgments like "lying is wrong," "honesty is a virtue," and "pleasure is good" address these three normative ethical questions.

Here are four metaethical questions we might ask about our three normative ethical answers—"lying is wrong," "honesty is a virtue," and "pleasure is good":

(1) If we judge that they're true, are we believing them, or having some other mental state regarding them like emotion or desire?
(2) If the judgments are beliefs, are they beliefs that objective wrongness, virtue, and goodness exist?
(3) If they're beliefs in objective moral properties, are these properties really out there making our beliefs true, or are our beliefs systematically false because they're absent?
(4) If they do exist, are they empirically accessible things we might discover within space and time?

Five of the most-discussed metaethical views can be illustrated in terms of when and whether they answer "no" to one of the four above questions. Non-cognitivists hold that moral judgments aren't beliefs, but instead are something like emotion or desire. Relativists hold that moral belief can be true about non-objective wrongness, virtue, and goodness, which consist in relations to an individual or culture's attitudes. Error theorists (like Matt) hold that moral beliefs are all false because they're about objective moral facts, which don't exist. Non-naturalists (like Spencer) hold that many moral beliefs are true, because there are moral facts that science can't discover. Naturalistic realists (like me) hold that many moral beliefs are true, because there are moral facts that science can discover.

Most metaethical views can be mixed and matched with normative ethical views, without generating any contradiction. If you judge that lying is wrong, you can be a noncognitivist and take your judgement to be a desire or emotion. You can be a relativist and regard it as a belief that will be true if your culture feels that lying is wrong. You can be a non-naturalist and regard wrongness as a property of lying that isn't empirically observable within space and time. You can be a naturalist and regard this wrongness as something that is empirically observable within space and time.

Only error theory contradicts the judgment that lying is wrong. It entails that nothing is wrong, and that all judgments of wrongness are false beliefs. It contradicts any moral judgment (apart from judgments with negations like "lying isn't wrong"). Error theory therefore has the most radical implications for normative ethics, contradicting all our intuitive judgments that things are right, good, or virtuous.

Matt explains why he holds this position: "Moral facts are strange and hard to square with a naturalistic picture of reality. And we have no evidence that moral facts exist. So we should not believe that they do" (119). He joins other error theorists in accepting moral skepticism, the view that we aren't justified in believing that there are any moral facts. No science has discovered moral wrongness, and as it's not clear how the objective reasons that it seems to require could fit into a scientific picture of the world, our overall scientific evidence suggests that there is no moral wrongness. That means that nothing is wrong, including lying.

If we give up all moral belief as Matt suggests, where does that leave us? Error theorists can offer ways to retain morality in a diminished form, perhaps by maintaining social fictions of rightness and wrongness, and regarding "lying is wrong" as a truth about fiction like "Gandalf was a wizard." But it's not clear how mere fictions could retain the significance that objective moral facts are supposed to have. Matt offers the more sensible suggestion that giving up our moral beliefs wouldn't change our lives all that much. We'd still care about others because do so regardless of whether it's morally right. We would generally avoid lying because honesty is the best policy, because we don't want to hurt others with lies, and because we just don't like to lie.

While Matt seems right that much of what we consider moral behavior could go forward without moral belief, moral facts might make their absence felt on specific issues like the possibility of great moral heroism. Works of epic fantasy like *The Lord of the Rings* draw some appeal from the vast moral significance of the heroes' goals. The hobbits' quest is heroic because saving their world from destruction is of great moral value. Those of heroic dispositions in our world might seek quests of such vast moral significance. But if error theory is right and heroic moral significance is as unreal as hobbits, it can't be achieved even by saving all life on this planet from destruction. Those seeking a quest of great moral significance won't find it in saving all life on this planet, any more than in being good at bowling. The impact of error theory and the importance of surprising metaethical conclusions might be felt on a variety of issues like this.

The other metaethical views have more subtle effects, shaping normative ethical discourse to make different conclusions more or less plausible. Non-cognitivism and relativism deny the existence of objective moral facts as error theory does, but regard moral judgment as a state of mind that need not correspond to objective moral facts. They therefore generally permit us to retain our present moral judgments, and make it hard to justify fundamental changes in these judgments. Non-naturalism and naturalistic realism agree that objective moral facts exist, and disagree about their epistemological and ontological status. While they can be articulated to support intuitive normative ethical theories, distinctive commitments regarding the nature of moral facts can lead these theories to surprising normative ethical conclusions. The rest of this foreword will consider these various metaethical views and their normative ethical implications.

Non-cognitivists regard moral judgment as a state of mind other than belief—perhaps desire or emotion. Cognitivism is the view that moral judgments are beliefs, and non-cognitivism is the only one of the five metaethical theories discussed here that denies it. Non-cognitivists can regard judging that lying is wrong as desiring that people not lie or having an emotion like guilt about lying. Since the clearest linguistic expressions of belief are declarative sentences, non-cognitivism suggests that moral judgments are more clearly expressed by exclamations or commands like "Hooray!" or "Go away!" Non-cognitivists might take "Lying is wrong", which seems to attribute the property of wrongness to lying, as better expressed by "Don't lie!" or "Boo lying!" Non-cognitivist avoidance of ontological commitment makes it impossible for moral judgments to be true or false in any robust sense, as emotions, desires, "Hooray!"

and "Go away!" aren't true or false. These mental states and linguistic expressions need not correspond with reality as beliefs and declarative sentences should, leading non-cognitivism to a "no" answer to the titular question of *Is Morality Real?* Non-cognitivism makes the idea of real moral rightness and wrongness hard to understand, since reality doesn't make desires or emotions true by corresponding with them.

Even after we accept its implication that there are no moral facts, non-cognitivism lets us continue making moral judgments as we always did. It treats moral judgments as things that need not change to correspond better with reality, leaving few constraints on normative ethical theory. What one may believe is constrained by evidence and reality; desire and emotion need change with our evidence or correspond with reality. Perhaps non-cognitive mental states constrain each other in some way, or perhaps some other states constrain them. Non-cognitivism eliminates an important kind of justification for changing our moral judgments or adopting a new normative ethical theory, letting us judge what is right and wrong the same way we always have.

Relativists deny that moral facts have to be objective, and regard actions as morally wrong if some individual or culture has the right sort of negative attitudes towards these actions. Many forms of non-moral value have a relativist character, depending on individual or cultural attitudes. Which foods are delicious is relative to individual taste. Which clothes are fashionable is relative to a culture's fashion sense. Beauty is proverbially in the eye of the beholder. Opponents of relativism often hold that moral value must be universal and objective, unlike fashionability, deliciousness, and beauty. Universal and objective moral standards would be useful for judging whether the values of one's society should reformed, and resolving disputes between cultures. Metaethical debates between relativists and their opponents often concern whether morality must be universal and objective, or whether value relative to individual or cultural attitudes is enough to make morality real.

Relativism guides us to normative ethical theories that correspond with individual or cultural moral attitudes. Theories invoking individual attitudes treat the moral facts as different for different people depending on individual taste, making them easy for each individual to know, like facts about which foods are delicious. These theories can resemble non-cognitivism in denying the possibility of moral improvement that corrects errors in our most fundamental moral attitudes. Theories invoking cultural attitudes make morality like fashion—differing between cultures, accessible to those who know a culture well, and potentially under the control of the powerful. A theory of what's fashionable in a culture must correspond with the culture's fashion sense; a relativist theory of what's morally right in a culture must similarly correspond with the culture's moral sensibilities. Reformers seeking to change their culture's most fundamental moral values then are automatically wrong, since morality is defined by these values, and to reject them is to be immoral.

Those who reject noncognitivism and relativism, as Spencer, Matt, and I do, regard moral judgments as beliefs about objective moral facts. We therefore face the question of whether morality is real—whether there are objective moral facts, which would make moral judgments true. If morality isn't real, Matt is right and error theory follows. The true normative ethical theory then will be a purely negative one: nothing is right or wrong.

If morality is real, the true normative theory will be a description of the moral facts. Both Spencer's non-naturalism and my naturalistic realism treat morality as real in this way. Both can be articulated to allow preservation of current moral judgments, but if the moral facts have a surprising structure, they can suggest that a deeply counterintuitive moral theory is true. Contemporary non-naturalists like Spencer articulate their theory to support intuitive normative ethical theories, though distinctive assumptions about the nature of non-natural facts could give normative ethics a different and perhaps counterintuitive structure. Naturalistic moral realism is more likely to lead to surprising discoveries about morality that contradict ordinary intuition, as the empirical facts about many things can surprise us.

Non-naturalists like Spencer hold that many ordinary moral judgments are true, because they're right about moral facts that empirical investigation of the universe can't discover. Wrongness is a property of lying, making it a fact that lying is wrong. While some things about lies are empirically observable within space and time—when and where a lie was told, and how loudly the liar told it—non-naturalists regard wrongness as different. Scientific examination of lies can reveal when, where, and how loudly they're told, but it can't reveal their wrongness. The wrongness of lying isn't discovered by empirically investigating lies using our senses or scientific instruments, but by reason itself. When we think about whether lying is right or wrong, it intuitively seems to us that it's wrong. Many other facts of philosophical interest are widely held to be known by intuition, including facts about mathematics and about what would happen under different laws, as it's hard to see how these facts can be empirically observed in space and time. Non-naturalists hold that moral facts are similar.

Since contemporary forms of non-naturalism take the moral facts to be discovered by ordinary intuition, they support a highly intuitive normative ethical theory. Spencer's view seems to be along these lines, as he avoids any especially distinctive commitments regarding the structure of non-natural moral reality. Past non-naturalists like Immanuel Kant had distinctive views about moral reality that suggested moral theories with occasionally counterintuitive commitments. Kant argued that our autonomy was the source of all our moral obligations, and that one could never be truly autonomous in telling a lie. He believed that lying is wrong even to deceive a murderer and save someone's life, which many people in his time and ours find surprising. Instead of deriving all moral truth from a single source like autonomy of the will, Spencer and other contemporary non-naturalists allow for a plurality of fundamental moral facts, giving them the flexibility to accommodate more of our intuitions. They can therefore say that lying is generally wrong, but that the rightness of saving a life can outweigh the wrongness. Since intuition provides our knowledge of all these moral facts, the resulting normative ethical theory will be highly intuitive.

Naturalistic realists think that there are objective moral facts, and regard them as empirically observable in space and time. They differ about how these facts are known. Analytic naturalists think the true moral theory can be discovered by analyzing moral concepts, and empirically investigating the world to see what corresponds with the analyses. Some recent synthetic naturalists suggest that the moral facts can be known by discovering what systematically causes our use of moral terms, as this will be what our terms refer to. My own view is that we should study which psychological processes reliably lead us to true belief and which don't, discover which processes generate our moral beliefs, and retain only those beliefs formed by reliable processes.[1] A common feature of

---

1 Sinhababu, Neil (2022). The reliable route from nonmoral evidence to moral conclusions. *Erkenntnis* (doi:10.1007/s10670-022-00631-w).

all these naturalistic realist views is that they don't make moral knowledge depend simply on intuition. There is some suitably empirical method for discovering the moral truth—analyzing moral concepts and seeing what they apply to, studying the causal relations to moral concepts, or assessing the reliability of the processes generating moral belief.

Whether naturalistic realism provides an intuitive normative ethics will depend on whether these empirical methods deliver intuitive results. Some naturalistic realists make intuitive results more likely by treating intuition itself as a process of belief-formation that empiricism can allow. Maybe intuition is simply part of conceptual analysis, or perhaps it's some other type of empirical process that is reliably correlated with the moral truth. But if we empirically discover that many processes generating intuitive moral beliefs are unreliable, perhaps by discovering that they generate lots of false nonmoral beliefs, we might accept a counterintuitive moral theory that gives up these intuitively appealing but dubious moral claims. I regard the emotional processes generating many of our intuitive moral beliefs as unreliable, and think the only independently reliable process generating moral belief is introspection of immediate experience, which reveals that pleasure is good and displeasure is bad. This leads me to ethical hedonism, with all its counterintuitive consequences.

Metaethics is interesting partly because of its consequences for normative ethics. What sorts of things goodness, rightness, and virtue are, and what sort of methodology will reveal them to us, depends on the answers to metaethical questions. Non-cognitivism and contemporary intuitionist non-naturalism agree with current normative ethical methodology in favoring ordinary intuition. Relativism treats individual or cultural moral attitudes as constitutive of morality, and can therefore render the moral principles intuitive to an individual or culture immune to fundamental challenge. Some forms of naturalistic realism favor intuition, while others can support counterintuitive theories. Error theory has the most counterintuitive consequences, requiring us to give up all our moral beliefs.

The answers to metaethical questions shape the methodology of normative ethics. In doing so, they suggest different answers to questions about what is good, right, and virtuous. Those interested in the answers to these normative ethical questions, as well as those interested in metaethics for its own sake, are encouraged to read this book.

Part I

Introducing Metaethics

Chapter 1

Fact or Opinion?

Matt Lutz and Spencer Case

Contents

Suppose that Francis and Judith disagree about abortion. Francis thinks that a fetus is morally a person, so that killing fetuses unjustifiably is literally murder. Abortion should be illegal in all but the most extenuating circumstances, such as when it's necessary to save the life of the mother. Judith, on the other hand, doubts that fetuses have the same moral status as born infants. Moreover, even if fetuses have such status, their right not to be killed doesn't override the woman's right to choose what to do with her own body. Judith concludes that abortion isn't essentially different from other forms of healthcare and that there should be few legal restrictions placed on it, if any. Perhaps the government should even subsidize abortion providers.

Let's say that Francis and Judith are discussing abortion—civilly, if that doesn't shatter believability—in a public space like a coffee shop. Russ and Sharon, who are seated at a nearby table, overhear them. This inspires a new conversation. Rather than taking sides with Francis or Judith, Russ and Sharon debate the nature of the conversation that they overhear. Russ thinks that Francis and

DOI: 10.4324/9781003183174-2

Judith are disagreeing over a matter of fact that isn't determined by anyone's feelings or beliefs. Their moral judgments are attempts to describe the world. Given that they're disagreeing, at least one person must be wrong, and perhaps they both are—a moderate position on abortion might be correct. But it's also possible that Francis or Judith has got the issue pretty much right. Sharon disagrees. She thinks that morality is "all just a matter of opinion." The disagreement between Francis and Judith could continue indefinitely without resolution even if neither is making any errors in reasoning, and each fully understands the other's position. There's no objective fact of the matter.

The dispute between Francis and Judith is a "first-order" moral disagreement, or rather a cluster of first-order disagreements. That's to say they disagree about what ought to be done. Should pregnant women be allowed to terminate their pregnancies if they desire? Should we prefer "pro-life" politicians or candidates who are more supportive of "reproductive freedom"? The debate between Russ and Sharon, by contrast, concerns "second-order" moral questions, or "metaethical" questions, which are about the nature of first-order moral disputes and the assumptions behind them. Examples include: are moral assertions like "abortion is wrong" and "the rich ought to aid the poor" supposed to describe reality or do something else (e.g., express the speaker's emotions)? If they do attempt to describe reality, then do any of them describe it accurately? How could we know, and what would make those assertions true? Russ is inclined toward moral realism, while Sharon is disposed toward anti-realism.

The terms *moral realism* and *moral anti-realism* seem to have originated in the twentieth century in Anglo-American philosophy. That's relatively recent by the standards of the history of Western philosophy, which goes back thousands of years. Nevertheless, the positions that these terms refer to have been debated since at least the fifth century BCE in ancient Greece. Some scholars believe that ancient Egyptians discussed metaethical questions even earlier (DeLapp 2020). Metaethical questions have also been independently considered in non-Western philosophical traditions—in Chinese, Indian, and Islamic philosophy, for example (Liu 2007; Kjellberg and Ivanhoe 1996; Davis 2013; Al-Attar 2010). The status of moral truths seems to be one of the perennial questions of philosophy, alongside questions about the existence of God, and how (and whether) we're able to acquire knowledge. It'll probably continue to be debated as long as there are humans, and maybe intelligent beings of a different sort, alive in the universe. We aren't conceited enough to think that our discussion will settle the issue once and for all, but we're confident that this book can deepen your understanding of the issue.

> The debate between moral realists and anti-realists is a debate about the nature of morality: are there real answers to ethical questions that don't depend on human opinions or not? It's one of the oldest and most universal debates in the history of philosophy.

1.1   What Is Morality?

We'll give a fuller characterization of moral realism and anti-realism shortly. Before we do that, though, we need to say a bit about what morality is. Here we have to tread carefully. If we say too much, then we'll prejudge the investigation. What morality is ultimately depends on the outcome of the moral realism/anti-realism debate. On the other hand, if we say too little, it won't be clear what the debate is about. Presumably, you already have some notion of morality since 'morality' is an ordinary language word and not some bit of academic jargon. In this section, we want to draw attention to a number of important features of our ordinary concept of morality that realists and anti-realists mostly agree on.

One preliminary terminological note: some professors make a fuss about the distinction between ethics and morality. We don't. We'll use 'ethics' and 'morality' interchangeably throughout the book. This is how they're used in ordinary discourse, and in a lot of scholarship, too.

1.1.1   Morality Is Normative

Philosophers studying metaethics typically distinguish between normative and descriptive claims. To a first approximation, descriptive claims say how the world *is* (while descriptive facts are facts about the way the world is), and normative claims say how the world *ought to be* (while normative facts are facts about the way the world ought to be). However, realists insist that some normative claims accurately describe the world, so we can't assume that "descriptive" and "normative" are exclusive categories without prejudging this debate against realism. Nonetheless, we intuitively recognize a difference between normative and descriptive terms. 'Ought' is a paradigmatic normative term; 'good,' 'bad,' 'right,' 'wrong,' and 'rational' are normative terms as well. These terms seem different from paradigmatic descriptive terms like 'large,' 'pink,' and 'shiny.' Some words, such as 'happy' and 'courageous' don't clearly belong on either list. Perhaps we should say that they're partly normative and partly descriptive. Some philosophers call such words "thick" normative terms (Väyrynen 2021b).

Is there any other way to define normativity other than by giving putative examples of normative terms? Unfortunately, we don't see one. **Normativity** is a difficult concept to explain, not because it's complicated but because it's apparently basic. To say that someone ought to do something, or that he has a reason to do it, isn't to say that he *will* do it. It's to say ... well, that he *ought* to do it, or that he has a reason to do it. We're close to conceptual bedrock here. It's hard to say much more than this without simply saying the same thing in different words, or adding emphasis, e.g., that he *really should* do it. Sometimes philosophers say that normative terms are "action guiding," though we think that this amounts to another way of saying the same thing. The concept just has to be grasped with the aid of examples, and by getting clear on what it *isn't* (see Parfit 2011, ch. 24).

Descriptive morality refers to the moral practices and beliefs of a group of people, as an anthropologist might document them. For instance, it might be true that members of a certain community believe that walking on sacred land is morally forbidden and that participation in seasonal warfare is required for adult males. Group members who flout these norms are punished. The claims made in the last two sentences are claims about descriptive morality, not normative moral claims. They don't purport to say how anyone ought to behave. Suppose that one of this community's rules is that during seasonal warfare male warriors should rape female captives. You probably think this rule is immoral and that the warriors should disregard it even if they're shamed for doing so. If so, that's a belief about **normative morality**, and normative morality is what interests moral philosophers. Note that the word "normative" has different specialized meanings in different disciplines. Social scientists sometimes use the word to refer to what is considered normal within a community. This is simply a description of the community's norms. So when a social theorist calls an action normative, she's making a descriptive claim, not a normative one. This can be confusing!

Understanding the descriptive/normative morality distinction heads off a common source of confusion. Philosophy students often say that "what's moral in one culture might not be moral in another culture." This remark is perilously ambiguous. It could be interpreted to mean that moral beliefs differ between cultures. So understood, it's an uncontroversial observation about descriptive morality. It could also be interpreted as the normative claim that there's no right or wrong beyond what our respective cultures label as such. That position is a form of relativism, which we'll discuss in Chapter 2. The danger lies in conflating these two claims and thinking that the fact that the world contains diverse *descriptive* moralities entails that relativism is true. It entails no such thing.

1.1.2 Morality Is Authoritative

Morality purports to be important. Many philosophers accept **moral overridingness**, the idea that moral considerations trump all competing considerations about what to do (Stroud 1998). The play *Fiddler on the Roof*, which is set in a Jewish village in Czarist Russia, dramatizes the idea of overridingness. When confronted with difficult choices, the main character, Tevye, thinks to himself (audibly, so that the audience can hear): "On the one hand... but on the other hand..." metaphorically weighing the reasons until he thinks they've been fully considered. At a pivotal point in the plot, he considers whether to accept the marriage of one of his daughters to a Christian, which he didn't authorize. But this would compromise his commitment to his religion: "If I try and bend that far, I'll break. On the other hand ... There is no other hand. No, Chava! No!" (Stein 1964, 94–95). In Tevye's mind, his religious obligations are overriding. Likewise, for those who accept moral overridingness, when we're deliberating about what to do and we discover that one and only course of action is permissible, then that settles it. We must obey morality; there's no "other hand" to consider.

The TV series *Breaking Bad* provides a more recent example from pop culture. The story details the moral decline of anti-hero Walter White, a high school chemistry teacher who decides to "cook" and sell methamphetamine to help his family financially (or at least that's how he rationalizes his actions). In an early episode, White finds himself in a predicament when a vicious drug supplier called "Krazy-8" ends up imprisoned in a basement. White can't keep him there indefinitely, and so he has to decide whether to release Krazy-8 or kill him. Krazy-8 insists that White has no choice but to release him since the alternative would be "cold-blooded murder." White, who hasn't yet descended into depravity, is reluctant to kill Krazy-8 but fearful of the consequences of releasing him. He makes a list of considerations for and against killing Krazy-8. Beneath "Let him go" he writes: "It's the moral thing to do," "Judeo-Christian principles," and "You are not a murderer." Beneath "Kill him" he writes: "He'll kill you and your entire family if you let him go" (Gilligan et al. 2008).

If morality is overriding, and if killing Krazy-8 would be wrong, then Krazy-8 is right: White has no (acceptable) choice but to release him. As with Tevye, there's no "other hand" to consider. If we take this view, then we might see the roots of White's moral decline in his willingness to consider reasons "on the other hand" when he already knows what morality demands of him. Another possibility is that White's initial assessment that letting Krazy-8 go would be "the moral thing to do" is mistaken and killing Krazy-8 wouldn't be wrong in these circumstances. Perhaps the killing would be a justifiable act of self-defense, albeit of an unusual kind. A third possibility is that killing Krazy-8 would be morally wrong, but White's non-moral reasons to protect his family and himself outweigh his moral duty not to kill Krazy-8. White *morally* shouldn't kill Krazy-8, but *all things considered* White should kill him. Only this last interpretation is incompatible with moral overridingness.

We take no stance on whether morality is overriding. But we do insist that morality purports to have significant authority, even if moral requirements don't override competing considerations in every circumstance. Moral concepts have a certain intuitive "feel" to them. Part of this "feel" is a sense of their gravity. Morality *matters*. A psychopath who generally knows how to use words like "right" and "wrong" in ordinary ways, but who doesn't think that rightness or wrongness should weigh very heavily in his own or anyone else's decision making, seems to not grasp these concepts. Perhaps moral requirements can be overridden by competing considerations, but if so, it takes a lot to trump them, and this doesn't happen very often. Morality doesn't exist unless moral obligations are usually authoritative. If we discovered that "moral" obligations may be shrugged off, then we'd have discovered that morality isn't real.

> Morality is *normative*: it's an account of what we ought to do, not an account of what we actually do or what we believe we ought to do. It's also *authoritative*. Morality matters. Moral reasons weigh heavily in practical deliberation—if they exist.

1.2 The Content of Morality

There seem to be normative domains besides morality. Prudential reasons concern the reasons we have to pursue our self-interest. Epistemic (i.e., knowledge-related) reasons are the reasons we have to form beliefs in such a way that they're candidates for knowledge. When you tell your friend "you shouldn't believe that crazy conspiracy theory you found doomscrolling on Twitter," you're telling your friend to pay attention to his epistemic reasons. So then what's distinctive about morality? This (of course) is a matter of debate. Without being too controversial, we can identify a core web of concepts that have a moral "feel" to them:

- *Virtues and vices*. These are morally significant states of character. Virtues, which are good states of character, include courage, generosity, kindness, honesty and perhaps loyalty. Vices, bad states of character, include cowardliness, rashness, stinginess, cruelty, dishonesty, disloyalty, and envy.
- *Rules*. This is probably what most people first think of when they hear the term 'morality': the "Thou shalts" and the "Thou shalt nots." Morally you shouldn't kill, steal, lie, etc. Rules can also be positive: you should help those in need, tell the truth, and develop your talents when you reasonably can.
- *Value*. Things that are valuable are worth pursuing and promoting. Things that are intrinsically valuable are worth pursuing and promoting for their own sakes. If something has moral value, then we morally ought to pursue it for its own sake. Plausible examples include happiness, knowledge, virtue, and beauty; the opposites of these things would be disvaluable.

What do rules, character traits, and values have in common that gives them *moral* significance? "Concern for others" is a tempting answer. Commonsense moral rules restrain actions that harm others. If we care about promoting value in the world, we're going to end up helping others. Things are a little bit more complicated with the virtues, since many ethicists, taking cues from Aristotle, think that becoming a virtuous person is an essential part of what it is for *you* to flourish as a human being. Still, they generally understand one's individual flourishing to benefit others (it's good to be around people who are kind, honest, etc.). However, understanding morality to be all about other people rules out the possibility of morally wronging oneself. Gratuitous self-harm seems wrong. We say things like "People who cheat only cheat themselves," and criticize people for self-deception. These remarks sound like moral criticisms. We think that it'd be a mistake to rule out the possibility that we have moral obligations to ourselves by the way we define 'morality.'

Here, we think, is a better suggestion. We take it that morality presupposes that we have duties to others of some sort, even if not all moral duties are other-directed. So we can say that morality concerns *normative reasons of the sort that underlie our duties towards others*. This allows us to remain neutral both on what those duties are, and on whether we also have moral duties to ourselves. First-order moral theories purport to tell us what sorts of reasons underlie our other-regarding duties. For example, according to eighteenth-century philosopher Immanuel Kant, we ought to avoid stealing because stealing treats people as "mere means"—that is, as instruments or things instead of as agents who deserve respect. We can also treat ourselves as mere means, Kant thought. This was his reason for thinking that suicide is morally wrong (Kant 1785/2018, 42). So the duty not to kill oneself counts as a self-regarding moral duty for Kantians, and it's a moral duty for the same reason that we have a duty not to kill others. Similarly, consequentialists say we shouldn't do anything that reduces the amount of value in the world. That's why we shouldn't harm others or ourselves.

This leaves plenty of room for non-moral reasons. If Spencer and Matt each want the last ticket to a concert they'd equally enjoy, both would have a prudential reason to try to get it before the other. There's probably nothing *moral* at stake here. Similarly, it seems like if you have evidence that it's going to rain today, you should believe that it's going to rain and take an umbrella when you go out. These sorts of normative reasons don't have a particularly moral feel to them. That's partly because the stakes aren't high and partly because these sorts of reasons don't underlie our obligations to others. It may be that, in the final analysis, epistemic reasons and mundane practical reasons are species of moral reasons after all, but it would take a lot of philosophical work to show this.

> Morality concerns virtues and vices, value and disvalue, and obligations and duties. Moral duties are typically other-regarding. Self-directed moral duties, if they exist, are of the same kind as other-regarding moral duties.

1.3   Realism vs. Anti-realism

That's what morality is, in a nutshell. So what does it mean to be a *realist* or *anti-realist* about morality? Our gloss earlier was that moral realists think that morality is a matter of fact, whereas anti-realists think morality is just a matter of opinion. This needs refinement. There can be opinions about matters of fact, and facts about opinions. More precisely, **moral realism** is the view that (1) moral judgments represent the world as containing moral facts or properties, (2) there are moral facts, and (3) those moral facts are stance-independent. **Moral anti-realism** is the denial of one or more of these claims.

Let's consider **stance-independence**. When we say that a fact is stance-independent, we mean that it doesn't depend on the stances of any agent. A *stance* is a belief or attitude, or a complex mental state composed of both. Some facts are stance-dependent, and some are stance-independent. Facts about the economic values of currencies are stance-dependent. When people value the U.S. dollar more or less, its economic value increases or decreases accordingly. If people believed the dollar to be worthless, then it would *be* worthless. Facts about the economic value of a currency depend on people's beliefs and attitudes about the currency's value. That makes those facts stance-dependent. By contrast, the fact that a hydrogen atom has one proton in its nucleus doesn't depend on anyone's beliefs or desires. That's what makes it stance-independent.

Before we say how this applies to moral facts, we need to distinguish two kinds of moral claims: *pure* moral claims and *impure* moral claims. Impure moral claims entail non-moral, descriptive claims; pure moral claims don't. For example, compare "It was wrong for Jill to have stolen" with "Stealing is wrong." "It was wrong for Jill to have stolen " entails that Jill stole something, which is a descriptive claim, and so "It was wrong for Jill to have stolen" is an impure moral claim. "Stealing is wrong" doesn't entail that Jill stole. Nor does it entail that anyone else has stolen or will steal anything, or any other descriptive claims. So that's a pure moral claim. Impure moral claims are made true in part by descriptive facts: if it's true that it was wrong for Jill to steal, then this is made true in part by the fact that Jill stole. Mundane as that observation might seem, it matters for how we should define the difference between realism and anti-realism. For consider the following claim: "Natasha's admiration of murderers is evil." If this claim is true, it's made true in part by facts about Natasha's moral stances, i.e., her admiration of murderers. Thus, it's a claim whose truth depends on someone's attitudes. Such claims are compatible with realism. Everyone agrees that some impure moral facts are stance-dependent. Realists say that *pure* moral facts are stance-independent.

We're especially concerned with independence from moral beliefs and attitudes here. Moral beliefs are beliefs about morality. The beliefs that the criminal justice system is unjust, that eating meat is wrong, that we should keep our promises, and that courage is good are all moral beliefs. Moral attitudes include being disgusted by some travesty of justice, or feeling warmly toward someone who has acted admirably. Usually moral attitudes come along with moral beliefs; the belief that an action is unjust is often accompanied by a feeling of outrage. The coincidence of moral attitudes and moral beliefs is so common that many philosophers think it's impossible to have moral beliefs without having any corresponding moral attitudes (more on that later).

If it's a stance-independent moral fact that humiliating others for amusement is wrong, then it's a fact that humiliating others for amusement is wrong, and not because anyone disapproves of it or believes that it's wrong. Moral realists hold that there are pure moral facts that don't depend on human attitudes or beliefs. Anti-realists deny this. That's the debate in a nutshell.

1.3.1 Why the Realism/Anti-realism Debate Matters

There are practical reasons to worry about the outcome of the realism/anti-realism debate. Peter Singer (1972) famously argued that people living in developed countries morally must give nearly all their disposable income to rescue the world's poorest people. If there are no moral facts, then we apparently don't need to worry about satisfying stringent moral obligations. If moral facts are real, but stance-dependent, then all moral obligations might be escapable. Maybe if enough people changed their stances toward charitable giving we'd no longer have such duties. But if there are stance-independent moral facts, and Singer is right about our obligations to others, then we can't evade some moral obligations even in principle. (We shall see in §2.3, however, that one form of anti-realism, Kantian constructivism, agrees with realism that some moral obligations are inescapable.)

There might also be non-practical reasons to worry about the debate. Joshua Blanchard (2020) observes that some philosophical disputes generate "philosophical angst." Many people feel that the outcomes of certain philosophical questions are inherently important, even when there's no clear practical upshot to them. Some think it matters a great deal whether or not we have free will, or whether any of our beliefs qualifies as knowledge. The realism debate also generates philosophical angst on both sides. Realists generally think it matters that the things they take to be paradigmatically evil, like slavery and genocide, really are evil. Some anti-realists find the idea that there are inescapable moral obligations to be downright tyrannical! Not everyone feels this way. Just as philosophers disagree about philosophical issues, they disagree about what issues are angst-inducing. Some profess not to see what's at stake in the free will debate; others feel the same way about metaethics.

The authors of this book are split on this. Spencer feels angst over the realism/anti-realism issue, but Matt doesn't really. That's not unusual: realists often feel that accepting anti-realism means giving up something of deep importance, while anti-realists typically deny this, and labor to dispel the illusion, as they see it, that adopting their position requires them to bear a heavy cost. One skirmish in the larger war between realists and anti-realists is over whether and why the war matters to begin with! We'll return to this in due time.

1.4 The Tolerance Distraction

Some people think that the realism/anti-realism debate matters because realism is an intolerant position whereas anti-realism is tolerant. If there's a truth of the matter about the moral status of abortion, then either Francis or Judith is wrong, period. So if we want to be tolerant, then we should reject realism, which rudely implies that some people are Just Plain Wrong in ethical matters, and others are Right. Mary Midgely wrote that during a discussion about the meaning of 'morality' one of her students exclaimed: "But surely it's *always* wrong to make moral judgments!" (2017, vii). However, questions of tolerance have no bearing on this debate. The idea that tolerance gives us a reason to reject realism confuses the existence of stance-independent moral truths, a metaethical question, with various first-order moral questions about how we should coexist amid moral disagreement. Midgley's student is making an ironic mistake: to say that it's wrong to make moral judgments is to make a moral judgment! Tolerance is good, at least to a certain degree. That's no objection to realism. Most realists probably agree. Believing there's a right answer to a question is compatible with being humble. Even when we're sure we have the right answer, it can be unkind to bluntly tell people that they're wrong, or impose your view on others.

It's also possible for an anti-realist to be intolerant. Suppose Fred thinks right and wrong are matters of personal preference, and that there's no further fact of the matter about what preferences are right or wrong. That certainly qualifies Fred as an anti-realist. But Fred needn't have any preference for tolerating people who disagree. So Fred might be as intolerant as any dogmatic realist. He may even excuse his intolerance by pointing out that, really, there's nothing wrong with being intolerant!

So tolerance is compatible with realism and intolerance is compatible with anti-realism. Questions of how tolerant we should be are a distraction from the issues at hand.

> The debate between moral realists and anti-realists is over whether or not there are stance-independent pure moral facts. This debate matters because it may have practical implications and because the question itself is a source of philosophical angst. The debate has no implication for how tolerant you should be.

Chapter 2

Anti-realism

Matt Lutz and Spencer Case

Contents

In the next two chapters, we'll look at varieties of realism and anti-realism and some of the major arguments for and against these different views. This will provide you with a basic vocabulary and sense of the major debates that have structured metaethics over the last century, and prevent you from developing too narrow a perspective on the central debate of this book. There are more varieties of realism than Spencer's, and more varieties of anti-realism than Matt's. Every view we discuss here has contemporary defenders, many of whom are brilliant philosophers with sophisticated views and subtle responses to the various objections we'll survey here. We don't mean to suggest that a view is hopeless just because neither of us accepts it. However, to keep things brief, we'll just go deep enough to explain the essences of the various views, what the main debates are, and why we'll be setting aside the views that we both reject.

Moral realism, recall, is the view that (1) moral judgments represent the world as containing moral facts, (2) there are moral facts, and (3) those moral facts are stance-independent. Accordingly, there are three basic ways to be a moral anti-realist. First, you might think that there are no moral facts at all. Second, you might think

DOI: 10.4324/9781003183174-3

that there are moral facts, but those facts are all stance-dependent. Third, you might think that moral judgments do not represent the world as containing moral facts. Let's consider each of these possibilities in turn.

2.1 Error Theory

Error theory is the easiest form of anti-realism to explain. As the name suggests, error theory implies that a fundamental error lies at the core of moral thought and language. Moral judgments are judgments about the moral properties that different actions, individuals, or states of affairs have. The judgment that slavery is morally wrong, for instance, describes slavery as having the property of being morally wrong. But moral properties don't, and perhaps couldn't, exist. This means that there are no moral facts, and so our moral judgments are systematically untrue. More formally, error theory is the conjunction of two claims:

> **Cognitivism:** Our moral judgments represent the world as being a certain way and thus are about moral facts.

> **Non-negotiable error:** There are no (substantive) moral facts.

Cognitivism is an intuitive view about moral judgments. According to cognitivism, to judge that giving to charity is good is to think of giving to charity as having the property of goodness. Moral language reflects this function. The word 'good' refers to the property of goodness, just like the word 'brown' refers to the property of brownness. So when we say "giving to charity is good," we attribute the property of goodness to all acts of giving to charity. And if all acts of giving to charity do have the property of goodness, then it's a fact that giving to charity is good, and so this judgment is true. However, the error theorist thinks that there are no moral properties, and therefore no substantive moral facts. And so all substantive moral judgments are untrue. By "substantive," we mean facts that presuppose, or entail, the existence of moral properties. And we say "untrue" because some error theorists think that the error in moral language is so deep that moral claims *aren't even false*. But we'll set this complication aside.

Error theorists are like the atheists of metaethics. According to atheists, the word 'God' refers to God, but God doesn't exist. Therefore, statements about God, like "God created the universe" are untrue, though meaningful. This isn't to say that there are no true sentences that include the word 'God.' It's true (in the eyes of the atheist) that God doesn't exist. It's true that monotheistic religions believe in a single God. And it's true that *if* the Son of God exists, *then* God exists. But any sentence that implies that God exists is untrue. Similarly, for the error theorist, any sentence that implies the existence of moral properties is untrue. So our moral judgments are systematically in error. If we realize that we commonly make an error when we make moral judgments, a reasonable way to respond is to go on making moral judgments, but do so without making any errors. The moral error theorist says that this can't be done. The error in our moral judgments is "non-negotiable," which means that the error is so central to our moral concepts that to abandon that error would be to abandon making moral judgments entirely. In the previous chapter, we suggested that morality is non-negotiably normative and authoritative: if we learn that there is nothing that is authoritatively normative, then we wouldn't have learned that morality isn't authoritatively normative, we'd have learned that there's no such thing as (normative) morality. Similarly, some atheists think that the existence of evil in the world proves that there can't be an omniscient, omnipotent, omnibenevolent being. If they're right, then this doesn't imply that God isn't omniscient, omnipotent, and omnibenevolent. It implies that God doesn't exist; a God that isn't omnipotent is no God at all.

The view that there are no moral properties (even though our moral language suggests that there are) is an old view; some versions of Buddhist ethics and Daoist ethics can be understood as versions of error theory (Dockstader 2018; 2022). Contemporary error theory was first formulated by the Swedish philosopher Einar Tegen, but Tegen's work has been little discussed outside Sweden (Olson 2014, ch. 3). It was only with the work of the Australian philosopher J. L. Mackie (1977), who coined the term "error theory," that the view gained prominence in the analytic tradition of philosophy that currently prevails in the English-speaking world.

Since cognitivism is so plausible, the main task for the error theorist is to argue that moral beliefs are non-negotiably wrong, and Mackie provided several influential arguments for that conclusion. The **relativity argument** proceeds from the observation that moral practices differ between cultures and epochs. The best explanation of this moral variation, Mackie thought, is that our moral beliefs and attitudes reflect our ways of life, not objective moral truths. Thus, we have no reason to believe in any objective moral truths. And since Mackie thought that objectivity is a non-negotiable feature of morality, he adopts error theory rather than some other form of anti-realism.

The **queerness argument**, which is really a family of arguments, maintains that we shouldn't believe that moral properties exist, because if they did, that would be *queer*. In this context, "queer" just means "weird"; with all the social-political meaning that the word 'queer' has acquired since 1977, when Mackie initially published *Ethics: Inventing Right and Wrong*, we might now prefer a different term. But the label has stuck. Mackie argues that the existence of moral properties would be weird in four different ways; each of these four arguments has been much discussed in the last five decades.

First is the **motivation argument**. Mackie writes that "An objective good would be sought by anyone who was acquainted with it … just because the end has to-be-pursuedness somehow built into it" (1977, 40). Mackie thinks it's clear that nothing could be intrinsically motivating in this way. However, it's not clear why Mackie thinks that morality *itself* is intrinsically motivating. The view that moral *judgments* are intrinsically motivating is popular and plausible. But if there's anything weird here, it seems to be about the nature of moral judgment, not the nature of moral facts. (As we'll see, the observation that moral judgments are intrinsically motivating is the basis of the main argument against cognitivism.)

Second is the **supervenience challenge**, which Mackie adopted from the work of R. M. Hare (1952). The challenge begins with the observation that moral differences imply non-moral differences. If two pictures are exactly identical, it's nonsensical to say that one is good and the other is bad. If St. Francis is morally virtuous, then someone with the same character must be morally virtuous as well. The challenge is to explain why this would be the case. There have been many ways of developing this challenge over the years, but we don't think that any version of it amounts to much. Whatever supervenience is, the existence of moral laws can easily explain it (Enoch 2011, ch. 6.2). Anti-realists might demand that these moral laws themselves be explained—but explained how? By more general moral laws? Once we identify the most general moral laws, our explanations have come to an end and the challenge is answered. We see no reason to think that this explanatory project can't be carried out.

Third is the **epistemological queerness argument**. If we know about moral facts, it would have to be in some very strange sort of way, "intuition," which is different from how we know about other kinds of facts. This is an important worry, but it seems to us that the best way to understand this argument is as an argument that moral knowledge is impossible, not an argument that moral facts are strange. We'll look at the possibility of moral knowledge later.

The final queerness argument is the **categorical normativity argument**. This proceeds from the observation that moral facts are normative, as we noted in Chapter 1. But more than this, they're *categorically* normative. Categorical normativity is normativity that's independent of our desires. If you have a categorical reason to do X, or if you categorically ought to do X, that means that you are, in some normative sense, *bound to do* X, and this is not because of any goals, desires, or attitudes that you have. Categorical normativity is contrasted with hypothetical normativity, which is normativity that *does* depend on our desires. ("Hypothetical" in this context just means "conditional," and "categorical" means "unconditional." Conditional on what? Our desires.) "Desires" is used broadly to refer not just to passing urges, but to the variety of wants, cares, and values that agents can have. If you care about dealing honestly with others, you have a hypothetical reason to do so.

Immanuel Kant introduced this distinction between categorical and hypothetical normativity in order to attack his intellectual *bête noire*, David Hume. Hume famously declared that reason is the "slave of the passions," meaning that practical reasoning, reasoning about what to do, is—and could be nothing more than—reasoning about how to get what we want (Hume, *Treatise*, 2.3.3.3.). Kant objected that Hume's position left no room for morality. If we morally ought to do something, then correct reasoning will yield the conclusion that we ought to do it. But this isn't reasoning about how to get what we want. If we morally ought to do something, we ought to do it *no matter what* (Kant 1785/2018, 28). Mackie agrees with Kant about moral concepts: moral oughts seem to be independent of our desires. But he agrees with Hume about metaphysics: all oughts derive from our desires. To say that something is categorically valuable implies that it's to-be-pursued.

To say that something is categorically obligatory implies that it's to-be-done. To-be-done-ness and to-be-pursued-ness are unique properties—some, like Mackie, would say suspiciously strange.

A point of clarification is in order. Sometimes philosophers say that Hume's theory is an account of *instrumental* normativity since all practical reasoning is about how to satisfy our desires. But the hypothetical-categorical distinction isn't the same as the instrumental-intrinsic distinction. There's such a thing as categorical instrumental value. If, say, pleasure is categorically to-be-pursued, then in a sense anything that is indispensable for promoting pleasure will be both categorically and instrumentally valuable: instrumental because it's for some further end, and categorical because our duty to promote that end doesn't depend on our desires. Similarly, someone sympathetic to Hume could say that desire-satisfaction is intrinsically valuable, since it's not instrumental to anything further, and that our reasons to satisfy our desires are hypothetical reasons, since they're desire-dependent. In short: the hypothetical-categorical distinction is about desire-dependence, whereas the instrumental-intrinsic distinction concerns whether our reason to do something derives from some further value. Mackie's queerness objection targets categorical normativity.

Mackie's queerness arguments are supposed to show that stance-independent moral facts would be unacceptably strange. And since moral judgments concern facts like these, all of them are untrue. That's the case for error theory. The primary case against it is simple: error theory has *highly* counterintuitive implications. Error theory entails that no substantive moral judgment is true. The worst actions you can think of aren't wrong. The best things you can think of aren't morally good. The best people you can think of aren't virtuous. Hitler wasn't evil, and he did nothing wrong. These conclusions are so repugnant that many philosophers regard error theory as a non-starter. We'll both have much more to say later about this argument against error theory and strategies for resisting it.

According to error theory, moral judgments describe an objective moral reality and are therefore the kinds of things that can be true or false. But because there's no objective moral reality, all substantive moral judgments are untrue. There are several arguments for error theory, the most important of which is the categorical normativity argument. The biggest problem for error theory is that it has highly counterintuitive first-order implications.

2.2 Relativism

While error theorists say that there are no moral facts, **moral constructivism** is the view that there are moral facts, but they are stance-dependent. The most well-known constructivist view is **moral relativism**. According to the relativist, basic moral facts depend on stances that can vary from person to person or from society to society. In this way, moral facts are like legal facts: what's legal in one society might be illegal in another society. Similarly, what's right in one society might be wrong in another society. Note that we say that basic moral facts *can* vary between people and societies, not that they *do*. Most self-described relativists would say that they do vary, but this isn't essential to the view. If a plague wiped out all societies but one, so there was once a plurality of moral frameworks but now just one, we wouldn't say that relativism was once true but became false. Metaethical classifications shouldn't depend upon the course of history.

Before we continue, we should be extra clear about what relativism *isn't*, since there are many potential points of confusion in the vicinity. Moral relativism isn't the common empirical view that descriptive morality varies from society to society, or between individuals (see §1.1.1). Relativism also isn't the view that morality is inflexible to the point that we shouldn't lie to deceive a would-be murderer in pursuit of a victim, or stealing food to avoid starvation. An ambiguity in the word "absolute" can confuse people on this point: saying that morality is "absolute" can mean that morality is stance-independent or that it admits of no exceptions. Relativists reject absolutism in the first sense but not necessarily the second sense. Thinking that moral rules aren't absolute in this way doesn't make you a relativist. Finally, we also distinguish relativism from what Midgely (2005) calls "moral isolationism." This is the idea, common among anthropologists, that we can't morally judge other cultures because we can never know enough about them to make informed moral judgments.[1] Whereas moral isolationism is a thesis about moral knowledge, relativism is a thesis about the nature of morality itself.

As we see it, then, the essence of relativism is the idea that moral facts exist and that they're stance-dependent in a way that makes them contingent. Gilbert Harman, one of the most prominent philosophers to describe himself as a relativist, characterizes relativism this way:

> My moral relativism is a soberly logical thesis—a thesis about logical form, if you like. Just as the judgment that something is large makes sense only in relation to one or another comparison class, so too, I will argue, the judgment that it is wrong of someone to do something makes sense only in relation to an agreement or understanding ... Just as it makes no sense to ask whether a dog is large, period, apart from any relation to a comparison class, so too, I will argue, it makes no sense to ask whether an action is wrong, period, apart from any relation to an agreement.
>
> (Harman 1975, 35)

For Harman, relativism is a "soberly" *logical* thesis about the meanings of moral terms to the effect that those terms refer to different properties when they're used by people who have different stances. So is relativism a thesis about language or reality? It's both. If moral facts depend on our stances, then this has implications for how moral language works. Someone with one stance will use moral language to talk about one set of facts, while someone with another stance will use moral language to refer to a different set of facts. This is how things work with the property of being illegal and the word 'illegal.' Different things will be illegal in different jurisdictions, and for this reason the word 'illegal' will mean different things in different jurisdictions.[2]

---

1 See Edgerton's critique of "adaptivism" (1992, ch. 2). Adaptivism is the view that every culture, viewed in the proper scientific light, is well-adapted to its environment. Thus, if some culture seems maladaptive, this just goes to show that we aren't viewing them in the proper scientific light.

2 As we've described things here, the moral relativist is a "contextualist" about moral language. In recent years, a new linguistic theory known as "relativism"

Relativist views vary along two dimensions. The first is whether moral facts are identical to facts about our stances, or whether moral facts are distinct from facts about our stances, though determined by those facts. If moral facts are identical to facts about our stances, then sentences about morality are synonymous with sentences about our stances. So we'll call the first view *semantic relativism*. We'll call the view that moral facts are distinct from but determined by facts about our stances *substantive relativism*. The second dimension is whether moral facts are identical to (or determined by) facts about an individual's stances, or facts about the stances of a group. This is the difference between *individual relativism* and *group relativism* (of which "cultural relativism," the view that cultural groups determine the moral facts, is a common form). This schema generates four varieties of relativism (Table 2.1).

According to an individual-semantic relativist, if I say that something's good or bad, I just mean that I have some attitude toward or against it. Edward Westermark was a relativist of this kind; he took "is wrong" to mean "belongs to the class of actions toward which I tend to take up an impartial attitude of angry resentment" (1932, ch. 5).

The group-semantic relativist thinks that moral claims refer to whatever the relevant group—typically, one's society or

Table 2.1 Four kinds of relativism.[3]

	Semantic	Substantive
Individual	Thomas Hobbes, E.A. Westermark	Protagoras(?)
Group	Ruth Benedict, Gilbert Harman	Protagoras(?) David Wong

has been developed, and this has led some to think that, properly, a moral relativist should be a linguistic relativist about moral terms as well (see Stojanovic 2017 for discussion). We're sticking with a contextualist understanding of moral language because (a) that is how moral relativism has traditionally been understood and (b) we have doubts about the coherence of linguistic relativism.

3 We borrow this schema from Tim Perrine.

culture—approves or disapproves of. Anthropologist Ruth Benedict seems to have been a relativist of this kind. She writes:

> We recognize that morality differs in every society and is a
> convenient term for socially approved habits. Mankind has
> always preferred to say, "It is morally good," rather than "It is
> habitual," and the fact of this preference is matter enough for
> a critical science of ethics. But historically the two phrases are
> synonymous.
>
> (Benedict 2001, 87)

The seventeenth-century English philosopher Thomas Hobbes
articulated a form of relativism that seems to be a hybrid between
individual-semantic relativism and some sort of group relativism.
Morality within society is "made up" by judges, arbitrators and
other officials, Hobbes thought; however, individual-semantic
relativism is true in "the state of nature"—i.e., outside of society:

> Whatever is the object of any man's appetite or desire is what he
> calls 'good', the object of his hate and aversion he calls 'evil' or
> 'bad', and the object of his contempt he calls 'low' and 'incon-
> siderable'. For the words 'good', 'evil', 'bad' and 'contemptible'
> are always used in relation to the person using them. Nothing
> is simply and absolutely—i.e. just considered in itself—good or
> bad; there is no common rule of good and bad to be taken from
> the nature of the objects themselves.
>
> (Hobbes 1651/2017, ch. 6)

Moral relativism avoids some of the more counterintuitive implications of error theory. Killing isn't permissible; it's forbidden, and
that's a moral fact. Its stance-dependence doesn't make it any less of
a fact. That a hundred-dollar bill is currency is a stance-dependent
fact, but that doesn't mean that it's not "really" currency. It really is!
(If you don't agree, please send one to us.) Similarly, relativists say
that killing really is wrong and the wrongness of killing depends on
our stances. Relativism also provides a retort to the "relativity" argument for error theory: moral beliefs vary between individuals and
societies not because there are no moral facts as Mackie believed, but
(at least partly) because the moral facts themselves vary in this way.

The main problem with semantic relativism, be it individual
or group, is that it's not clear how we're supposed to understand

moral disagreement (or agreement, really). If individual-semantic relativism is correct, then when Yuri says, "Giving money to charity is good," that means "I (Yuri) approve of giving money to charity." And when Xiao says, "Giving money to charity isn't good," that means "I (Xiao) don't approve of giving money to charity." Thus, Yuri and Xiao aren't really disagreeing, at least not if "disagreement" implies that the disagreeing parties are saying contradictory things. Similarly, they wouldn't be disagreeing if Yuri said that it was 3:00 p.m. in New York, and Xiao said it was 4:00 a.m. in Beijing the following day, which is the same time in two different time zones. But Yuri and Xiao *are* apparently disagreeing about the morality of charity. So individual-semantic relativism can't be correct.

Group-semantic relativism also faces a further problem. Suppose Jenna lives in a society of meat-eaters who think that vegetarianism is weird, but that she's convinced that eating meat is wrong. When Jenna says, "Eating meat is wrong even though my society doesn't disapprove of eating meat," she's critiquing her society. But if group-semantic relativism is true, then Jenna's sentence means, "My society disapproves of eating meat even though my society doesn't disapprove of eating meat." This sentence is contradictory, but Jenna's assertion isn't.[4]

Substantive relativism might seem better positioned to answer these challenges since, according to the substantive relativist, sentences like "Giving money to charity is good" aren't *synonymous* with any claim about what an individual or group approves of. Nonetheless, these sentences will be made true by moral facts that depend on stances, and so, since Yuri and Xiao have different stances, they'll be talking about different moral facts. So, potentially, they'll both be saying something true. But if they're both saying something true, then they're not contradicting each other. So the same problem arises.

Substantive relativism also has confusing metaphysical implications. Consider a society whose culture celebrates everything that you (and most people in your society) regard as morally

---

4 Individual-semantic relativism faces a version of this problem if it turns out that we have stances that we don't know we have. Huemer (2005, ch. 2) develops a similar objection against certain forms of expressivism.

reprehensible: slavery, rape, murder, arbitrary discrimination and the like. From the point of view of people in that society, these things are good. Not only is this a counterintuitive conclusion—possibly as counterintuitive as any of the implications of error theory, if not more so—we're left wondering what to say about this society. Is it good or bad? Both? We might say that it's evil-for-us, but not evil-for-them. But what does it mean for a person to be evil-*for-someone*? Is this just a description of what someone's attitudes are? If so, substantive relativism doesn't seem like a *normative* view of morality at all. If relativism amounts to the view that moral disagreement exists, then it's philosophically uninteresting.

David Wong's "pluralistic relativism," a form of group-substantive relativism, is the most interesting and defensible version of relativism we know of. Wong understands morality to be "partly a system of rules that human beings have evolved in order to work and to live together" (1995, 383). There are, however, many possible arrangements by which human beings might work and live together. Some of our values are in such tension with one another that they can't be simultaneously realized, even in principle. For example, no society can always maximize both individual freedom and the common good. Circumstances like the COVID-19 pandemic will eventually force tradeoffs. Biology doesn't provide humans with specific guidance on how to weigh values; hence, "universally valid criteria yield merely a skeleton of a morality" that culture fleshes out into specific moralities (ibid., 389). The moralities of specific cultures determine how value tradeoffs are to be made, e.g., where the balance lies between individual autonomy and collective interest. Different moralities are inconsistent with one another, but equally true in the sense that they all qualify as moral systems (see also Copp 2009).

Wong tries to get around the disagreement problem by distinguishing between two forms of agreement and disagreement: pragmatic and what we'll call "alethic," meaning "pertaining to truth." People who participate in different moralities can disagree pragmatically, meaning that their preferred choices of action, and attitudes, conflict. So if someone from the northern part of the pre-Civil War U.S. thinks slavery is wrong, and someone from the south thinks it's right, they really do disagree in this sense. But the two disagreeing parties need not have disagreeing beliefs. After all, one says that "Slavery is wrong-in-the-north" and the other says, "No, it's right-in-the-south." Alethic disagreement is only possible for those whose moral stances are similar enough that their moral terms mean roughly the same thing. Decide for yourself whether this resolution is satisfactory.

According to relativism, moral facts depend on stances. This view validates the legitimacy of different individuals' or cultures' moral views, but it has implausible implications about how moral language works. It also validates moral views that you probably don't want validated.

2.3   Kantian Constructivism

Anti-realist philosophers are often motivated by the idea that moral properties don't exist "out there" in the world, independently of ourselves and our attitudes. If moral facts exist, they must come from ourselves and our attitudes. Yet if we ourselves generate all the moral properties, we can in principle evade our moral obligations by changing our minds. Acknowledging the stance-dependence of morality means sacrificing the universal and inescapable nature of moral obligations which realists are keen to vindicate.

Kantian constructivists think that there's a way to thread this needle: basic moral facts can be stance-dependent and yet still be universal and inescapable for all rational agents. It's important that we're talking about *rational agents* here. Rocks don't have moral obligations; trees can do no wrong. Morality only applies to those individuals—humans, certainly, but perhaps also aliens or artificial intelligences or others—who can deliberate about how to act and then act as a result of that deliberation. If moral facts depend on stances that are constitutive of the very nature of rational agency, then moral facts are both stance-dependent and universally binding on all rational agents.

Kantian constructivism comes from the work of Kant and has many contemporary defenders, notably Christine Korsgaard (2009). Kantians argue that respect for oneself is necessary for all rational agents because rational agency is the basis of all actions. It's incoherent to act without valuing the rational agency that makes action possible. So there's a universal attitude of self-respect among rational agents. And if we value ourselves *as rational agents*, then we're rationally required to equally value all others *as rational agents*, since all rational agents are equal with respect to their rational agency. We must therefore treat all rational agents as beings with value, who matter. In sum, rational agency is the basis of morality. Everyone is owed respect on the basis of their rational agency, and we'll recognize that we owe each other this respect insofar as we're rational ourselves.

Not only is this a compelling way to capture the thoughts that motivate both realism and anti-realism, it directs us towards some appealing and influential conclusions in first-order ethics. We should treat everyone equally because we are all rational agents. This means we shouldn't make an exception for ourselves: we should treat others the way we want to be treated. And this is all grounded in a rationally required attitude of universal respect for everyone as a rational agent, unaffected by trivial contingent matters like wealth, race, or sex. As John Rawls (1971) famously argued, this has political implications as well. When we are making laws and designing political institutions, we should do so in a way that everyone could agree on if they were ignorant of those trivial contingent matters and thinking of one another only as rational agents with interests that matter.

Alas, there are problems. First, it seems possible for people to fail to respect or value themselves. People apparently can lack self-respect, and such people still seem to count as rational agents. We wouldn't want to say that they're exempt from moral requirements because they don't respect themselves. A typical Kantian response is that any agent without the right kind of self-respect doesn't *really* count as a (capital-R-and-A) Rational Agent, where a Rational Agent is *defined* as someone with the right kind of self-respect. We're not convinced. The fact remains that many human beings won't count as Rational Agents. Why should we care about what it takes to be a Rational Agent, particularly if many humans aren't Rational Agents? For a development of this objection, see Enoch (2006).

Second, even if I must value my own agency, that doesn't entail in any obvious way that I must value others' agency. My own agency has an important feature that no one else's agency has—it's *mine*. I must act through my own agency and not someone else's. Therefore, if I'm required to value my own agency because it's the basis of my own actions (as Kantians say), then the basis of my self-respect is particular to myself and doesn't generalize to others.

Third, even if I'm rationally required to respect all other agents, this doesn't mean that I *do* respect all other agents, only that I *should* respect all other agents and *would* do so if I were perfectly rational. Perhaps I irrationally value only myself, or just me and my friends. A Kantian might reply that morality is grounded in the attitude of universal respect that everyone *should* have. But a Kantian who responds in this way has abandoned the constructivist idea that our moral facts are determined by our attitudes and is instead determined by the general, stance-independent normative fact that we should respect all rational agents. Perhaps Kantianism can succeed, but only at the cost of giving up on constructivism.

> Kantian constructivism is a version of constructivism that attempts to ground morality in stances that are constitutive of rational agency. It's unclear whether there are any such stances and, if there are, whether those stances could ground morality.

2.4   Non-cognitivist Expressivism

We introduced the idea of moral cognitivism in the section on error theory. This again is the view that moral judgments represent the world as being a certain way and that moral language serves to express moral judgments so sentences containing moral language describe the world as being a certain way. For instance, "Stealing is wrong" represents stealing as being wrong. Pretty intuitive, right? As we noted, though, not everyone accepts it. According to **moral non-cognitivism,** moral judgments don't represent the world as being a certain way and the function of moral language isn't to describe the world.

What do moral judgments do if they're not representational? Recall that, in our discussion of Mackie's "queerness" arguments, we noted that there seems to be a very close connection between motivation and action: If you sincerely judge that you ought to do something, you'll be (at least somewhat) motivated to do it. But how can a simple representation of the world as being a certain way motivate you all by itself? Non-cognitivists think that representations can't motivate all by themselves; but desires can. So we should think of moral judgments as some sort of *desire-like attitude*. There are lots of accounts of what that desire-like attitude is. Simple versions of non-cognitivism say that moral judgments are simple emotions of approval or disapproval (Ayer 1936, ch. 6). More complicated versions of non-cognitivism hold that the attitude that is expressed is a distinctive kind of motivational attitude (Blackburn 1984), or the acceptance of a system of norms (Gibbard 1990), or a comprehensive-yet-conditional plan of action (Gibbard 2003). In all cases, the nature of moral judgment is described in such a way that it can explain the intimate connection between moral judgment and motivation. This is an important point in non-cognitivism's favor.

What about moral language? Many non-cognitivist proposals have been offered up over the years, but by far the most popular proposal, which we'll focus on here, is that moral language *expresses attitudes*. This view is known as **expressivism**.[5] Suppose you stub your toe, feel pain, and want to communicate that you are in pain. You could say, "I feel a sharp pain in my toe." You could also say, "Ouch!" Anyone who sees you stub your toe and hears you say "Ouch!" knows how you feel. But "Ouch!" doesn't mean the same thing as "I feel a sharp pain in my toe." That sentence *reports* that you're in pain whereas "Ouch!" *expresses* your pain. English contains other exclamations like "Ouch!" If we want to express our enjoyment of a good meal, we can say, "Yum!", which isn't the same as saying, "I'm enjoying the meal." If we want to express our desire that the Yankees win the game, we can say, "Go Yankees!", which isn't the same as saying, "I want the Yankees to win." If we want to express our attitudes of approval or disapproval, we can say "Hurray!" or "Boo!", which, again, are different from saying,

---

5 Expressivism isn't just a view about the meaning of moral language. Expressivists hold that *all* language serves to express attitudes. The difference between moral language and other kinds of language is that moral language serves to express "desire-like" attitudes, while other kinds of language express "belief-like" attitudes.

"I approve" or "I disapprove." There's a difference between *reporting* an attitude and *expressing* an attitude. The expressivist says that moral language serves to *express* (rather than report) our moral judgments (which are, again, a kind of motivating attitude). This is what distinguishes individual-semantic relativism from expressivism. For the individual-semantic relativist, "Stealing is wrong" means something like "I disapprove of stealing." It *reports* your attitude. For the expressivist, "stealing is wrong" is like "Boo to stealing!" It *expresses* the attitude.

What do expressivists say about metaphysics? As a rule: not much, because the expressivist thinks that moral thought and language aren't in the business of describing the world. This allows her to evade some of the most unpalatable commitments of error theory. The error theorist says that moral sentences are untrue because they purport to accurately describe the world but fail at this task. The expressivist also holds that moral sentences don't accurately describe the world, but denies that language is riddled with error. Moral language can't be on the hook for failing to hit a target it was never aiming at in the first place.

Expressivism can also evade one of the biggest problems for relativism, the disagreement problem. Relativists struggle to explain how people with different stances can disagree, since they're not really contradicting one another; they're talking past one another. We noted that Wong's solution to this problem was to say that moral disagreements are pragmatic, and not alethic, i.e., not about how the world is. He borrowed that strategy from expressivists. For the expressivist, Yuri and Xiao's disagreement about whether it's good to give to charity must be pragmatic and not alethic since sentences like "Giving to charity is good" don't describe anything (Stevenson 1944).

Nice theory. But does moral language really work that way? There's some reason to think it does. Moral language is frequently—arguably, primarily—used to signal practical stances, and to encourage others to share those stances. That's a different kind of speech act from *describing*, and so it would make sense if the meaning of moral sentences was to express attitudes of practical commitment and encouragement rather than to express a belief that describes reality as being a certain way. But there's also good reason to be skeptical. The grammar of moral sentences looks to all the world the same as the grammar of other declarative sentences that merit a cognitivist analysis. When I assert "Murder is wrong," I seem to be saying something *about murder*—that it's wrong—rather than expressing disapproval of murder. I *have* that attitude, of course. But it doesn't seem to be the meaning of the sentence "Murder is wrong".

Surface grammar can be misleading, but the problem is deeper than grammar. The key problem for expressivism is known as the **Frege–Geach problem**, which is named after two philosophers, Gottlob Frege and Peter Geach. Frege, who wrote in the late nineteenth century, observed that language must be compositional. **Compositionality** is the feature of language whereby sentences get their meanings from the meanings of the words that make up those sentences, and complex sentences (i.e., sentences that are made up out of simple sentences) get their meanings from the meanings of the simple sentences from which they're made. Geach, who wrote in the mid-twentieth century, argued that it's hard to explain how language could be compositional if expressivism is true.[6] The Frege–Geach problem is immensely complex, and we're afraid it's impossible to give a full explanation of the problem here. For a remarkably accessible introduction to the Frege–Geach problem, see Mark Schroeder's *Non-Cognitivism in Ethics*, particularly Chapters 3–7. What we'll present here is just a large and prominent chunk of the problem.

Consider the following sentence:

1   If it's fun to steal, then it's fun to get your little brother to steal.

This is a complex sentence, with a conditional logical form. Conditional sentences contain two simpler sentences as parts, one in the antecedent and one in the consequent. (1) contains both the sentences "It's fun to steal" and "It's fun to get your little brother to steal." The meaning of (1) depends on the meanings of those two sentences. More specifically, it states that there's an *entailment* relation of some kind between those two sentences: If the sentence in the antecedent is true, then the sentence in the

---

6   This point was noticed earlier by Ross (1939, ch. 2), but somehow Geach's name got stuck to this idea rather than Ross's. We'll follow common usage and refer to "the Frege–Geach Problem," but readers should be aware that Ross is smart and awesome too.

consequent is true as well. (1) might be false. There might be no such entailment; perhaps stealing is only fun if you do it, and you get no vicarious thrill from getting others to do the same. Still, that there's such an entailment is what (1) says. The fact that (1) states the existence of such an entailment is what makes it capable of featuring in arguments like:

1   If it's fun to steal, then it's fun to get your little brother to steal.
2   It's fun to steal.
3   Therefore, it's fun to get your little brother to steal.

There might be problems with that argument, but one virtue it has is that it's *valid*: the truth of the premises guarantees the truth of the conclusion. Reasoning from the premises to the conclusion is a good way to reason. And this is in virtue of the fact that (1) asserts an entailment between (2) and (3).

Now consider the following sentence:

4   If hurray to stealing!, then hurray to getting your brother to steal!

This sentence doesn't make sense. It's gibberish. (4) has the same logical form as (1)—it's a conditional—but the antecedent and the consequent are exclamations rather than descriptions. Because the antecedent and consequent don't describe the world as being any particular way, we can't really say that (4) states an entailment between those two sentences. We can't say that (4) says that if the antecedent is true then the consequent is true as well, because the antecedent and consequent aren't the kinds of sentences that can be true. Accordingly, the following argument is a bad one:

4   If hurray to stealing, then hurray to getting your brother to steal!
5   Hurray to stealing!
6   Therefore, hurray to getting your brother to steal!

This argument isn't valid. Even though it might look as though it has the same logical form as the first argument, the truth of the premises doesn't guarantee the truth of the conclusion because the premises aren't the kinds of things that can be true or false and the key conditional premise, (4), is gibberish. Consequently, you can't reason from it to get to (6).

Now consider:

7 If stealing is wrong, then it's wrong to get your little brother to steal.

That sentence makes sense, for all of the reasons that (1) makes sense. And consider the argument:

7 If stealing is wrong, then it's wrong to get your little brother to steal.
8 Stealing is wrong.
9 Therefore, it's wrong to get your little brother to steal.

That argument seems to have all the same virtues as the first argument. Whether or not it's sound, it's valid because the premises entail the conclusion. And reasoning from the premises to the conclusion is sensible; this is the sort of argument you might encounter in any discussion of ethics.

If expressivism is true, then the meaning of (7) should be more like the meaning of (4) than the meaning of (1). But it's not: (7) seems more similar to (1) than (4). Again, this isn't just a matter of grammar. All of the virtues that we attributed to (1) and the argument (1–3) hold in virtue of the meanings of the sentences involved. All of the vices that we attributed to (4) and the argument (4–6) hold in virtue of the meanings (or lack thereof) of those sentences. So not only should (7) have a meaning that is similar to (4) if expressivism is true, the sentence (7) and the argument (7–9) should have the same crippling vices as (4) and (4–6). But they do not. The problem isn't just that (7–9) looks more like (1–3) than like (4–6). The problem is that (7–9) has the same virtues that (1–3) has, but the expressivist can't explain why.

Expressivism struggles to give an account of the meaning of sentences when they're embedded in other sentences, for example when they're the antecedent or consequent of a conditional. Furthermore, valid arguments always involve logically complex sentences, and the validity of the argument comes from the meaning of the logically complex sentences. Expressivism struggles to explain why valid arguments are valid and why reasoning in accordance with a valid argument is good reasoning. So expressivists don't only have to explain why moral sentences look like descriptive sentences. They also have to explain how moral sentences function in embedded contexts and in valid argument constructions given that moral sentences aren't descriptive sentences. This is difficult because, as the contrast between (1–3) and (4–6) illustrates, the obvious accounts of embedding and validity depend on the assumption that the sentences in question are descriptive. It's not clear how to develop compositional semantics for non-cognitivism. Many attempts have been made to solve this problem over the years; none have attracted many followers. The Frege–Geach problem remains a devilishly tricky problem for expressivism.

You might think that you've spotted a way out for the expressivist. Perhaps the expressivist could interpret (7) to mean: "If I don't approve of stealing, then I wouldn't approve of getting your brother to steal." Alas, that isn't consistent with expressivism; that's *individual-semantic relativism*. Recall that the difference between the individual-semantic relativist and the expressivist is that relativists say that moral language *reports* our attitudes, whereas expressivists say that moral language *expresses* our attitudes. The Frege–Geach Problem is the problem of coming up with a system of compositional semantics for expression.

2.4.1 Contemporary Complications

Throughout this section, we've been assuming that, for the expressivist, the *entire* meaning of a moral sentence is the expression of an attitude. But perhaps moral sentences have complex meanings with two parts: one part cognitivist, the other part expressivist. This view is **hybrid expressivism**. A hybrid expressivist might say that "Stealing is wrong!" both reports *and* expresses your disapproval of stealing.[7] Because there's no problem with explaining the compositionality of descriptive sentences (like (1) above), hybrid expressivists can explain the compositionality of the descriptive parts of complex moral sentences. But how can a hybrid expressivist deal with the expressive part of the meaning of the sentence? Consider

---

7 Stevenson (1944) proposed something like this. Other hybrid expressivists will have different accounts of what the cognitive meaning and the expressivist meaning are.

the complex sentence "it's not the case that stealing is wrong." If the expressive content takes *narrow scope*, then "it's not the case that" would modify both the descriptive content of the sentence and the expressive content of the sentence. But what does it mean to negate the expressive content of the sentence? This is just the Frege–Geach problem; so no progress has been made. For this reason, most hybrid expressivists will claim that the expressive content takes *wide scope*, meaning that "it's not the case that…" modifies only the descriptive content of the sentence, leaving the expressive content unchanged. That is, both "Stealing is wrong" and "It's not the case that stealing is wrong" express the same attitude. But what attitude could plausibly be expressed by both of those sentences? Hybrid expressivism is interesting, but it's not clear that it helps with the biggest problems for expressivism (Schroeder 2009).

One last complication is worth mentioning. We said that expressivists tend to avoid discussing moral facts and that they deny that moral claims could be true or false. This was the case historically, but not anymore. Many contemporary expressivists have been drawn to a program known as **quasi-realism,** which is an attempt by expressivists to "earn the right" to say everything that realists do. Quasi-realists typically begin this project by accepting deflationism about truth. Deflationists deny that truth or falsity are metaphysical categories; for a deflationist, "It's true that stealing is wrong" is just a long-winded way of saying "Stealing is wrong." The expressivist will happily say "Stealing is wrong" with the understanding that, in doing so, she's expressing disapproval of stealing. By accepting deflationism, then, she can also say, "It's true that stealing is wrong." She's now "earned the right" to speak about the truth and falsity of moral claims.

The quasi-realist project doesn't stop there. It's plausible that if it's true that P, then it's a fact that P. So if the quasi-realist earns the right to say "It's true that stealing is wrong," then she earns the right to say "it's a fact that stealing is wrong." This would mean saying that "fact" isn't a meaningful metaphysical category either, but expressivists can be happy with that; they're generally suspicious of metaphysical categories (Blackburn 1988). We've characterized the debate between the realist and the anti-realist as being about whether or not there are stance-independent moral properties that make moral statements true. But a quasi-realist could deny that "stance-independent property" is a meaningful metaphysical category. So a quasi-realist could say that "Wrongness is a stance-independent property that the act of stealing possesses" is also just a long-winded way of expressing disapproval of stealing. But if the quasi-realist succeeds in her project of "earning the right" to say everything that a realist says, is quasi-realism really a form of anti-realism? After all, if there's nothing that a realist will say but a quasi-realist will deny, wouldn't a successful version of quasi-realism end up being a version of realism (Dreier 2004)? Both the view itself, and how we should categorize it, are subjects of ongoing controversy.

> Expressivism is the view that moral sentences serve to *express* your moral attitudes. This view avoids the problems of error theory and relativism, but at the cost of adopting an incredibly complex and controversial program that revises our basic understanding of how language works. Quasi-realism supplements this with a non-metaphysical account of truth to allow expressivists to say their moral assertions are true. But it gets hard to say what, exactly, distinguishes quasi-realism from realism.

2.5 Moral skepticism

Moral skepticism is the view that it's impossible for us to know anything about morality. Moral skepticism is consistent with realism as we've defined it: it's possible for there to be stance-independent moral facts that are unknowable. Nonetheless, realists generally aren't skeptics, and moral skepticism is frequently viewed as a threat to realism. Indeed, some define realism as the view that there are moral facts *we can know about* (Cuneo 2007, ch. 1). That's because moral skepticism threatens everything realists care about in metaethics.

First, moral skepticism makes realism practically useless. If moral skepticism and realism are both true, then there are some kinds of actions that are morally obligatory and that all agents absolutely *must* do—but no one knows what they are. Sure, *maybe* genocide is wrong, and kindness and charity are good. On the other hand, maybe genocide is morally required, and kindness and charity are serious moral deficiencies. Who knows? The universe is a great mystery. We noted in §1.3.1 that there are two kinds of reasons to worry about the outcome of the realism/anti-realism debate: practical reasons and philosophical angst-related reasons. The existence of *unknowable* moral facts would be practically useless, and knowledge of their existence might even exacerbate philosophical angst. Second, moral realists want to provide us with good reasons for thinking that realism is true. Moral skepticism probably makes this impossible. If we can't know whether any actions are wrong, not even those that realists point to as paradigmatic examples of wrong actions, then it's going to be hard to argue for realism!

Metaphysics, the branch of philosophy that concerns being, is often driven by epistemology, the branch which concerns knowledge and justified belief. The things that we should believe exist are the things that we have reason to believe exist. We can be confident that round squares don't exist because it's impossible for something to be both round and square. But plenty of things that we don't believe exist—unicorns, dragons, demons, honest politicians—aren't *self-contradictory*. We just don't have evidence for them. Similarly, moral anti-realism is often grounded in moral skepticism. Many anti-realists don't believe in stance-independent moral facts largely, or even wholly, because they think there's no good reason to believe in them.

The most common arguments for moral skepticism take off from two of Mackie's arguments we've already discussed: the epistemological queerness argument and the relativity argument. The epistemological queerness argument proceeds from the worry that moral knowledge would have to come from a weird faculty of moral intuition. It's easy to see how that metaphysical concern could be given a skeptical twist. Moral knowledge, if it exists, must come from this faculty. But that faculty doesn't exist, or if it does, the intuitions it generates don't give us knowledge. Therefore, moral knowledge doesn't exist. According to the relativity argument, moral disagreement is best explained by culture, not moral facts; the best explanation for disagreement is that moral facts don't exist. Again, it's easy to see how this can be given a skeptical twist. Disagreement doesn't prove that there are no moral facts, but it might indicate that our moral judgments are unreliable in a way that deprives us of moral knowledge.

Evolutionary debunking arguments are another source of doubt (see Street 2006; Joyce 2007; Lutz 2018). These arguments proceed from the observation that our moral thinking is the product of

Darwinian forces. Helping friends in need gives us a warm, fuzzy feeling, and we usually judge this to be praiseworthy. A population of people who aid each other will be better able to survive than a population of callous egoists. The warm fuzzy feeling, and the moral judgments associated with that feeling, are therefore likely the product of evolutionary pressures. But evolutionary pressures are distinct from moral considerations. If we discover that we're inclined to judge that giving to friends is the right thing to do because of evolution, and not because it's the right thing to do, then this discovery should undermine our confidence in that kind of judgment. If similar things can be said about all moral judgments, then skepticism follows.

Arguments against skepticism mirror arguments against error theory. Just as it strikes many as absurd to suggest that killing innocent people for fun isn't wrong, it seems equally absurd to suggest that we don't know this is wrong. So many philosophers consider skepticism to be a non-starter. Matt is a moral skeptic and Spencer, a realist, considers skepticism to be the strongest threat to realism, so we'll return to these issues.

Moral skepticism is the view that moral knowledge is impossible. While skepticism is compatible with realism, realists are almost never skeptics—and for good reason. The arguments for skepticism are similar to the arguments for error theory. Moreover, if we can't know what's right and wrong, then defenses of realism seem pointless, even if realism turns out to be true.

Chapter 3

Realism

Matt Lutz and Spencer Case

Contents

In the previous chapter, we looked at the different varieties of moral anti-realism. In this chapter, we'll look at different varieties of realism.

3.1 Moral Naturalism

Arguably, the most important metaethical disagreement between moral realists is over **moral naturalism**, the view that moral properties are natural properties. So what's a natural property? There are a variety of views about this. Without surveying them all, we'll simply plump for the one we think is best. We understand a natural property to be a property that can be investigated empirically, i.e., by ordinary observation and the use of scientific methods (Lutz and Lenman 2018). Examples of natural properties include the properties of being red, of being round, of weighing 50 grams, and of being composed primarily of hydrogen.

Some natural properties are substantially more complex than others, and some require sophisticated methods of observation to detect. It took humans until the latter half of the nineteenth century

DOI: 10.4324/9781003183174-4

to figure out that they could investigate the composition of distant stars by looking very carefully at the light they emit. Are moral properties the sort of thing that we can empirically investigate, at least in principle, perhaps with the aid of observational methods that haven't yet been discovered? This question divides moral naturalists from non-naturalists.

Although this characterization of natural properties is common (see, e.g., Shafer-Landau 2003, ch. 3; Smith 1994, 17; Copp 2007, 27–28), it seems to run two questions together: "What sort of properties are moral properties?" and "How can we know whether some moral claim is true?" The claim that moral properties are natural properties looks like an answer to that first question. But when we gave a characterization of "natural properties," we said something that looks a lot like an answer to the second question. We can unify these questions if we think that only one kind of property can be empirically investigated and so deserves the label "natural." To say that moral properties are natural, then, is to say that they're properties of the kind that we can empirically investigate. Thus, to know whether moral properties are natural, we need to know both (a) what properties we can investigate empirically and (b) whether moral properties are properties of that kind. This is a tricky position to be in, since (a) is a contentious question in epistemology and the philosophy of science. Unfortunately, whether or not moral properties count as "natural" depends on how we answer that question.

We offer the following answer to the first question: A traditional view, going back at least to Descartes's *Meditations* (Descartes 1641/2017, 79–80) holds that our experiences give us knowledge of mind-independent properties if those properties have the power to *explain* our sensory experiences. For instance, the property of being round has the power to explain why I have a round experience when I look at something round, like a ball. I have that experience *because* the ball is round. If the ball were a different shape, I wouldn't have had that experience. That's why my experience is evidence that the ball is round. We can say the same thing about all natural properties, including the more complex and difficult-to-study properties that the contemporary sciences reveal to us. We know that typical white dwarf stars are composed primarily of carbon and oxygen by observing the light from those stars through a spectroscope. The light observed in a spectroscope looks the way it does because of the star's composition. If the star had a different composition, then the refracted light would look different. That's why my experiences would give me evidence about the star's composition. So a natural property is one that has the power to make a difference as to what sensory experiences we have, and thereby explain our experiences.

If moral properties can impact our experiences in ways that we can investigate through empirical methods, then they're natural. (To head off a possible counterexample: any kind of "magic" we can imagine that can be empirically investigated in a systematic way just would be a part of the natural order in virtue of that fact, and not really supernatural). This doesn't imply that moral knowledge is trivial if naturalism is true. Our ability to construct a spectroscope and understand what the colors of the refracted light we observe in it mean about the chemical composition of the light source depend on our knowledge of optics, the relations between matter and electromagnetic radiation, and the mechanics of how the materials that make up a spectroscope work, etc. The same might be true of moral properties. Perhaps we can only empirically investigate morality via elaborate experimental setups. Constructing those experimental setups might require extensive theoretical knowledge in physics, psychology, sociology, and even moral theory.

3.1.1   Analytic Naturalism

Moral naturalists say that moral properties are natural properties. This might be because moral terms can be defined in natural terms. To see how this might work, consider the term 'vixen.' We can define the term 'vixen' as 'a female fox;' 'a female fox' is just what the term 'vixen' *means*. This mundane observation has interesting implications. Some words can be defined in terms of other words, and so some words seem to be more fundamental than other words. 'Vixen' is a non-fundamental word. We can define 'vixen' in terms of 'female' and 'fox,' but it's hard to define 'female' in terms of 'vixen.' The fact that the word and concept 'female' is more fundamental than the word and concept 'vixen' doesn't mean that 'female' is itself a fundamental term. It doesn't matter for present purposes whether 'female' can be defined in still simpler terms. What matters is the general framework. We can't go on analyzing words into more basic terms forever; there must be some fundamental terms. Non-fundamental terms, such as 'vixen,' can be analyzed in other terms. Fundamental terms, such as 'red,' can't be.[1]

So are any moral terms fundamental, or can all moral terms be defined in non-moral terms? If no moral terms are fundamental, then as we keep analyzing our language, we'll eventually arrive at a point at which everything is stated in fundamental terms, and none of those fundamental terms will be moral terms. The view that moral terms can be defined in descriptive terms is known as **analytic naturalism**, or **analytic descriptivism**.[2] Because moral terms can be analyzed in descriptive terms, the moral properties to which those moral terms refer can be identified with the properties that those descriptive terms refer to. Since (it's widely assumed that) descriptive terms refer to natural properties, this means that moral terms refer to natural properties.[3] Thus, moral properties are natural properties. If a moral term, M, can be analyzed in descriptive terms, D, then the pure moral claim "All Ds are M" will be true in virtue of the meanings of D and M. Claims that are true in virtue of their meanings are known as analytic claims. That's why the view is called "analytic naturalism."

1   The word 'red' has a dictionary entry, of course, but dictionaries generally attempt to define 'red' by giving examples of red things or else by talking about the band of the electromagnetic spectrum taken up by red light. Neither of these is a definition in the sense we're interested in here. A list of red things isn't a definition of 'red,' and the claim that redness is a portion of the electromagnetic spectrum is a synthetic property identity claim, about which more shortly.

2   The view that moral terms can be analyzed into normative-but-not-moral terms is sometimes called *normativism*. Normativists aren't analytic descriptivists, but we can't say more than this, because different normativists say different things about the nature of normative terms and normative properties. Some normativists are Kantian constructivists, others are non-naturalist realists, and others are synthetic naturalists. The issues that confront these different varieties of normativism mirror the difficulties that confront constructivism, non-naturalism, and synthetic naturalism in general.

3   This assumption is common but problematic. Descriptive terms are "is" terms, as contrasted with normative "ought" terms (see §1.2). And natural properties are those properties that can be studied by the sciences, which are (plausibly) the properties that can explain our experiences. But there are plausibly descriptive terms that refer to non-natural or supernatural properties. The terms 'angelic' or 'conscious' are descriptive, but it's dubious whether being angelic or being conscious are natural properties.

The strongest argument against analytic naturalism, advanced by twentieth-century British philosopher G.E. Moore, is the **open-question argument**. Moore may not have been the first to make this argument, but he made it famous. He asks us to compare the following two questions:

1   This fox is a vixen; but is it a female?
2   This is pleasurable; but is it good?

(1) answers itself. 'Vixen' just means 'female fox,' so anyone who understands the meanings of these words can see that the answer must be "yes." A "no" answer would be contradictory. So we say that (1) has a "closed feel." Yet if we know that something is pleasurable, that doesn't obviously settle whether it's good. Unlike (1), (2) has an "open feel:" it seems like we could deny that a pleasurable thing is good without contradicting ourselves. People can rationally disagree about the answer to this question while agreeing about its meaning. There's a general lesson here: *any* question of the form "X has descriptive property D, but does it have property M?" will seem open. This means that we cannot analyze any moral term 'M' in terms of any descriptive term 'D.' Therefore, analytic naturalism is false (Moore 1903, §13).

The most straightforward defense of analytic naturalism is to say that this argument overgeneralizes. The conclusion that *no* moral term could be defined in *any* descriptive terms is an awfully strong conclusion to draw from a single example! The open-question argument thus seems to advance a conclusion that's stronger than its premises support. This worry wouldn't evaporate if we added one or two (or ten) further supporting examples. If a moral term can be defined in descriptive terms, there's presumably one correct definition (and maybe a handful of other equivalent definitions), but an infinite number of incorrect definitions. So no matter how many incorrect definitions I give for some moral term 'M,' I can't be certain that there's no correct definition of 'M' out there that I haven't tried yet (Finlay 2014, ch. 1).

Sharon Rawlette has argued that, while (2) might have an open feel, the closely related (2*) does not:

2*   This is pleasurable; but is it good in some way?

(2*) answers itself because 'pleasurable' means 'a good way for things to feel.' Thus, it can be analytic that some things (particularly, pleasure) are good *in a way*. The question only remains open if we ask whether something is good *all things considered*, as (2) does (Rawlette 2020, ch. 4). Yet it's not clear that being good *in a way* matters from the standpoint of morality. If a toaster has the ability to make nicely brown toast, that's good *in a way*, but that has nothing to do with morality (compare Thomson, 2008, ch. 1). Similarly, the pleasure that an ax murderer gets from plying his grisly craft *feels* good, but that pleasure isn't obviously *morally* good. (Rawlette would say that this pleasure is morally good, but that it's outweighed by the suffering of the victims.)

Nevertheless, as the example of the good toaster reminds us, we often use terms like 'good' in non-moral ways. It's the *moral* use of these terms that ethicists are interested in, and it's the moral use of value terms that seems to resist analysis in descriptive terms. This is because moral terms have, while descriptive terms lack, a distinctive moral "feel" that we tried to characterize in Chapter 1. If moral terms inherently have a different feel from descriptive terms, then that's a good reason to think that any question of the form "X is D, but is X M?" will feel open (Wittgenstein 1969; Enoch 2011, ch. 5). The term 'M' will have that special feel to it, but 'D' won't, and thus the question will remain open. Of course, the analytic naturalist might insist that if we only locate the *right* definition of the right moral term, we'll find a 'D' that captures all the moral feel of 'M.' How compelling this response is depends in part on how distinctive you think the feel of moral terms is.

3.1.2 Synthetic Naturalism

Synthetic naturalism combines moral naturalism with the view that at least some moral terms are unanalyzable in descriptive terms. Hence, there are no analytic claims of the form "If X is D, then X is M." This doesn't mean that synthetic naturalists deny that some of that form are *true*. Synthetic naturalists might even agree with stronger claims, like "X is D *if and only if* X is M." But they deny that any claims like this are *analytic*.

Synthetic naturalists like to explain their view using the example of 'water' and 'H_2O.' Those two terms refer to the same thing. But 'H_2O' isn't the *definition* of 'water,' or vice versa. Though H_2O is mentioned in some dictionary definitions of 'water,' we didn't discover, and couldn't have discovered, that water is H_2O by analyzing the meaning of the word 'water.' We established this empirically.

Before the crucial experiments were conducted, you could understand the meaning of 'water' without knowing that water is H_2O. So 'X is water if and only if X is H_2O' (or, more colloquially, 'Water is H_2O') isn't the *definition* of the word 'water.' It's a *synthetic property identity claim*.[4] Thus, the synthetic moral naturalist says, it's possible that there's a synthetic property identity claim of the form 'X is M if and only if X is D.'

However, synthetic naturalists don't need to say that there are synthetic property identity claims. In a synthetic property identity claim, like 'water is H_2O,' two different terms refer to the same thing. Analytic naturalists and the kind of synthetic naturalist that we discussed in the last paragraph both say that there are descriptive terms that refer to moral properties like goodness. But other naturalists say that only one word or phrase refers to goodness, and that word is 'good.' Why would we expect otherwise? This is fully compatible with naturalism. Naturalism isn't the view that we can use descriptive words or phrases to refer to moral properties; it's the view that moral properties are natural properties. And on our understanding of natural properties, this means that moral properties have the power to explain our experiences and thereby be empirically investigated. So if you ask a naturalist, "If you think that goodness is a natural property, what natural property is it?" a naturalist can respond "Goodness is goodness, which is a natural property." That might not be the most informative answer, but it's consistent. Naturalists who respond in this way tend to call themselves "non-reductive naturalists," although this label has been the source of endless confusion.[5] Jonathan Dancy (2006) and Pekka

---

4   See Chapter 3, footnote 1.
5   "Reductive naturalism" is a common phrase in metaethics, but it's used in a variety of ways, which makes it impossible for us to give a proper definition of the phrase. There are two main problems. The first is that 'reduction' is sometimes used to refer to a *metaphysical relation* and sometimes to a *linguistic relation*. Some philosophers in the 1980s developed a view that they referred to as "non-reductive naturalism" because they rejected analytic naturalism and so rejected the idea that moral terms could be *linguistically* "reduced" (Boyd 1988; Sturgeon 1988). However, because many philosophers can't help but think of reduction as a metaphysical relation, the non-reductive naturalists have occasionally been understood as advancing a metaphysical thesis of dubious coherence. The second, related problem is that there's no agreement on what metaphysical relation "reduction" is supposed to refer to (compare Rosen 2010). We'll avoid

Väyrynen (2021) call this view **"one-term naturalism,"** as opposed to the "two-term naturalism" that endorses (analytic or synthetic) property identity claims. Those are better labels.

Synthetic naturalists don't need to worry about the open-question argument, which purports to show that no pure moral claims are analytically true. However, synthetic naturalism has its own problems. Synthetic naturalists hold both that some moral terms are fundamental and that they refer to natural moral properties. *How* do fundamental moral terms refer to moral properties? To answer this, they need to consider the more general question: how do fundamental terms in general refer to things? The most common answer to this question is the **causal theory of reference**, according to which fundamental terms refer to whatever properties causally regulate their use within a community of language users. For example, 'red', which seems to be a fundamental term, refers to redness because redness is the property that causes normal English-speakers to say—and think—things like "That's red." Similarly, 'good', another fundamental term, refers to goodness because goodness is the property that causes English-speakers to say things like "That's good." Goodness doesn't just have the power to explain our experiences, it also has the power to explain our use of the term 'good,' and that's why 'good' refers to goodness.

Unfortunately, this solution gives rise to a version of the disagreement problem for relativism that we looked at in Chapter 2. Consider two different communities that make diverging moral judgments. Why do their moral judgments differ? Because they take different things to be good or bad. Their judgments about goodness and badness are causally regulated by different things—different things cause them to say (and judge) things like "That's good." And therefore, according to the causal theory of reference, the word 'good' will mean different things for them. 'Good' in the mouth of someone from community A will refer to whatever property causally regulates community A's use of the term 'good.' 'Good' in the mouth of someone from community B will refer to whatever property causally regulates community B's use of the term 'good.' Those properties aren't the same. Thus, if someone from A says,

---

talking about "reduction" anywhere in the main text; it has become a confused term which serves only to propagate other confusions.

"X is good" and someone from B says, "X isn't good," they're not talking about the same property, and aren't really disagreeing with one another. We call this the **causal relativism problem**. (It's commonly known as the "Moral Twin Earth problem" because it was first illustrated with a thought experiment called the "Moral Twin Earth" thought experiment; see Horgan and Timmons 1992).

The causal relativism problem is usually thought to be a problem about the possibility of disagreement, but the problem isn't just about disagreement. One version of the disagreement problem for relativism stresses that it's possible to question your own attitudes or the attitudes that are present in your society. "I approve of X, and so does everyone else in my society, but is X really good?" is an intelligible thought. It's possible to conclude that X isn't really good even though you and everyone else approves of X. Similarly, "X regulates my community's use of the term 'good'; but is X really good?" seems intelligible. And, equally, it seems coherent to conclude that X isn't good even though X causally regulates our use of the term 'good.' The fundamental problem is that the causal theory of reference makes whether or not something is good a matter of social conventions regarding what will cause us to judge something is 'good' (Sinhababu 2019). Intuitively, it's possible to live in a society whose beliefs about morality and tendencies to call things "good" are systematically unreliable. Any view that accepts the causal theory of reference will therefore be vulnerable to the same objections that plague relativism.

Synthetic naturalists can respond to the causal relativism problem by rejecting the causal theory of reference. But then they need to explain how fundamental terms refer to things. That's a heavy burden to take on, and naturalists haven't yet developed a promising alternative account of the reference of fundamental terms in general, or fundamental moral terms in particular, that could allow them to address this issue.

Taken together, the open-question argument and the causal relativism problem constitute a major problem for naturalism. The open-question argument prevents us from saying that moral terms are analyzable in descriptive terms. But the causal relativism problem prevents us from saying that moral terms are unanalyzable and refer to the properties that causally regulate our use of those terms. So what do moral terms refer to, then, and how do they do it? Without an account of how moral terms could refer to natural properties, or an accompanying account of how we can know which natural properties moral properties refer to, moral naturalism remains problematic.

> Moral naturalists say that moral properties are natural properties. Analytic naturalists say that this is because moral terms can be analyzed in descriptive terms and, because descriptive terms refer to natural properties, so do moral terms. The biggest challenge for analytic naturalism is the open-question argument. Synthetic naturalists say that moral terms can't be analyzed in descriptive terms, but moral terms still refer to natural properties. The most common account of how moral terms refer to natural properties is provided by causal theory of reference, but this leads to the causal relativism problem.

3.2   Moral Non-naturalism

We turn now to **non-naturalist moral realism**, or **moral non-naturalism**. On this view, moral facts are *sui generis*, i.e., "of their own kind." While it's common for non-naturalists to explain their view in these terms, we're uncertain whether this lends much clarity. (Can you think of something that isn't the kind of thing that it is?) What non-naturalists have in mind when they say that moral facts are *sui generis* is the idea that moral facts aren't natural facts. Nor are they supernatural facts that are made true by the commands of a deity (more on that later). They're a third—unique—kind of thing. Just as metaethical naturalism is closely linked with empiricism, non-naturalism is linked with **rationalism**, the view that we have substantive knowledge that goes beyond what we learn by our senses (synthetic *a priori* knowledge, in philosopher speak). Non-naturalists generally think that moral intuition is an important source of information about reality. Indeed, Huemer (2005) calls non-naturalism "intuitionism."

Non-naturalists typically combine arguments for moral realism with arguments against naturalism. So far, we've looked at several different varieties of both anti-realism and naturalism, and surveyed the major objections to those various views. Non-naturalists tend to agree with those objections, leaving non-naturalism as the only realist view on the table. This is more than just an argument by elimination, however. Both moral naturalism and the various forms of anti-realism are in tension with various deep-seated intuitions about morality. Moral naturalists struggle to capture the distinctive normative feel of morality, and anti-realists struggle to account for the fact that some moral claims, like the claim that needless cruelty is bad, seem to be straightforwardly, objectively, authoritatively *true*. Non-naturalism captures those intuitions.

Alas, there's no such thing as a free lunch, and these advantages come with a hefty price tag (at least in the eyes of critics). Most obviously, non-naturalism entails abandoning **naturalism**, the idea, roughly, that all properties we can know about are natural properties. Many philosophers find naturalism appealing because of its simplicity: we have no good reason to go beyond science into the realm of weird entities that we know about via mysterious faculties. Non-naturalists reply that they don't reject science, but there are more things in Heaven and Earth than are dreamt of in naturalist philosophies. Nevertheless, even non-naturalists will want to keep some non-naturalistic entities at arms' distance. Some non-naturalists will welcome the existence of aesthetic facts, souls, and libertarian free will into their metaphysics. But what about God, angels, auras, and a faculty that directly bears witness to spiritual truths (see Plantinga 2000)? Most non-naturalists will find some of these things hard to take seriously. Naturalists can easily avoid disreputable association with spooky things because they don't accept anything non-natural. It's a bit more awkward for non-naturalists to argue against the inclusion of these things into their metaphysics since they have no objection to non-natural properties as such.

There are three general strategies that non-naturalists have pursued for answering these challenges. The first we might call the "robust realist" strategy. **Robust realists**, like David Enoch (2011), Erik Wielenberg (2014), and Stephanie Leary (2017), attempt to provide constructive accounts of the nature of moral properties that can answer the most pressing metaphysical and epistemological challenges to non-naturalism. Robust realists seek to explain, for instance, how moral intuitions could be reliable indicators of moral truth, or why moral facts supervene on natural facts. Fully surveying all of the challenges to non-naturalism that have been developed over the years and the various avenues of response that robust realists have developed in order to answer those challenges would take us too far afield. But robust realist responses are unified in that they take these challenges seriously and attempt to answer them head-on by providing constructive explanations.

The second, somewhat more modest strategy for answering challenges to non-naturalism, is to appeal to what has been called the
"companions-in-guilt" defense, though we think it really should
be called the **companions-in-*innocence* defense** (it's a *defense*, after
all). This strategy attempts to show that arguments parallel to those
made against the existence of non-naturalist moral facts, or our
capacity to know them, would jeopardize some entities or knowledge that critics would likely say are "innocent." Here are two different ways the companions-in-innocence defense might be run,
depending on whether the non-naturalist is defending himself from
an epistemic or a metaphysical objection:

Epistemic companions-in-innocence

1   If we can't have knowledge of non-natural moral facts, then we
    can't have knowledge of X either.
2   But we do have knowledge of X!
3   Therefore, we can have knowledge of non-natural moral
    facts.

Metaphysical companions-in-innocence

1   If anti-realist arguments refute non-natural moral facts, then
    parallel arguments refute X facts as well.
2   Parallel arguments don't refute X facts (because there clearly
    are facts of that kind).
3   Therefore, anti-realist arguments don't refute non-natural moral
    facts.

Whether these arguments succeed or fail will depend on what
X is. Mathematical facts are among the most promising innocent
companions. Mathematical facts concern subject matters such as
numbers and idealized shapes, which are abstract and thus (possibly) not "natural" entities. And we seem to have knowledge of
numbers through a faculty of intuition that is *a priori*, meaning
that it derives conclusions independently of experience. So numbers
seem metaphysically and epistemically mysterious in the same ways
that non-natural moral properties are. But we shouldn't be skeptics
about mathematical facts or mathematical knowledge. It might be
hard to say what the nature of the fact that $2 + 2 = 4$ is, or how
that's the kind of fact that we can know. But of course $2 + 2 = 4$,
and of course we know that $2 + 2 = 4$!

In order for this argument to work, moral knowledge has to be analogous to mathematical knowledge, and moral facts have to be analogous to mathematical facts in all relevant respects. Whether the analogy holds depends on the outcome of some long-running debates in the philosophy of mathematics. The analogue of non-naturalist moral realism in philosophy of mathematics is known as mathematical Platonism, which is popular, but controversial. There are naturalist realists and anti-realists in the philosophy of mathematics as well. (For an overview of mathematical Platonism, see Linnebo 2018; for a defense of the companions-in-innocence objection, see Clarke-Doane 2020). If Platonism is false, then the analogy with mathematics doesn't help the non-naturalist realist.

Perhaps there's a better companion-in-innocence than mathematics, or maybe the analogy with mathematics is a good one. At any rate, what's distinctive about the companions-in-innocence strategy is that it doesn't directly try to provide a constructive answer to the skeptical challenges that beset non-naturalism. Instead, the companions-in-innocence strategy attempts to show that some constructive answer *must* be available, even if we don't know what it is. Although we might not be able to explain precisely how knowledge of moral properties is possible, it must be possible *somehow* because mathematical knowledge is possible, and moral knowledge is just like mathematical knowledge in all relevant respects.

The third strategy for responding to skeptical challenges is to endorse **quietism,** the view that the questions realists face about the nature of moral properties and how we could know about them are ultimately incoherent. Quietists thereby dismiss these problems. Quietism has a lot in common with, and has been influenced by, quasi-realism. Like quasi-realists, quietists re-interpret seemingly metaethical claims as first-order normative claims (Kremm and Schafer 2017). Those first-order claims are then justified by the methods of moral theory; no further meaningful questions can be asked about the status of moral facts.

T. M. Scanlon (2014) argues that it makes no sense to ask whether moral facts *really* exist because there's no such thing as a domain-neutral category of "existence." Everything that exists exists in its own way, and the standards of existence for that kind of thing are discerned through the methods of inquiry in the relevant domain. To illustrate, consider mathematical sets. Do sets exist? Set theorists say "certainly." They can give you rigorous proofs of the existence of certain sets that proceed from the accepted axioms of set theory. But what about those axioms? How do we know that they, and the proofs based on them, tell us anything about the way the world is, independently of how set theorists think? Scanlon maintains that these further questions are misguided. The ontology and methodology of sets are *internal* to the domain of set theory, and philosophers are simply mistaken if they think that there are more fundamental, external questions that we can ask about that domain. Similarly, says Scanlon, there are moral facts. It's a fact that killing is wrong. How do we know that killing is wrong? By the methods of normative ethics: intuition and reflective equilibrium. But what's the nature of those moral facts? In what sense do they exist? How do we know that those methods are reliable with respect to those moral facts? Scanlon claims it's a mistake to think those questions are meaningful.

Critics of quietism want to know how many domains there are and what distinguishes them from each other (Enoch and McPherson 2017). Why couldn't we say that there's a domain of "schmeasons", just as there's a domain of reasons, and that the truths about both are determined by the appropriate domain-internal standards? And why couldn't they conflict, so that we have "schmeasons" to do one thing and reasons to do something incompatible? It seems reasonable to ask what we Just Plain Ought to do in the event of such a conflict (Case 2016), but it's hard to see how a quietist could make sense of that question. We simply have two domains recommending two irreconcilable courses of action with no domain-independent standard capable of adjudicating between them. Andrew Sepielli (2020) calls this objection to quietism the *counter-normativity challenge*. Building on this critique, Dan Wodak (2017) argues that quietism allows for us to create new reasons "out of thin air" by positing them into existence. If that's right, then quietism is better classified as a form of constructivism, not realism. That's a problem because quietists advertise their view as one that can deliver everything realists appreciate about realism.

The quietists aren't going quietly in response to these objections. Scanlon (2017) and Sepielli (2020) independently fire back at the counter-reasons objection, along similar lines. They each argue that if "schmeasons" play the same psychological, motivational, and social role as reasons, then "schmeasons" talk is just "reasons" talk; hence, the terminology is redundant, and we have only one domain, not two. Scanlon (2017) also rejects the idea that any "super-domain" encompassing all first-order domains is presupposed in philosophers" talk about existence. There's (again) much more to say here; suffice it to say that it seems to us that the critics are right: quietists face insuperable challenges when it comes to specifying in a plausible way what domains we should accept and why. Once again, there's no such thing as a free lunch.

Moral non-naturalists deny that moral properties are natural; they're a distinctive kind of thing. This theory seems to do a good job of capturing some of our core conceptual commitments about morality. However, non-naturalism confronts sharp metaphysical and epistemological problems: what is that distinctive kind of thing, exactly, and how can we know about it? Non-naturalists can meet those challenges head on by providing constructive explanations, appeal to companions-in-innocence arguments to show that constructive explanations must exist (even if we're not in a position to give them now), or go quietist and reject the meaningfulness of those challenges.

3.3 What about God?

Some readers might be wondering when God is going to enter the picture. So let's discuss the view that basic moral truths are true because of what God commands. This view is known as **divine command theory** or **divine voluntarism**; we'll call it "voluntarism" for short. It's important to keep in mind that the voluntarist isn't committed to saying we can know moral truths only by divine revelation, or that basic moral truths are inaccessible to atheists, though the voluntarist might also say these things. Voluntarism leaves it open whether an atheist could uncover important moral truths without knowing that these truths depend on God or His will. Voluntarism is a view about what makes actions right or wrong, not about how we come to know about rightness and wrongness.

Voluntarism is widely held among religious people—many see it as the default position—and it has some sophisticated defenders. Nevertheless, it's not a popular view among philosophers, even those who believe in God. Philosophical discussion of voluntarism begins (and frequently ends) with Plato's dialog, *Euthyphro*, in which Socrates and Euthyphro discuss the nature of piety, or holiness, something Euthyphro claims at the outset to know a lot about (see the translation by Grube 1997). Euthyphro proposes that piety is "what the gods love." Socrates demands a clarification: "The point which I should first wish to understand is whether the pious or holy is beloved by the gods because it is holy, or holy because it is beloved of the gods." His question in a monotheistic and meta-ethical context would be: "Given that God commands all and only good things, does God command what He does *because it's morally good*—or are morally good things morally good only *because of God's commandments?*" And relatedly: "Does God forbid bad things because they're bad, or are they bad because He forbids them?"

This question, in any of these forms, has come to be known as the **Euthyphro dilemma**, and it's often regarded as a decisive objection to voluntarism. The trouble is this: If God commands what he does *because it's good,* then goodness must have an independent existence that God is responding to when He decides what to command us to do. That entails that voluntarism is false since God's commandments are supposed to explain why things are good and bad in the first place. Theists might also find the first option objectionable on theological grounds. Voluntarism, some believers worry, "contradicts the absolute sovereignty of God; it implies that there are realities other than Himself that do not owe their being to His creative activity" (Alston 1990, 318). Some believers might feel uncomfortable with the view that God created heaven and earth, but not right and wrong.

Voluntarists must take the second option: what's morally good (and bad) is so because of God's commandments. But if what's morally good is only good because God says it is, then there's no moral standard above God's commandments. If God didn't forbid rape, then rape wouldn't be wrong, and if God commanded rape, then it would be right just because He commanded it. You might think: Of course God wouldn't command rape! But why not? It can't be because it's wrong. Moral facts about the wrongness of rape can't explain why God forbids rape if the wrongness of rape is itself supposed to be explained in terms of God's commandments.

The voluntarist might bite the bullet and say that God's commandments really are morally arbitrary. Historically, surprisingly few philosophers have been willing to say this without qualification. William of Ockham (1285–1347 CE) notoriously claimed that God could have made theft and adultery morally right by commanding them (King 2006).[6] This position makes him an outlier among Christian philosophers, who generally think that such actions are intrinsically wrong. In her study of ethics in the classical period of Islamic philosophy (spanning roughly 700–1300 CE/80–680 AH), Miriam Al-Attar concludes that voluntarism "is not the prevailing theory in Islamic thought … Moreover, it has no special place in Arabo-Islamic cultural heritage, nor could it be supported by Qur'ānic evidence" (2010, 142). Some Islamic theologians in the Ash'arite school did think that God's commandments determine our moral *duties*. They generally conceded that God can't change basic value facts like "what's harmful is bad," though this seems to amount only to the claim that God doesn't contradict Himself, since "harm" is bad by definition.

The voluntarist might also say that God's loving character explains why He wouldn't command evil deeds (Kurtz and Craig 2009, 30). A *loving* God wouldn't command rape; moreover, God's character is eternal, so we can be sure He will never command such things. We find this response unsatisfactory. First, we can ask why God is loving. It can't be because *it's good to be loving*. That posits an independent moral standard, which puts us on the first horn of the dilemma. We might say that God has no reason to be loving; that's just a fundamental fact about His nature. But that seems to make God's love, and hence his love-based commands, morally arbitrary. Second, as Wes Morriston points out, even if God's eternal nature makes it impossible for God to command rape, it would nonetheless be true, according to voluntarism, that *if* God commanded rape, then rape would be morally good (2009, 253). That

---

6   There's a wrinkle here: Ockham thought that God couldn't make 'murder', 'theft', or 'adultery' permissible because these terms (or their Latin equivalents) imply wrongness. But God could make permissible all the actions these words *denote*. Strictly speaking, God can't make murder right because 'murder is wrong' is true by definition and God doesn't contradict Himself. But He could make any sort of killing morally permissible, or even obligatory, by commanding it.

implication is repugnant even granting that God would never issue such a commandment.

A different response is to "split the horns" of the dilemma. God neither commands what He commands because it's good, nor are things good because God commands them. Instead, God's commandments are good because God Himself *is the Good* (Alston 1990, 320–321; Craig 2009, 169–170). At this point, there's a new dilemma similar to the first, which Morriston calls the "son of Euthyphro" dilemma: Does God have the properties He has *because they're good*, or are they good *because they belong to God*? Morriston raises a different concern: "Why should it make any difference to the good-makingness of compassion, say, if there is (or isn't) a supremely compassionate God?" (2009, 253). The goodness of compassion seems independent of whether or not anything has that property to the maximal degree.

To end on a point about philosophical taxonomy: we chose to discuss voluntarism in the realism section, but it's not obvious how it should be categorized. The view on which God, or God's nature, is the standard of goodness seems like a version of realism since God's existence (if He exists) is a stance-independent moral fact. On the other hand, if God creates the basic facts about moral obligations by issuing commandments, then that seems like a version of anti-realism, since the moral facts depend on facts about God's moral stance. True, the basic moral facts on this view are independent of *human* stances. So if we understand "stance-independence" to mean "independence from human stances" then voluntarism counts as a form of realism. But we find that restriction to human stances arbitrary. The fact that voluntarism is arguably a version of constructivism is ironic given that proponents advertise voluntarism's supposed ability to vindicate ethical objectivity (Adams 1999, 256; Craig 2011). There's more to be said, but we'll leave the voluntarist to work out his own salvation—literally as well as figuratively.

Voluntarism is popular among typical religious believers. But unqualified forms of it are widely rejected among philosophers—even religious philosophers—on account of the Euthyphro Dilemma. We think even the most sophisticated versions of it can't overcome the Euthyphro objection.

3.4   Part I Conclusion

You should now understand what metaethics is about and have some sense of the dividing lines between various metaethical positions. It bears repeating that we've only provided a sketch of these debates so that you're prepared for what's to come. Nonetheless, we've indicated that we don't find some of these views very plausible. We both think that relativism makes a mess of moral language. Expressivism makes an even bigger mess of moral language. Kantian constructivists load too much into their account of rational agency. Naturalistic realism is going to have a hard time getting around the one-two punch of the open-question argument and the causal relativism problem. And then there's voluntarism; neither of us is a theist, but even if we were theists, we wouldn't try to ground ethics on God's commandments (though Spencer would be more sympathetic to the view that God simply *is* goodness). So we really agree on quite a lot.

But we don't agree on everything. Spencer is a realist. Matt is an error theorist and a skeptic. Now it's time for us to part ways and make the case for our respective views. The fun part of this book is about to begin.

Part II

Opening Arguments

A. For Realism

Chapter 4

The Moorean Argument

Spencer Case

Contents

Bertrand Russell once said that even though he gravitated toward moral anti-realism, he couldn't quite believe that bullfighting was only "wrong" because of how he felt about it (1944, 51). Like Russell, I'm compelled to think that some of my moral judgments are true for reasons independent of my reactions, just as I'm compelled to believe that my sensory perceptions aren't internally generated. When I reflect on the wrongness of the trans-Atlantic slave trade, I can't help but think that my mind has snagged on some protruding shard of reality. Unlike Russell at the time of that writing, I trust that intuition and embrace realism. In this chapter and the next one, I'll defend this position. The argument I'll defend in this chapter is inspired by "Moorean" responses to external world skepticism. This defense of realism isn't very original (for a precedent, see Brambraugh 1969), but I think it's no worse for that.

4.1 Moorean Anti-skepticism

If a logically valid argument with plausible-looking premises leads to a conclusion that seems unacceptable, then we may either reassess

DOI: 10.4324/9781003183174-7

our rejection of the conclusion or rethink our acceptance of the premises. Logically, one is as good as the other. But sometimes rejecting an argument's premises in order to avoid its conclusion is the only *reasonable* option. As eighteenth-century Scottish philosopher Thomas Reid observes:

> A traveller who has good judgment may mistake his way, and be led unawares onto a wrong route; and for as long as the wrong road in front of him is open and passable he may go on without suspicion, and be followed by others; but when the road ends at a coal-pit, he doesn't need much judgment to know that he has gone wrong, and perhaps to find out what has led him astray.
>
> (*Inquiry* 1.8)

Inconsistency is the surest philosophical coal pit, but some logically coherent views probably constitute coal pits as well. G. E. Moore, a twentieth-century successor to Reid, thought that we must reject philosophical views that are inconsistent with common sense knowledge. Moore's examples of common sense include his knowledge that he has a human body, that the Earth existed before he was born, and that he has interacted with bodies other than his own (1993, 107). What unifies this list? Of course, common sense beliefs are *common*: they're accepted with a high degree of certainty by almost every sane person, and not only in one culture or epoch. They're also frequently presupposed in ordinary human interactions, and highly credible.

Does the fact that a particular belief is a part of common sense explain why it's credible? This depends on what kind of account of common sense we want to give. On one kind of account, common sense beliefs are justified because they have some particular feature in common that explains their epistemic status. Moore's account is of this kind: "common sense" beliefs are justified, and non-negotiable, because they're starting points that everyone, including philosophers with revisionist views, must share in order to be understood, and maybe even to think at all (Vanrie 2021). The alternative is to define common sense beliefs in terms of their authority. According to Jonathan Fuqua, a "Common Sense Thesis" is a proposition that is "epistemically superior to philosophical skeptical arguments to the contrary" (2021, 6944; see also Kelly 2005, 81). David Lewis called such claims "Moorean facts" (1996, 549). Of course, if a

"Common Sense Thesis" or a "Moorean fact" withstands any philosophical argument against it, then the philosophical revisionist will say that whatever belief he wants to overturn never had that status in the first place.

I see no advantage in building philosophical invincibility into the definitions, and so I'll say that a "common sense" claim enjoys a very high degree of plausibility so that almost everyone, including the interlocutor, if he's being honest, accepts it. Conceivably, philosophical arguments could overturn common sense, but the revisionist has a heavy burden of proof to overcome. Now since I'm defining common sense as a body of beliefs that enjoys this strong-but-not-invincible standing, I can't *explain* the credibility of any particular common-sense belief by appealing to the fact that it's commonsensical. That would be circular. For dialectical purposes, that's OK, so long as my premises seem plausible to *you*. In the fullness of time, we'll want a complete story, particularly about how we come to know common sense theses that are neither true by definition, nor verifiable by observation. Here I'll say only that I think an important part of this story is a general principle of self-trust: we should accept what seems hard to deny unless we have good reason to think the appearances are deceiving.

Reid is remembered as a critic of Hume, but one of his most important arguments was in response to René Descartes. In *Meditations on First Philosophy*, Descartes tried to employ skepticism in a controlled way in order to locate the most incorrigible beliefs. He imagined that an evil demon was systematically deceiving him with false sensory perceptions, and, like a philosophical escape artist, tried to extricate himself from this skeptical straightjacket using pure reason. (Of course, he'd only do this if he knew the outcome in advance). Reid thought that this was irrational. Reason and the senses come from the "same workshop" (*Inquiry* 6.20). There's no reason to trust one and not the other. Neither the senses nor reason needs outside accreditation in order to be a source of knowledge. Doubting all of our faculties at once would make the straightjacket unbeatable (not even Descartes attempts this) while Descartes's selective skepticism is arbitrary. So we must trust *all* our mental faculties.

If we should trust our reason, we should trust our senses; and if we should trust both of these things, then we should trust our moral intuition, too. Michael Huemer's (2001; 2005, 99–101) principle of Phenomenal Conservatism is a more recent formulation of this basic idea. According to Phenomenal Conservatism, appearances are a basic source of epistemic justification; as a consequence, we should trust all appearances, whether they're sensory perceptions or intuitions, unless we have some reason to reject them. In another recent development of Reid's thought, Linda Zagzebski (2015) argued that the logic of the "workshop" argument extends to others' minds: if we should trust the faculties of our own minds, then we should usually trust those same faculties in the minds of others. If she's right, then it's foolish to dismiss things that seem true to almost everyone, in many different cultures and epochs. This strengthens the case for relying upon common sense: the fact that a claim seems clearly true to many minds, in many different circumstances, is good evidence of its truth.

Moore saw nothing improper about directly appealing to Common Sense to rebut radical philosophical doctrines. For instance, here's how Moore criticizes "Hume's principles" (don't worry about what those are):

> It seems to me that, in fact, there really is no better argument than the following. I *do* know that this pencil exists; but I could not know this, if Hume's principles were true; *therefore*, Hume's principles, one or both of them, are false. I think this argument really is as strong and good a one as any that could be used: and I think it really is conclusive. In other words, I think that [the implication that] if Hume's principles were true, I could not know of the existence of this pencil, is a *reductio ad absurdum* [proof of the absurdity] of those principles.
>
> (Moore 1993, 71–72)

The basic template of a **Moorean argument**, then, is:

Moorean argument

1 If [philosophical view], then [negation of some common sense claim].
2 But [common sense claim]!
3 Therefore, negation of [philosophical view].

If you find this groan-inducing like a bad pun, you're not alone. I'm reminded of a scene in *Raiders of the Lost Ark*, the 1981 adventure film that launched the Indiana Jones franchise. During a long chase sequence through the streets of Cairo, the hero, Indiana

Jones, played by Harrison Ford, encounters a baddie deftly bran-
dishing a saber; the audience is led to believe that this is the prelude
to an impressive fight scene. Instead, Jones, looking annoyed, pulls
out a pistol and simply shoots his antagonist.[1] The skeptic, like the
saber-bearer, has intimidating weaponry, but Moore says that we
can dispatch him with a single unsporting shot. Kant complains
that appeals to common sense are a cheap ruse "whereby the dull-
est windbag can confidently take on the most profound thinker and
hold his own with him" (1783/2004, 9). I don't fault the windbag
for bringing a gun to a knife fight, but Kant isn't the only philosopher who cries foul. Wittgenstein is also unimpressed:

> If you do know here is one hand [a reference to another of
> Moore's shameless appeals to common sense (1993, 147–170)]
> we'll grant you all the rest. When one says that such and such a
> proposition can't be proved, of course that does not mean that
> it can't be derived from other propositions; any proposition can
> be derived from other ones. But they may be no more certain
> than it is itself.
> (Wittgenstein 1969, 2–2e)

Well, perhaps we *should* grant Moore "all the rest." If proofs must
proceed from premises that are more certain than their conclusions,
then, necessarily, no arguments for our most certain beliefs could constitute "proofs." Are such arguments necessarily futile, then? Thomas
Kelly asks us to consider an ancient philosopher who is perplexed by
Zeno's argument against the possibility of motion (2011). What he
should do, Kelly says, is follow his *total evidence* where it leads. The
only way for him to do this is to reflect on all of his evidence, including his common sense starting points. Zeno's argument provides him
with evidence against the existence of motion, but his sensory perceptions outweigh that evidence. So this philosopher should run a
Moorean argument against Zeno's position. Eric Sampson writes:

> The whole point of advancing a Moorean argument is to invite
> a plausibility comparison between the premises in the argu-
> ments for the competing views, and this can be done only if we

---

1 The impressive fight was the original plan, but Ford was too sick to shoot that
scene (Kovach 2014).

have both arguments in view at the same time without supposing that one has some advantage in virtue of being advanced first in the dialectic.

(Sampson 2023, 197)

Does it matter that this reasoning is unlikely to persuade the hard-bitten skeptic? Let's step back and reflect on the point of debating skeptics. Michael Veber distinguishes between ambitious and unambitious anti-skeptical arguments (I'll speak of "projects" rather than arguments). The *ambitious* anti-skeptic project is to show that the skeptic should be "rationally persuaded" and not merely to satisfy ourselves that the skeptic must be wrong. Aristotle's argument in *Metaphysics* (Γ), which purports to show that the Principle of Noncontradiction skeptic is refuted by his own words, is a good example of ambitious anti-skepticism. The *unambitious* project is to show that we can reasonably reject skepticism, if only by appealing to premises that the skeptic rejects. Moorean anti-skepticism is unambitious. Veber thinks philosophers ought to be engaged in the ambitious project, quipping that "unambitious epistemology is a placebo treatment. It only works if you believe" (2019, 366).

Must we strive to meet such lofty standards? The skeptic's standards are higher than what we expect of our friends and family when we deliberate with them, of scientists when they publish, and of jurors who must reach verdicts "beyond reasonable doubt." So maybe adopting "ambitious" standards grants the skeptic too much, at least if we're assuming that the skeptic is a potentially rational interlocutor. I think the skeptic should be persuaded by paradigmatic examples of knowledge; if that's right, then Moorean arguments are appropriately "ambitious." As Kelly argues, if we're not skeptics ourselves, then we shouldn't find anything wrong with reasoning from non-skeptical premises (2008, 53–78). We shouldn't worry about persuading philosophical skeptics, since there aren't many around. Even if success at the ambitious project is ideal, the unambitious project might be a worthy second best. If we can't chase the skeptic out of his redoubt, we can at least take consolation in the thought that he can't evict us from ours. Maybe it's OK if this amounts to a placebo treatment. Placebos work!

In practice, we all accept this. At some point, we've all believed that an argument was unsound because of how unlikely its conclusion seemed, without having any independent motivation to reject any of its premises. Nathan Ballantyne recounts a conference presentation during which a presenter wrote some innocent-looking claims on the board and wouldn't proceed until he'd established that the audience accepted them. When he later revealed his thesis to be an "explosive" claim, many in the audience "felt they'd been tricked" (2019, 66). We're all like this audience. It doesn't matter how plausible the premises of an argument seem, we won't trust them until we're assured that they aren't leading us into a coal pit. If philosophers didn't reason this way, we'd expect to find many skeptics, since the strongest skeptical arguments are difficult to overcome. In reality, skeptics are rarer than hen's teeth. A non-skeptic who discovers a flaw in his anti-skeptical strategies almost certainly will adopt a different anti-skeptic strategy rather than embrace skepticism.

I suspect that philosophers are often biased against Moorean arguments. One reason for this is that Moorean arguments don't tell us where skeptical arguments go wrong. This is what philosophers most want to know, so it's easy to overlook what Moorean arguments *do* show. Another reason is elitism. We got a whiff of this from Kant's disparaging remarks about the "dull windbag": these arguments occur to ordinary people. Philosophers want to look smart. If a view obviously has a counterintuitive implication, then pointing it out doesn't make you look smart. If pointing out *precisely the same implication* requires impressive intellectual acrobatics, then it'll be considered a great comment in the Q&A line. Let's not lose sight of the fact that the purpose of philosophical inquiry is to arrive at the truth, not to broadcast one's own intelligence. Sometimes the propeller hat objection is the right one to make.

> We appear to have knowledge of "Moorean facts" and it's legitimate to appeal to this knowledge in response to skeptical arguments, even when we're not yet sure where those arguments go wrong. In practice, we all occasionally rely on similar patterns of reasoning.

4.2   Moorean Arguments in Metaethics

Hopefully, I've persuaded you that Moorean arguments can be legitimate counters to radical skepticism. Now I want to convince you that similar reasoning refutes moral error theory and skepticism:

Moorean parity

1   If Moorean arguments refute external world skepticism, then similar arguments refute moral error theory and skepticism. (*Equivalency*)
2   Moorean arguments refute external world skepticism. (*External success*)
3   Therefore, similar arguments refute moral error theory and skepticism.

If this argument is sound, then it refutes the two views I regard as the biggest threats to realism: skepticism and error theory. However, in order to complete the case for realism, we'll need to supplement *Moorean parity* with arguments against other anti-realist views. Chapter 2 provided arguments against those views that I find satisfactory; however, let me now add one anti-relativism argument to the pile:

Anti-relativism

1   If relativism is true, then nothing is objectively morally wrong (i.e., wrong regardless of what anyone says, feels, or thinks about it).
2   Some things are objectively morally wrong.
3   Therefore, relativism is false.

This argument relies on the intuition that some actions are *objectively* wrong. That's a bit more contestable than the claim that some actions are wrong, and so maybe not a candidate for the title of "Moorean fact." Nevertheless, it's plausible that rape would be wrong regardless of what anyone thought or believed. Recall that we define "objective" negatively: objective morality doesn't depend on beliefs and attitudes. Someone who thought that rape is wrong, but not *objectively* wrong, would be taking the position that its wrongness is stance-dependent. The relativist would have to add some story about whose mental states could determine whether rape is wrong, or wrong for a some group of people. I'm skeptical that such a satisfying account of this kind can be given; and, anyway, we've already seen that many problems bedevil relativism. So I'll proceed as though it's been refuted. If the objections to non-cognitivism and quasi-realism are compelling, then we can press the following argument:

Pro-realism

1 If realism is false, then nothing is morally wrong regardless of
   what anyone says, feels, or thinks about it.
2 [*Horrible action*] is wrong regardless of what anyone says,
   feels, or thinks about it.[2]
3 In judging that (2), I am ascribing a property to some action.
4 Therefore, realism is true.

The soundness of *Moorean parity* doesn't entail the soundness
of *pro-realism*. Nevertheless, if *Moorean parity* succeeds, then
pro-realism is going to look pretty good. So does it succeed? In
§4.1, I defended *external success*; let's now take a closer look at
the *equivalency*, the claim that if Moorean arguments work against
external world skepticism, they work in metaethics, too. Here's
how Shafer-Landau defends the analogy between moral and external world skepticism:

> We believe that there is an external world, a world of natural
> facts, because such a belief unifies a great deal of our particular
> experiences and beliefs, and presents itself as so plainly true as
> to be, for all practical purposes, irresistible …
>   Most of us think that this intractable disagreement [with skep-
> tics] is compatible with our being justified in believing that there
> is an external world. We think this because of the aforementioned
> unification and practical irresistibility of such a belief. I think a
> perfectly parallel case can be made on behalf of our confidence in
> the existence of moral facts. The atrocious immorality of certain
> actions just impresses itself upon us in a way that makes the aban-
> donment of such a conviction completely untenable.
>   (Shafer-Landau 2007, 327)

Moral beliefs and external world beliefs share two significant features, according to Shafer-Landau. Moral beliefs unify our moral

---

2 Read strictly, this rules out Kantian constructivism as well as relativism. Kantian constructivism doesn't have the counterintuitive implications of relativism, though we've seen in Chapter 2 that Kantian constructivism faces other
   objections. Anyway, since Kantian constructivism is the closest to realism of all
   anti-realist views, I'm less worried about refuting it.

intuitions in the same way beliefs about the external world unify our experiences. The belief that harming others without good reason is wrong unifies many categories of wrongful action. Murder, rape, theft, and deception have this in common. And moral intuitions and judgments, like perceptual experiences, can be so compelling that they seem subjectively *irresistible*. This point is worth dwelling on at length so we can be clear about just how "irresistible" some of them seem. Here are some actions that are incontrovertibly evil. (Be warned: these real examples are *very* bad; you might want to skip the bullet points and take my word for it):

- On March 12, 2006, a group of American soldiers deployed to Iraq gang-raped a 14-year-old girl, Abeer Qassim Hamza al-Janabi, and murdered her along with three members of her family. The massacre made orphans of two younger brothers (Frederick 2010).
- On February 1, 2008, jihadist terrorists in the same conflict planted remote-controlled bombs on two mentally handi-capped women and then detonated them in a pet bazaar, killing over 70 people (Associated Press, 2008).
- According to the testimony of British abolitionist Granville Sharp, in the latter part of the eighteenth century, slave own-ers in the Caribbean islands forced their slaves to wear iron devices in their mouths so that they couldn't eat the sugar cane they were made to harvest. They used another contraption to force open the mouths of slaves who refused to eat or tried to kill themselves by eating dirt. These devices could be heated to torture non-compliant slaves (Schama 2007, 56).
- On April 6, 2019, a 19-year-old Bangladeshi woman, Nusrat Jahan Rafi, was doused with kerosene and set on fire. She died in a hospital four days later. Apparently, this was in retaliation for her refusing to withdraw an allegation of sexual assault against the headmaster of her madrassa (Sabbir 2019).

I'm counting on you to agree with me that these are grossly immoral actions. Fortunately, some human behavior is as com-mendable as these actions are hideous:

In 1943, Leopold Socha, a Polish sewer worker, discovered a secret tunnel out of the ghetto in the city Lvov, where impris-oned Jewish people were awaiting execution. Rather than reporting it to the Nazis as they required him to do, he helped a group of Jews plan their escape at great risk to himself. Had the Nazis discovered him, they would have likely killed Socha and his family. Despite this peril, Socha helped a group of 20 Jews hide in the sewers. He delivered food and other provisions, which required him to move through a kilometer of narrow pipe each delivery. The group remained in the sewers at Socha's mercy from June 1, 1943 to July 28, 1944. Thanks to his efforts, ten of the original group survived.

(paraphrased, Miller 2018, 26–30)

I can't withhold admiration for Socha's courage and compassion any more than I can withhold revulsion toward those evil actions. Both are irresistible in the sense that Shafer-Landau described. Now, assuming we're on the same page about the moral statuses of these actions, ask yourself which of these possibilities is most likely:

(a) Your current sensory experience of reading this page, seeing everything else in your visual field, and all your other sensory perceptions of your environment, is illusory. Soon you'll wake up in a different environment and realize that what you're now experiencing was a vivid dream or hallucination. (Really pause to gauge how certain you are that you aren't now experiencing this kind of illusion).

(b) Your current sensory experiences aren't misleading you, but tomorrow you'll have an epiphany that will lead you to the realization that none of the actions described in the bullet points are morally wrong, or even criticizable, and this won't be in virtue of learning new information about these incidents. (Again, really pause and reflect on the likelihood of this scenario).

To be clear: I'm only asking you to compare your confidence in your most certain moral judgments with your confidence in your ordinary sensory perception. I'm not asking you to consider any further philosophical question, such as whether some objective fact makes your moral judgment true. Hence, the intuitions I'm trying to elicit testify against error theory and skepticism, but not relativism.

My intuition is that (b) is less likely than (a). So it seems to me that moral intuition can be compelling enough to rival the senses when they're operating in near-ideal conditions. In persuasiveness, moral intuition even rivals basic logical intuition, which is the epistemic gold standard if anything is. Consider your confidence in the principle of noncontradiction: no proposition of the form "P and not-P" can be true. Acceptance of this principle is near the center of my web of belief, meaning that I'd abandon most of my other beliefs rather than accept true contradictions (Quine and Ulian 1970). But if for some strange reason I had to choose between my belief that the Nazi Holocaust was morally wrong and my belief that there are no true contradictions, I'd become reconciled with "dialetheism," the idea, endorsed by some logicians, that some contradictions are true (Priest, Berto, and Weber 2023). I can more easily imagine that some article in a logic journal contains a convincing argument that true contradictions exist than that some ethics paper contains a compelling argument for the moral rectitude of the Holocaust.

I cannot compel anyone to share my intuitions. Nor am I suggesting that this kind of "irresistibility" is epistemically invincible. My point is more modest: if you find that your moral intuitions are as compelling as this, then you should take them seriously. If we want to avoid skepticism in domains other than morality, then I think we have to say that intuitive compellingness counts for something. With that in mind, compare some claims that feature as premises in the most sophisticated arguments for moral skepticism and error theory:

- Categorical normativity is ontologically or epistemologically "queer" (Mackie 1977, ch. 1; Joyce 2001, ch. 7).
- We have no way of reliably distinguishing between the scenario in which moral realism is true from the skeptical scenario in which it's false (Lutz 2021).
- Moral facts aren't part of our best explanations for empirically observed events, *and* if they're not, then we have no good reason to posit them (Harman 1988).
- The best explanation for persistent moral disagreement is that there are no objective moral facts (Mackie 1977, ch. 1).

Though some philosophers find these claims plausible, I think they're *much* less certain than the clear-cut moral claims we've discussed. Moreover, the philosophical cases for each of these claims rely on intuition no less than our moral beliefs do. If we're going to rely on intuition—as we *must*, at some point—then it makes sense to favor more compelling intuitions over less compelling ones. As philosophers, we still need to figure out where anti-realist arguments go wrong, but like Kelly's perplexed ancient philosopher, we can be sure that they do go wrong somewhere in virtue of our compelling evidence against their conclusions.

Perhaps some anti-realists simply feel that objective moral truth is inherently *weird*; it's this intuition, not any of these premises, that's doing the heavy lifting for them. Is there anything that the realist can say to defuse concerns about "weirdness"? Perhaps. He might point out that *many things* appear to be fundamentally different from everything else—e.g., time, space, matter, information, minds, songs, people, numbers, and symbols (Huemer 2005, 200)—and that all of these things seem pretty mysterious upon reflection. The world's a mysterious place. You might recognize this as a version of the "companions-in-innocence" defense: unique, even *mysterious*, entities are all around us, and this doesn't seem like a compelling argument for skepticism in other domains. Thus, there's no reason to think that morality is especially suspect.

The realist can also remind his interlocutors that he's a realist about the moral senses of "ought" and "good" that we ordinarily talk and think about. Few philosophers truly seem to reject moral truths in day-to-day life. This includes Matt, who shares many of my moral convictions. Philosophical skeptics of morality typically don't lack moral commitments; rather, they suffer from cognitive dissonance. As Moore wrote: "The strange thing is that philosophers should have been able to hold sincerely, as part of their philosophical creed, propositions inconsistent with what they themselves knew to be true; and yet, so far as I can make out, this has really frequently happened" (1993, 115). Errant philosophical doctrines lead them to disavow their moral beliefs in narrow contexts like philosophy classrooms, but (thankfully) not in the wider world. They should reject these errant doctrines and fully embrace the moral beliefs that they intellectually hold at arm's distance.

Some moral beliefs seem as certain as our beliefs about the external world. Some moral intuitions appear as compelling as sensory perceptions. Thus, some moral beliefs seem to rest on "Moorean facts" of the same caliber as we can use to resist external world skepticism. If that's right, then we can refute error theory and skepticism, and even argue for realism, using arguments similar to those that Moore employed against non-moral skeptics.

4.3   Undermining Defeaters

Undermining defeaters reduce the extent to which beliefs are justified, or prevent them from counting as knowledge, by casting doubt upon the evidence that supports them, or the reliability of how they were formed. Suppose a cross-examination exposes an accuser as an unreliable witness. This doesn't show that the accused is innocent, but it *undercuts* testimonial evidence for his guilt. Now the case for realism relies on the testimony of moral intuition. If the anti-realist can show moral intuition to be an unreliable witness, the case for realism will be similarly undercut. So let's consider three putative undermining defeaters that might discredit moral intuition.

4.3.1   Science Has Rebutted "Common Sense"

It's surprising that whales are biologically more like bears than fish, but probably nothing in science is as counterintuitive as quantum mechanics, which describes the behavior of matter the size of atoms and smaller. Quantum mechanics is perhaps the most well-confirmed theory in the physical sciences, but there's deep disagreement about its metaphysical implications. The so-called *many-worlds interpretation* "entails that people (along with other objects) are constantly branching into innumerable copies" (Lewis undated). Since all of the major interpretations have comparably strange implications, it seems likely that the true interpretation, whatever it is, will as well. This highlights that common sense has its limitations, but I don't think that this is good grounds for moral skepticism.

First, we shouldn't overlook the fact that scientific inquiry routinely *confirms* many common sense beliefs. This is easy to forget because it's so obvious. There aren't going to be headlines that proclaim: "Scientists discover object permanence." Indeed, scientific inquiry presupposes much common sense. You can't get very far investigating without relying on your knowledge of the existence of a relatively stable world populated with people whose perceptions and testimony are basically reliable. Scientists are ordinary people who rely on common sense to get by, and much of their reasoning in scientific context may be seen as extensions and refinements of common sense, attended to with uncommon rigor.

Second, many putative examples of science overturning common sense are unconvincing. McPherson points to the implication of atomic theory that "the volume of ordinary objects is made up of empty space" as an instance of a scientific discovery that overturns supposed Moorean facts (2009, 14–15). Rinard argues that special relativity, which has the counterintuitive implication that time is relative rather than absolute, overturns common sense (2013). However, neither of these is a clear example of science overturning any part of what Kelly (2008, 54) calls the "Hard Core" of common sense, which roughly corresponds to the propositions that Lewis classified "Moorean facts." Practical affairs don't presuppose beliefs about the metaphysical natures of physical objects, space, and time. People seldom think of these things; when they do, the beliefs they form are hardly among their most certain convictions. We thus have grounds for doubting whether the ideas these theories refute were ever really "common sense" to begin with.

I suspect that when ordinary folks say that a brick is solid, and not mostly empty space, they mean something like, "You can't see through it, you can't pass your finger or any other medium-sized objects easily through it, and if you rap your knuckles on it, you'll hit something hard"; and when they say, "Time and space are absolute" they mean something like, "If two people start a race at the same time, then there will either be a tie, or one will finish ahead of the other."[3] Given the context of ordinary life, which takes place within shared frames of reference, this is true. The beliefs that there are physical objects with which we can interact, and that time and motion exist, are better candidates for "common sense" beliefs. Atomic theory, quantum mechanics, and relativity don't threaten those beliefs. If we understand ordinary beliefs about the world to be metaphysically modest, then it's not clear that relativity and quantum mechanics overturn them.

We can often understand counterintuitive scientific findings as qualifying common sense, rather than debunking it altogether. An analogy with the senses is helpful here: We don't expect our senses to function reliably in environments far removed from what we're used to, such as the insides of caves. The thought experiments that physicists have dreamed up to test theories describe circumstances very distant from anything our ancestors ever experienced; for instance, putting one twin on a spaceship that flies around at the speed of light while the other twin remains on Earth. Scenarios like

---

3 Thanks to Eric Sampson for this point.

this outrun our intuitive headlights, but that shouldn't cause us to give up on intuition altogether. We can concede that common sense has limits and still maintain that the burden of proof falls on the skeptic who rejects it.

I conclude that scientific progress hasn't shown that common sense in general, or moral intuition in particular, is too feeble to serve as premises in Moorean arguments.

4.3.2 Disagreement as a Defeater

The disagreement objection, in a nutshell, is that there's much more disagreement about morality than in other domains, especially science and mathematics. Moreover, where there's disagreement in science and mathematics, there's usually in principle a straightforward method for confirming who's right. By contrast, it's hard to imagine any procedure by which moral disagreements could be definitively resolved. Seemingly no empirical observation or logical proof could settle any moral dispute. This should make us doubt our moral intuitions and the judgments based on them. Mackie (1977), Quine (1981), Harman (1988), and Wright (1992) have each pressed versions of this objection.

Realists may respond by considering non-moral disagreement. Suppose someone tells me that he sees an enormous spider hovering a hundred feet above the ground. I tell him that I don't see it; he responds that my senses, not his, are malfunctioning. I tell him there's no record of any such sightings. He retorts that he's heard of previous sightings; so perhaps my memory is faulty. I could find passers-by who could serve as witnesses to side with me, but I'd be bringing them to convince him, not because I'm in doubt. (And I'd have to trust my own senses to know that I was speaking to others, wouldn't I?) Nor would I change my mind if the next several people I spoke to reported seeing the spider. If enough witnesses claimed to see it, I might really begin to doubt my senses, or my sanity, or conclude that I'm the victim of an elaborate prank.

Returning to ethics: the belief that there's nothing wrong with recreationally kidnapping and killing children is—I'd say—about as absurd as the belief in the giant floating spider. If I'm allowed to "stand my ground" against the person who says he sees the spider, then I should be allowed to do the same against people who have morally insane opinions. This is an extreme case, of course; there's often something to be said for the other party's opinion, as when two people disagree about abortion. Note, however, that this sort of moral disagreement won't, and shouldn't, bring anyone to moral skepticism. In the same way, disagreement about whether the animal that just ran across the road is a coyote or a fox won't, and shouldn't, bring anyone to external world skepticism.

The disagreement that could potentially threaten moral skepticism would have to be radical and it would have to occur between parties who are trustworthy, or at least apparently trustworthy. Notice that the more radical a given disagreement is, the more likely I am to have grounds for doubting my interlocutor's trustworthiness. The person who claims to see the giant spider doesn't cause me to doubt my senses because I think he's insane, and I think this because of his report. Psychopathic moral views are plausibly disqualifying, at least when it comes to the trustworthiness of an agent's *moral* opinions. On the other hand, moral disagreement with people who have sane views isn't comprehensive enough to generate skepticism about morality generally. It's thus difficult to see how any sort of moral disagreement could be used as a premise in a persuasive argument for moral skepticism.

Moral disagreement with many others, or even everyone else, might undermine my justification. It'd certainly undermine my confidence; I'd have a hard time believing I'm the only sane person around, even if that were true. Humans are social creatures, intellectually as in other respects. It's hard for us to "fly solo" for long. As with perception, however, it'd take *a lot* of disagreement to shake some of my moral beliefs. And it might still be most reasonable for me to conclude that something had corrupted everyone else's moral intuitions, just as in the spider case it might be most reasonable for me to conclude that I'm being pranked. I'm tempted to say that it would still be rational to stand my ground on the wrongness of murder even if no one else I interacted with viewed it as wrong. But I'm not sure about that. Fortunately, the moral disagreement we actually encounter isn't so comprehensive.

What about moral disagreements between societies and cultures? We should first note that cross-cultural moral disagreement isn't as pervasive as some people seem to believe. The "Golden Rule" to treat others as you would want to be treated is endorsed in many cultures, and every major religion. Philosophers are often dismissive of the Golden Rule because it appears simplistic, trivial, or susceptible to counterexamples (e.g., "a sadist is a masochist who follows the Golden Rule"). However, Harry Gensler (2013) argues that such counterexamples rely on misapplications of the Golden Rule, and that the rule, correctly understood, is both substantive and action-guiding. Anthropologist Donald Brown writes that

> In spite of anthropology's professional charge to study all cultures, which uniquely qualifies the discipline to both identify and verify universals, some anthropological practices have not been congenial to the study of universals. Notably, anthropological attention has been riveted more surely by differences between societies than by their commonalities.... Innate universals have tended to be neglected (in extreme cases, their existence was even denied).
>
> (Brown 2004, 49–50)

Anthropologists' bias against universals seems to have originated as an overreaction against the ethnocentrism that prevailed earlier (Edgerton 1992, ch. 1). As a corrective, Brown compiled a list of over 400 universals of culture, society, language, behavior, and psyche to which there were no known exceptions. The moral universals on his list include resistance to perceived abuse of power, disapproval of stinginess, admiration of generosity, redress of wrongs, proscription of rape and murder, taboos against mother–son incest, and the conceptual distinction between good and bad (Brown 1991, ch. 6; Pinker 2002, appendix on Brown's list). Other scholars have pursued the theory that there's a universal moral grammar analogous to Noam Chomsky's universal grammar in linguistics (Chomsky 1988, 152–153; Mikhail 2007, 143–152).

Some caution is in order. As Brown notes, social scientists have studied only a small sample of all the societies that have existed, so exceptions might emerge. There's also variation in how different cultures understand and apply these "universal" norms. All societies forbid murder and rape, but some don't consider killing disabled infants to be murder. Different societies certainly disagree about what sexual encounters constitute "rape." Nonetheless, in every culture Brown was aware of, taking human life, exercising power over others, and having sex were considered morally significant activities. We all seem to recognize that not everything goes when it comes to these things.

There's reason, moreover, to think that Brown's list understates cross-cultural moral agreement. Brown includes only things accepted in all known societies, omitting those accepted by an overwhelming majority of societies, but not all (the Golden Rule, for example). And superficial disagreement can mask underlying agreement. The ancient Greek historian Herodotus reports that the Persian King Darius summoned a group of Greeks and a group of Indians. He asked the Greeks how much money it would take for them to eat their dead parents. They were horrified and said no amount would be enough. The Indians, whose custom was to eat their dead parents, were similarly repulsed when Darius asked them how much money they'd have to be paid to burn their parents as the Greeks did (*Histories*, Book 3). When you're king of Persia, you can mess with people like that. The Greeks and Indians agreed that parents' bodies deserve respect; they just had different customs about how to pay respects. It's hard to tell how much apparent moral disagreement may be subsumed under fundamental agreement.

Consider one apparent case of moral divergence that philosophers have discussed. In the late 1940s, philosopher Richard Brandt joined a group of anthropologists on their investigation of the Hopi, a Native American tribe in Arizona. Brandt was disturbed by some of the ways that the Hopi treated animals. Children would sometimes be given small animals as "pets" which they played with roughly, often tied to a string. Sometimes they tied birds to trees and threw rocks at them until they died. Brandt interrogated the elders: did they find this morally troubling? Some reported that they didn't, despite believing that the animals felt pain. They told him that it was a game for children, and there wasn't much else to say about it (1954, 213–234). Allan Gibbard, a student of Brandt's, worried that Brandt's observations seemed to show

> that we and the Hopi he consulted are both coherent in our respective views. No argument from premises they accept would conclude that they are wrong in thinking that the chicken's pain doesn't matter, and no argument from premises that we accept would conclude that we are wrong in thinking that the chicken's pain does matter ... [B]ut there's an asymmetry, we are convinced: the chicken's pain does matter, and so on this issue, we are right and they are wrong ... All this makes us come out as embarrassingly dogmatic ...
>
> (Gibbard 2017, 743)

Gibbard omits some qualifying details because he's interested in the hardest cases of inter-cultural moral disagreement. But do we really find such fundamental disagreement between "Westerners" and the Hopi? Brandt begins the section of his book dealing with animal cruelty by saying: "The Hopi say that hurting animals is wrong. But their behavior raises some doubt about how strongly they disapprove. The reader can judge for himself from what follows" (Brandt 1954, 213). Some informants found the treatment of "pets" objectionable. Brandt reported that the Hopi believed "One is obligated to avoid injuring other sentient beings. Thus one should not be mean to children or cruel to animals ..." (ibid., 214) and "Hopi disapproval of cruelty to animals seems weaker than that of a large segment of white American opinion" (ibid., 245). Apparently, they had some cognitive dissonance about the moral standing of animals. That should sound familiar to contemporary Westerners, who imprison people for cruelty to pets but usually don't think twice about agricultural practices that doom tens of billions of animals a year to miserable lives and deaths in factory farms. Brandt also catalogs about two dozen moral principles he thinks the Hopi and "Westerners" (he seems to have in mind primarily American whites) agree about (ibid., 247–250).

Might there be better examples? Robert Edgerton's *Sick Societies* contains vivid descriptions of cultures with beliefs and practices that will strike many readers as absurd and repugnant, including some spectacularly misogynistic societies (1992, 82). But what reports would we need in order to be confident we had a case of *intractable* moral disagreement? Would all members of the society need to have attitudes and beliefs fundamentally opposed to ours, or only a majority? If there were a discrepancy between their espoused beliefs and their behavior, which should we take to be the most reliable indicator of their "true" moral beliefs? In short, it's far from obvious what kind of disagreement should trouble the realist, and what sorts of observations we'd need to make in order to confirm that there are many instances of it (see Moody-Adams 1998, ch. 1).

Suppose for the sake of argument that the people in some societies are indifferent to misogyny or animal cruelty and that this disagreement truly is irreconcilable. What then? We should, it seems to me, "stand our ground" against them just as we would against a morally depraved individual. The fact that a serial killer doesn't share our moral judgments that recreational rape, torture and murder is wrong shouldn't cause us to doubt this. We don't consider him trustworthy about morality because his moral views and behavior are psychopathic. We should say the same about people who are members of a psychopathic culture: they aren't trustworthy because of this malign cultural influence. This is literally dogmatic, but, *pace* Gibbard, it doesn't seem embarrassing to me. Fortunately, cross-cultural disagreement is rarely so profound that we can't find any shared premises from which to productively argue.

4.3.3   Evolution as a Defeater

Many moral skeptics believe that evolution undermines moral beliefs (Street 2006; Lutz 2018). Evolution could explain why it seems like there are moral facts even if there aren't any (e.g., cooperation increases survival, and "wrong" actions hinder cooperation). By way of illustration, suppose I showed you that what appeared to be a tree near you is actually a hologram I can turn on and off with my cellphone. After that demonstration, it'd be unreasonable for you to insist that you *know* you're looking at a real tree. Even if I'd only given you evidence that some of the (apparent) trees around a particular tree are holograms, that would undermine your justification for trusting your eyes about this one. Insisting that you know that this tree is real, and therefore not a hologram, is bullheadedness.

This illustrates why appeals to what seems obvious don't have the final word, epistemically, but it also suggests that the bar for overturning sensory perceptions in near-ideal conditions is high. Demonstrations like this don't come along every day. The evidence that this tree might be a hologram would have to be substantial to make it reasonable for you to doubt your eyes. Suppose you're in a park you've never been in before when you read a news article that said the military has developed technology that could potentially produce holograms of that kind. That wouldn't be enough evidence to make it reasonable for you to suspend judgment about the existence of the trees in your vicinity. For that, you'd need to have more specific information, e.g., credible evidence that the military is running tests of this technology in your area and (perhaps additionally) seeming to remember that there wasn't a tree there before.

The moral of the story is that the would-be evolutionary debunker must do more than show that evolution *could* explain away our moral intuitions. He must provide substantial evidence that it *does* explain them away. He must also take care to tell a debunking story with the right level of generality. The evolutionary debunking challenge fails if it only shows that some of our moral intuitions are untrustworthy, or if it targets all moral knowledge but at the same time jeopardizes important non-moral forms of knowledge that the moral skeptic presumably wants to retain. Suffice it to say, it's not going to be easy to avoid these pitfalls.

I've considered three supposed "undermining defeaters" that allegedly show that we can't trust moral intuition. The first is that science undermines common sense generally. This is overstated; scientific discoveries sometimes qualify common sense, but don't give us reason to reject it as altogether useless. Moral disagreement doesn't undermine moral judgment to the extent that should bring us to moral skepticism. Finally, evolution doesn't undermine moral judgment. It's going to be difficult to provide a "debunking" story that's strong enough to induce moral skepticism that doesn't also lead to broader skepticism.

Chapter 5

A Foothold for Realists

Spencer Case

Contents

One way to respond to skepticism that stops short of the rejection of all knowledge whatsoever is to ask the skeptic for a limiting principle: "Why doesn't your case for skepticism about X apply to skepticism about Y, which would be absurd?" If there's no way to avoid absurd forms of skepticism once we accept X-skepticism, then we should reject X-skepticism. In metaethics, the realist can press the moral skeptic with similar reasoning:

Normativity dilemma (skepticism)

1 Either the reasoning that supports moral skepticism supports normative skepticism, or it doesn't.
2 If it does: the case for moral skepticism is weak, since parallel reasoning leads to a false conclusion (normative skepticism).
3 If it doesn't: some normative knowledge is relatively safe from skeptical challenges, and the moral realist can treat this knowledge as a companion-in-innocence to resist moral skepticism.
4 Therefore, the realist can resist moral skepticism.

DOI: 10.4324/9781003183174-8

Could a parallel argument allow the moral realist to resist anti-realism? It depends on what form of anti-realism we're talking about. Some expressivists are prepared to extend their analysis of moral language to all normative language; indeed, that was the original idea. And once we've accepted Kantian constructivism about morality, accepting Kantian constructivism about normativity generally doesn't put us in a worse position, as far as I can tell. So expressivists and Kantian constructivists might have nothing to fear in denying the counterpart to (2) in the above argument. However, I think a parallel argument *is* forceful against error theory and relativism. For present purposes, I'll set relativism aside to focus on the version of the argument that targets error theory:

Normativity dilemma (error theory)

1   Either the reasoning that supports moral error theory supports normative error theory, or it doesn't.
2   If it does: the case for moral error theory is weak, since parallel reasoning leads to a false conclusion (normative error theory).
3   If it doesn't: the realist can appeal to the undisputed normative facts as companions-in-innocence to resist moral error theory.
4   Therefore, the realist can resist moral error theory.

This argument has what I take to be the surest sign of a good philosophical argument: thoughtful critics who reject the conclusion are divided over which premise to reject, and/or why they should be rejected. Moral error theorists are divided about whether to accept normative error theory (thereby rejecting (2)), or to reject it and deny that this is a concession to the realist (thereby rejecting (3)). This argumentative strategy allows the realist to effectively counter the arguments for moral error theory and skepticism. But the realist should want to do more than show that non-skeptical realism hasn't been disproven. Realists tend to argue as if they're the kings of the hill and it's the job of the skeptic or anti-realist to knock them off. They tend to take for granted, in other words, that realism deserves the presumption of truth, so that the realist case is proven by rebutting the anti-realists and skeptics (Enoch 2017). It'd be nice if the realist could argue offensively and show that he could make it to the top of the hill without starting there. The following is my best attempt to construct an argument that will (sort of) do that:

Foothold argument

1   There are knowable normative truths.
2   If (1), then it's reasonable to think that there are some knowable truths about non-hypothetical normativity.
3   If (consequent of 2), then it's reasonable to believe that there are some knowable truths about moral normativity.
4   If (consequent of 3), then it's reasonable to believe that some of those moral truths are objective (i.e., realism is true).
5   Therefore, it's reasonable to believe that moral realism is true.

I call this the "foothold argument" to underscore how the realist has a dialectical foothold once it's conceded that normative error theory and skepticism are false. If those views are false, then there's a normative aspect to reality that we can know about. That concession gets us on the road to realism—and the further we go, the harder it'll be for the anti-realist or skeptic to argue against taking the next step. The argument is modest in that it purports to show only that realism is *reasonable*. By this I mean something stronger than "not disproved" but weaker than "proven": that it's at least a philosophical live contender and somewhat likely to be true.

I'm going to belabor (1) a bit because the foothold is so important. Then I'll turn my attention to (2) and (3). The arguments for (4) are just the arguments against constructivism we've already considered, which I won't recite again here.

5.1   The Foothold: Normative Error Theory and Skepticism are False

To begin with (1): There are knowable normative truths. This means that there are knowable truths about what's good or bad, what we should do, and/or what we should think. Accepting this means rejecting normative error theory, the view that there are no true substantive statements about normativity, and normative skepticism, the view that we can't know about such things. These views are unpopular for good reason. Both have *extremely* counterintuitive implications. Accepting normative error theory means embracing all the absurdities of moral error theory, plus these:

•   There's no reason for anyone to choose any course of action over any other course of action.

- Excruciating pain isn't bad for the person experiencing it; it's never any worse for anyone than the most complete happiness.
- No belief is any more reasonable or unreasonable (justified or unjustified, rational or irrational, etc.) than any other belief.
- It's no better for you if all your desires are fulfilled than if they're all frustrated.
- Either no one has any interests, or else people have interests but have no reason to promote them.
- No state of the world is any better or worse than any other state of the world.

Normative skeptics are committed to epistemic corollaries that seem just as bad: we don't know whether we ever have any reason to prefer one course of action over another, whether excruciating pain is bad for the person experiencing it, etc. Given that the consequences of these views are so unpalatable, it's understandable that many moral error theorists and skeptics decline to extend their error theory or skepticism to normativity generally. Mackie thought that values are subjective—and for that reason, he thought, not properly *moral*—not that they don't exist at all, or that they're all unknowable (1977, 17–18). Joyce (2001) is likewise a moral skeptic, but not a normative skeptic. Matt, we'll see, takes a similar position to Mackie and Joyce. These philosophers will grant me the foothold and challenge later steps in the foothold argument. For now, let's focus on the philosophers who seem willing to reject (1) despite its counterintuitiveness.

Brendan Cline is a thoroughgoing normative error theorist.[1] Stan Husi's "meta-normative skepticism" also amounts to normative error theory by a different name (2013, 424–449). Christopher Cowie seems sympathetic enough to normative error theory that he'd be willing to adopt it if a defense of moral error theory required it.[2] Bart Streumer argues that normative error theory is true, though with the twist that it's unbelievable—including to himself (2013, 194–212; 2017, 155–188). Even if no one accepted normative error theory or skepticism, it would still be worth considering

---

1 It's often the case, though, that those who argue for total error theory rely on epistemic arguments, so that they could be understood as skeptics as well.
2 Cowie (2019) rejects the analogy between epistemic and moral judgments but also says the error theorist could embrace total error theory.

whether there was anything more that could be said against those views besides that they're very counterintuitive. The fact that these positions have sophisticated defenders makes the quest for a further argument against them more urgent. What can the realist say to such opponents who aren't deterred by counterintuitiveness?

The strongest refutation we can hope for is one that proves that the target view is contradictory. We're unlikely to find such a refutation of normative error theory or skepticism. The views that there are no facts about what's valuable, or what we should do or think, or that we couldn't know the answers to these questions, are apparently consistent. Maybe we could think of some further implication of these views that's even more repugnant than those already mentioned. Even if we could, normative error theorists and skeptics would probably accept these as well. Philosophers refer to accepting the counterintuitive consequences as "biting the bullet." I've heard that the saying arose because in earlier times British soldiers flogged for disobedience were given lead bullets to bite on to help withstand pain. Color me skeptical: biting on a lead bullet itself sounds pretty painful to me! In any event, the phrase "biting the bullet" has become what George Orwell called a "dead metaphor" (Orwell 1981). I propose a fresh, living one: the philosopher who accepts a prickly consequence "embraces the cactus." Normative error theorists and skeptics seem prepared to embrace any and all cactuses that their views commit them to embracing.

If we want to persuade these tough antagonists, and we're not content to rely on Moorean arguments, there's one move left to make. Philosophers who accept counterintuitive positions can usually say that we have *the most reason* to accept their conclusions, that we *should* resist the temptation to go with our guts. Normative error theorists and skeptics can't consistently say these things. They must awkwardly recommend their views to us without saying that we *should* believe them. I doubt they can engage in philosophical dialectic without at least *implying* this. We can hardly avoid offering reasons to others in ordinary speech, even if we don't explicitly draw attention to the fact that this is what we're doing. That remains true for those who want to convince us that there aren't any knowable reasons to do or believe anything.

Indeed, these interlocutors must assume that knowable normative reasons exist before the debate begins. The error theorist is *committed* to denying that normativity exists, and affirming anything that follows from that. This is to say more than that we expect him to say certain things; it's to say that he *ought* to. Someone who doesn't take himself to be committed in this way isn't really a normative error theorist. But the normative error theorist who *does* see himself as having commitments of any sort has inconsistent beliefs. The normative skeptic is gored on the horns of a similar dilemma, provided that we understand skepticism of some domain to mean that we *ought* to suspend judgment about a certain kind of propositions. That's not the only way you could think of it. Skepticism could also be the view that doxastic states of a certain sort fail to constitute knowledge, without making any normative recommendations, though it seems to me that this kind of skepticism is toothless: so what if a given belief fails to constitute knowledge, if that's no reason for me to suspend judgment about it?

So even if normative error theory and skepticism are logically consistent doctrines, *being* someone who holds one of those positions necessarily implicates you in some sort of deep inconsistency or incoherence. Moore—yes, that Moore—noticed that there's something paradoxical about utterances such as "It's raining, but I don't believe that it is" and thoughts that have that content (Moore 1993, ch. 6). The sentence is consistent, but the second half undercuts the first half. If you don't believe it's raining, then you can't sincerely assert that it is. Likewise, it's hard to see how you could believe any philosophical theory unless you thought there were some reasons for accepting it that you could come to know about. Many philosophers, including anti-realists, recognize that normative error theory and skepticism seem self-defeating:[3]

- Stan Husi (2013, 429): "Skepticism [about normative reasons] appears to be cutting off the very justificatory branch it sits upon, seeking to engage [in] a dialectical enterprise while denying its currency."
- Bart Streumer (2013, 197): "The property of being a reason for belief, in the sense of a consideration that counts in favor of a belief, is a normative property. If the error theory is true, this

---

3 Susanna Rinard (2018, 240–266) argues that external world skepticism is self-defeating. Rinard points out that considering arguments for skepticism requires us to rely on memory. Arguments parallel to those that the skeptic employs to unseat perceptual justification also undermine memory. I think a similar argument could be made against normative skepticism, but I leave that project for another day.

property does not exist. The error theory therefore entails that there is no reason to believe the error theory."

- David Copp (1995, 46–47): "Paradoxically, if one thinks that an argument proves normative skepticism to be true, he cannot consistently hold that the argument justifies belief in normative skepticism."

I see two main avenues of response: "softline" and "hardline". The *softline* response is to try to diffuse the paradox and show that it could be reasonable to accept normative error theory or skepticism. The *hardline* response is to fully embrace the cactus and say: "Sure, it can't be reasonable to believe the position in question, but so what? It's true anyway." Let's consider each in turn.

Jonas Olson sometimes seems to take the softline approach. He attempts to dissolve the paradox by distinguishing between "reducible" reasons that boil down to descriptive facts that are consistent with error theory, and "irreducible" reasons that aren't. Only the latter are a problem since "there need be nothing metaphysically queer about there being a reason for writers in English not to split the infinitive since, in one sense of 'reason' this is just for there to be a rule of grammar according to which splitting the infinitive is inappropriate" (2014, 121). The same goes for other convention-based reasons: "the point here is that moral error theorists need not deny that there are standards of correctness in logic and reasoning because these reasons are reducible" (ibid., 138). This response enables us to say that normative error theory is reasonable provided that we understand "reasonable" to mean something wholly non-normative. For instance, we might understand beliefs to be reasonable just in case evidence indicates their truth.

It's important for us not to be confused about the meaning of "reducibility" here. As philosophers ordinarily use the term, to say that A is reducible to B is to say that A exists, and that it's nothing "over and above" B. The normative error theorist can't say this about normative properties. Normative properties, for the error theorist, can't be identical to any existing properties. To take an analogy in the philosophy of mind, if you say "the mind is reducible to the brain," you're saying that the mind *exists*—as the brain. The analogue to normative error theory in philosophy of mind is eliminativism, the view that the mind doesn't exist (Churchland and Churchland 1998). Eliminativism isn't compatible with reductionism.

We could understand the normative error theorist to be making a conceptual point: "reasonable" just means "strongly supported by evidence"; since normative error theory is strongly supported by evidence (says the error theorist), it's *reasonable*. But then I can ask: Why should I proportion my beliefs to the evidence if I don't want to? My opponent can't give a reason without contradicting himself. So it doesn't matter whether normative error theory is "reasonable." You don't have, and couldn't have, any reason—in the ordinary sense of "reason"—to believe error theory. Consider:

(a)   There's no epistemic reason to believe my view.
(b)   There are epistemic reasons to believe my view—provided that we understand "epistemic reasons" to have no authority over what anyone should think.

(b) is no improvement over (a). If the error theorist asserts only the first part of (b), or asserts the whole of it only once and thereafter only says the first part, then it might *appear* as though he's avoided paradoxicality. However, once we keep in mind that the normative error theorist's view is only reasonable in a sense which we can rationally disregard, we see the prestidigitation exposed. It's no advantage to be able to call one's position to be "reasonable" or "epistemically justified" if these terms lack normative significance (Case 2020). The error theorist might respond:

> It's true that I don't accept any normative standards of reasonableness, or epistemic justification, and so from my perspective, my own view isn't reasonable or justified (how could it be, given that I'm a normative error theorist?). I'm just pointing out that my view satisfies *your* standards. You think it's reasonable to follow evidence where it leads, and by that standard, we should be normative error theorists, since normative error theory is what the evidence supports.

This "by your standards" response is a non-starter: normative error theory couldn't be epistemically justified according to *my* standards because I understand epistemic justification to be essentially normative, and because I think epistemically justified philosophical views must seem justified from the point of view of the person holding them. Any conception of reasonableness that doesn't capture that we *ought to be* reasonable is inadequate.

Imagine an atheist telling a Christian: "I don't believe that God is worthy of worship." Any being that isn't worship-worthy couldn't be God because of what "God" means. Charitably interpreted, what this atheist means is that the beings traditional scriptures call "God" *couldn't be* God. It's a similar mistake for the error theorist to say that the realist's standards support his view. The realist's standards rule out normative error theory from the get go by the fact that they're *normative* standards.

So much for the soft line. Let's now look at the "hardline" response. The normative error theorist taking this line concedes that his view is self-defeating in the sense described—it can't be made to seem reasonable from the first-person perspective—but denies that this is a problem. After all, normative error theory could be *true* regardless of whether accepting it is epistemically justified. Streumer is a hardliner. He not only accepts that normative error theory can't be reasonably believed, he argues that it *can't be believed at all*. Moreover, this is no problem for normative error theory, according to Streumer. Indeed, Streumer thinks it might even be a theoretical *advantage*. For present purposes, though, what matters is his weaker claim that we couldn't have a reason to believe it. Here's Streumer:

> Just as a theory can be true if we do not believe it, a theory can also be true if we cannot believe it. Of course, if we cannot believe a theory, we cannot sincerely say that this theory is true. But our inability to sincerely say that a theory is true does nothing to show that it is false.
> (Streumer 2013, 201; 2017, 129–137)

Whereas Husi (2013, 431) seeks a path to "faithful participation in the argumentative enterprise," Streumer seems unbothered by the thought that his own dialectical participation might be less than faithful: "Instead of showing that my arguments are unsound or that the error theory is false, this would merely show that I have insincerely put forward sound arguments and have insincerely told you the truth" (2013, 210–211). Streumer rejects David Lewis's "simple maxim of honesty [to] never put forward a philosophical theory that you yourself cannot believe in your least philosophical and most commonsensical moments [Lewis 1984, x]" on the grounds that "There is no reason why the truth could not be beyond our grasp" (ibid., 212). If Streumer doesn't mind keeping disreputable company, he might quote Thrasymachus, who tells Socrates: "What difference does it make to you whether I believe it or not? Isn't it my account you're supposed to be refuting?" (Plato, *Republic* 349a).

This is embracing the cactus, indeed! The hardliner is a more challenging antagonist for the realist because he's less concessive. In attempting to show that normative error theory is reasonable, the softliner seems to acknowledge that reasonableness is a desideratum, thereby giving the realist a foothold. The hardliner digs in and leaves the realist less to work with. It's a great dialectical position for those who can tolerate the costs (though few can). There may be no rejoinder available to the realist that proceeds from premises that the hardline normative error theorist will accept. That might be OK, so long as the realist can say something that could convince the average reasonable person. The realist should be able to accomplish this; presumably, a reasonable person must be on the side of whoever says that we can and ought to form our beliefs in a reasonable way.

As Streumer observes, realists who press the self-defeat objection appear to be making an *ad hominem* argument, and that's regarded as bad philosophical practice. Note, though, that this is a very unusual sort of *ad hominem* argument, one that would apply to anyone who adopted Streumer's position, including me. *I* would be insincerely defending a position that I didn't (and couldn't) believe in. I'd have adopted a view that couldn't seem reasonable from my own perspective. What's wrong with that? I think it's not enough to believe propositions that are epistemically justified, disbelieve their negations, and suspend belief when I don't have enough evidence one way or the other. I should also worry about *being a reasonable person*. And I can't be a reasonable person while knowingly adopting positions that I can't defend as reasonable, or engaging in philosophical dialectic in an insincere way. So I have compelling reason not to follow Streumer's reasoning.

Doesn't this "beg the question"? If "begging the question" amounts to asserting something my interlocutor denies, then I'm guilty as charged (assuming that I can be *guilty* of anything). To echo Streumer on unbelievability, why is this bad? The charge of question-begging is worrisome only when we're accused of *unreasonably* asserting something our interlocutors deny. The standard for the quality of a valid argument whose premises are contested isn't whether it persuades a given interlocutor, but whether it should persuade a *reasonable* interlocutor (Simmons 2020, 43–50). If the hardliner objects that I haven't given an argument against normative error theory, I'd reply that I have. I've shown that adopting normative error theory is incompatible with being reasonable, and that it's hard, and perhaps impossible, to argue persuasively against the claim that we should be reasonable.

One final point: Patrick Clipsham argues that normative error theorists are at a dialectical disadvantage because they can't claim that the realist violates any binding principles of rationality, whereas the realist *can* say that about the error theorist (2019). This point can be pressed further. Suppose after considering the arguments for and against normative error theory, we're uncertain about what to believe. How should we proceed? My suggestion, inspired by Blaise Pascal (1670/1958), is that we should consider what would be the best bet given our epistemic values. I value true and reasonable beliefs, and I disvalue false and unreasonable beliefs. Suppose for the sake of argument that you share these epistemic values.

If we're evenly divided about what's true, then, we should decide based upon what maximizes our chances for believing reasonably. The best-case scenario for normative error theory is that it's non-reasonable: there are no epistemic reasons against it, but also none for it.

If normative error theory is false, believing it might be very unreasonable, and rejecting it might be very reasonable. That means that we have nothing to gain and much to lose by betting for normative error theory. All things considered, then, we should bet against normative error theory. Indeed, *any* authoritative principle or value that we might appeal to in order to adjudicate the uncertainty must entail that normative error theory is false in virtue of the fact that it offers normative guidance of some kind (see Parfit 2011, 619; Beardsley 2022).

I conclude that we have excellent reasons to reject normative error theory. Similar reasoning should also lead us to reject normative skepticism, though I won't rehearse it here.

This section establishes a foothold for realists by demonstrating the high costs of embracing normative error theory or skepticism. Not only do these views have absurd implications, they're self-defeating in the sense that whoever accepts them can't consistently think she has a good reason for holding them (or at least a good reason that she'd be in a position to know about, in the case of skepticism). I considered two possible responses on behalf of the normative error theorist, and argued that neither should persuade a reasonable person.

5.2 The Instability of Moderate Error Theory and Skepticism

I'm going to proceed optimistically as though I've convinced you that there are some knowable normative truths. Now I need to convince you that it's reasonable to believe in categorical normativity, and moral normativity in particular—(2) and (3) in the Foothold Argument, respectively. Pursuant to that, it's useful to consider what might motivate someone with anti-realist leanings to embrace normative error theory or skepticism, despite the high costs of those views. We'll see that one motivation is that allowing hypothetical normativity through the door gives the realist an opening. I think they're right about that, though I draw different conclusions from that lesson.

Cline, who defends normative error theory under the label "global normative skepticism" (2018), raises three concerns about "moderate" error theory, by which he means moral error theory without normative error theory, thereby highlighting its instability. The first is something that I noted in Chapter 4: realism about non-moral normativity makes it harder to run evolutionary debunking arguments against moral judgment. It's hard for the skeptic to debunk moral knowledge without impugning knowledge of epistemic or practical reasons, since these are similar to moral reasons in many respects.

Second, moral error theorists generally reject moral knowledge because they reject categoricity. Moral error theorists who aren't normative error theorists leave an escape hatch for realists. Granting that skeptical arguments force us to choose between the existence of moral facts and the conceptual claim that morality is necessarily categorical, why must we stick with the conceptual claim? Realists could reject the claim that moral reasons are categorical to preserve the claim that moral facts exist (Finlay 2008; Cuneo 2014, 120–122; Cuneo and Case 2020). Some self-described realists do reject categoricity (Arvan 2019). Others would reluctantly accept this revisionism if they thought it was the only way to avoid error theory. By contrast, no such revisionist response could be made to the normative error theorist. If there's no normativity at all, not even hypothetical normativity, then it's game over for the realist, since even error theorists are "realists" about descriptive morality.

Third, just as moral realists are unable to explain the relationship between moral and natural properties (as Cline sees it), moral error theorists who accept hypothetical normativity can't explain why having a desire makes it the case that you have a *reason* to satisfy that desire, as opposed to a mere motivation. Cline contends that brute facts about non-moral normativity are just as mysterious as brute moral facts. Xinkan Zhao makes this point nicely:

> Suppose we find witches queer. It certainly does not alleviate the queerness by saying "The world as such doesn't contain witches, but *if* we make some sculptures in their shape and perform certain rituals, *then* they will come into being, with all their powers." This response doesn't make witches any more understandable than before; rather, it invites an entirely new burden of explaining why natural rituals can summon super-natural beings. The same can be said of reasons. It is hard to see why a change in our subjective states such as committing to norms can give rise to objective, normative reasons.
>
> (Zhao 2021, 865)

Cline's sword cuts both ways. The skeptic or error theorist might decide that hypothetical normativity is more troublesome than he realized, as Cline wants, *or* that accepting categorical normativity isn't as big a step from his current commitments as he'd supposed. The moral skeptic who stands his ground against the normative skeptic, or the moral error theorist who stands his ground against the normative error theorist, should be able to appreciate how the realist could reasonably stand his ground against *him*. If you accept normative facts and knowledge in order to accommodate practical and epistemic intuitions, and you recognize that all normativity is *a bit* mysterious, then it's hard to see firm grounds for opposing the realist, who extends his ontology a bit further and tolerates a little more mystery in order to accommodate important moral intuitions.

Joyce, the target of Cline's criticism, makes for a useful study. In *The Myth of Morality*, Joyce rejects categorical normativity, and with it all moral reasons, largely on the grounds that, like Mackie, he finds it mysterious how categorical reasons could motivate agents to act in accordance with them (2001, ch. 7). In later work, we find Joyce conceding for the sake of argument that epistemic reasons are categorical: apparently, you epistemically ought to believe ratio-nally regardless of whether this promotes your desires. He insists that this doesn't weaken his case against morality (note that in the following passage, by "instrumentalism" he means the view that all normativity is *hypothetical,* not that it's all instrumental, which would generate an infinite regress):

> But the fact that one might be a committed instrumentalist about practical reasons exerts zero pressure on one to be an instrumentalist about other areas. Instrumentalism about doxastic reasons is, on the face of it (and possibly at bottom, too) quite implausible. Instrumentalism about warrant for emotions is also easy to resist. The proponent of the argument from reasons for the moral error theory need not think otherwise.
>
> (Joyce 2019, 61)

Joyce is mistaken to think that accepting categorical epistemic reasons "exerts zero pressure" on what we should say about practical reasons. Non-moral categorical reasons can be a useful companion-in-innocence for the moral realist. Joyce insists that he can simply weaken the key premise in his argument to deprive the realist of this companion. Instead of asserting that there are no categorical reasons of any kind, his revised argument would assert that there are no categorical *practical* reasons. This looks question-begging, since "categorical practical reasons" is close to being the definition of moral reasons. Perhaps such reasons wouldn't count as "moral" if they never concerned the well-being of others; in that case, Joyce would owe us an argument as to why categorical practical reasons with this content are especially problematic. It's hard to see what that argument would be.

If we find that we can dispense with categorical epistemic reasons, then that lends credence to the idea that we can dispense with categoricity altogether. By the same token, if we find that categorical normativity exists somewhere, then it'd be less surprising to find it someplace else. Joyce can reject the widely held intuitions that moral duties are categorical (hence, a man has a moral duty to stop beating his wife even if he doesn't want to). But he needs a good reason to reject these intuitions. The most natural way is to argue that there are no categorical reasons, period. But Joyce instead suggests that the error theorist may relent and accept categoricity in order to avoid counterintuitive implications about epistemic reasons. This gives the realist another dialectical foothold. If you're going to relent to avoid counterintuitive epistemic implications, why not relent a little more in order to avoid counterintuitive *moral* implications?

Joyce compares the realist's epistemic companions-in-innocence response to his own "categorical normativity" argument with a compelling response to the atheist's argument from evil. Neither of these should be enough to change the error theorist's or the atheist's mind, according to Joyce, because there are so many other considerations in favor of those positions (Joyce 2019, 57–59). That might be true, but if the atheist were forced to concede that the argument from evil fails, then he'd be having a bad day of philosophical arguing. For everyone but Richard Dawkins, the case for atheism would look less compelling. The error theorist who gave up on the categorical normativity argument would be in the same position.

Prudential normativity provides another frequently overlooked companion-in-innocence (Fletcher 2018). Moral error theorists who aren't normative error theorists think that they have interests, that some things—like pleasure—are good for them to have and other things—like pain and suffering—aren't. Typically, they think prudential normativity is purely hypothetical: it's good for me to be healthy because that's what I want, and it's bad for me to be in pain because I don't want that. But once we accept that prudential normativity is real and needs to be accommodated in metaethical theories, the door is open for the realist to argue that some prudential reasons are categorical: you have duties to protect the well-being of your future self even if you'd rather "live for the moment." Depending on what theory of well-being you accept, it might be good for you to have knowledge and friendship whether or not you want them.

If you get this far, then it's also easy to see a bridge between categorical prudential reasons and categorical moral reasons: if your well-being matters, the well-being of others must matter, too. Here's an illustration. Suppose that you're at a dinner party and the host is serving some homemade salsa they canned last summer. You notice something alarming: the can has "popped"—a sign that the salsa wasn't properly stored and may have botulism, a deadly bacterium. Before you say anything, the guest next to you pours some salsa for himself and for you. Clearly, you have a reason not to eat the salsa. Just as clearly, you have a reason to warn the person next to you. The reason not to eat the salsa yourself is a "prudential" reason and the reason to warn your companion is a "moral" reason, but the two seem very similar! It's odd to think that the fact that the salsa may have deadly bacteria gives you a reason to avoid it, but doesn't give you a reason to warn the person next to you.[4] If your well-being gives you reasons for action, then so must the well-being of the person next to you.

In conclusion, I agree with Cline that the most principled place for the moral error theorist to make his stand is with the rejection of all normativity. Cline thinks hypothetical and categorical normativity fall together; I think it's much more reasonable to conclude that they *stand* together. This applies to moral skepticism, too: the most stable position for the moral skeptic to adopt is normative skepticism. To go beyond this is to trade theoretical parsimony—i.e., simplicity—for intuitive adequacy, leaving an opening for the realist to say that the moderate should trade more parsimony for more intuitive adequacy. I think that's a good trade.

> Once we reject normative error theory and skepticism and concede that some knowable normative reasons exist, it's hard to motivate the rejection of categorical normativity. If categorical normativity is mysterious, then hypothetical normativity is only marginally less so. It's even harder to find grounds to reject morality if we accept that epistemic normativity is categorical, as many philosophers have thought, or if it turns out that there are categorical prudential reasons.

5.3   Epistemic Entanglement

I'm going to present two further arguments, one in this section and one in the next one, each of which support (3): if it's reasonable to believe in non-hypothetical reasons (of some sort), then it's reasonable to believe in specifically moral reasons. Here's the first:

Epistemic entanglement[5]

1   *Entanglement premise.* If categorical epistemic reasons exist, then categorical moral reasons exist.
2   *Existence premise.* Categorical epistemic reasons exist.
3   Therefore, categorical moral facts exist.

---

4   I thank Tim Perrine for this example.
5   For a detailed presentation of this and another related argument, see Case (2019).

What did the philosopher say after moving to a new apartment? "There's a lot to unpack here." So let's unpack this, starting with (2). There are two ways one might reject it. The first is by denying that there are any epistemic reasons. I hope we've seen that's a dead end. The second is to say that epistemic reasons are hypothetical rather than categorical. This entails that epistemic reasons cease to be reasons proper when believing in accordance with them fails to promote our ends. Thus, a true believer in a cult would have no epistemic reason to carefully evaluate evidence that contradicted the cult's beliefs so long as she wanted to believe them badly enough. Of course, her refusal to confront the evidence might cost her dearly. But if she prioritized hanging on to those beliefs come what may, then on the present view we'd have to conclude that she wasn't being unreasonable. Surely, that's wrong—she's being very unreasonable! So we should accept (2). (See Kelly 2003).

The crux is (1): if categorical epistemic reasons exist, then categorical moral reasons exist. To see this, we must reflect on how the quality of an investigation bears on how we should epistemically evaluate whatever beliefs that the investigation yields. Consider someone who forms her opinions based on motivated reasoning and scours the internet for confirming evidence. These opinions are unjustified, or unreasonable, regardless of how well she proportions her beliefs to the evidence that she collects, in virtue of the fact that they resulted from an investigation that wasn't diligent.

Epistemic justification requires investigative diligence, it seems. How thoroughly must we search for our investigation to count as "diligent"? We can hold out for more evidence before making up our minds; at some point, though, the search for new evidence ceases to be worthwhile and continued suspension of judgment is irrational. I think how much investigation is needed depends on two factors: the stakes and the cost of acquiring more information. If a friend tells me that I'll like a certain movie, and he's generally reliable when it comes to my tastes, then his testimony and judgment are enough for me to justifiably believe that I'll like the movie. That's true even though I have other information easily available, such as online reviews, because the stakes are low. At worst, I've wasted 14 dollars and three hours.

Now suppose that same friend tells me that an old carbon monoxide detector is safe to use in my house. It's not clear that I'd be justified in believing that based on his testimony alone if I knew that a simple internet search would turn up relevant information. Since the lives of me and my family members are at stake, I should suspend judgment until I do more digging. To conclude, on the basis of this evidence in these circumstances, that the device is reliable would be *epistemically* unjustified because of the moral considerations involved. I think it would still be unjustified if I simply didn't care enough about my life and my family. I morally ought to take precautions, and this bears on what it takes for my investigation to be diligent enough to yield epistemically justified beliefs. If the costs of investigation were much higher—if I had to drive hundreds of miles and pay thousands of dollars in order to get more information about this device—then I might reasonably conclude that my friend's testimony is good enough to go on.

An investigation whose outcome has profound implications for others, but not for the agent's own goals or interests, is for epistemic purposes a "high stakes" investigation. In "The Ethics of Belief," W. K. Clifford asks us to imagine a ship owner who deceives himself into believing that his ship is seaworthy when it isn't, ultimately resulting in the deaths of all passengers on board. Clifford concludes that this man is responsible for these deaths because "had no right to believe" that his ship was seaworthy based on the available evidence (1878/1999). We can imagine a variation in which the owner perfunctorily inspects his ship, and still has no right to believe based on whatever evidence this halfhearted inspection turns up. On my account, that's because the stakes raise the bar for diligent investigation higher than what the shipowner has performed. If he'd known in advance that only an extraordinarily diligent and costly search might have turned up evidence of a problem, then we might have good reason to think that the ship owner's belief was epistemically justified, and that the ship owner himself is, for that reason, morally innocent.

The costs of inquiry are another point of moral-epistemic entanglement. To illustrate, there are moral and prudential constraints on how medical researchers should investigate a new drug about to be released on the market. Prudentially, they shouldn't spend more money researching the drug than it's expected to generate; morally, they shouldn't conduct cruel medical experiments on unwilling subjects in order to obtain more information. Their investigation wouldn't count as "negligent" if they operate within these constraints, though it would if they cut corners to avoid mere inconvenience. So in determining whether an investigation is diligent, we'd need to know what moral and prudential considerations are applicable. Since diligent investigation is relevant to the epistemic standing of beliefs, it follows that moral and prudential considerations bear on the epistemic standing of our beliefs.

Why couldn't those moral considerations be hypothetical instead of categorical? Because if moral reasons were hypothetical, then in many high-stakes cases, investigative diligence would be trivially easy to achieve. The shipowner's belief in the seaworthiness of his ship could count as justified by that standard, provided he's somewhat worse than he is in Clifford's original example and truly doesn't care about his passengers. Consider a psychopathic medical researcher who declines to conduct unethical experiments out of sheer laziness. This person's investigation could in principle count as negligent if he fails to undertake this step, assuming that conducting the experiments is the most cost-effective way of learning what he wants to know. Both these conclusions are perverse. An interlocutor who concedes that epistemic facts are intertwined with prudential facts but denies that this extends to *moral* entanglement would face similarly perverse conclusions.

An alternative is to accept epistemic purism, the view "the epistemic realm is independent of the practical realm and that our epistemic concepts are independent from our practical ones" (Kim 2017, 1). An agent's prudential and moral concerns aren't relevant to the truth of that agent's beliefs; hence, these things don't bear on epistemic evaluations. One epistemic purist, Trent Dougherty, writes, "Since [Clifford's ship-owner] owed a duty to the passengers to protect their safety, his lack of investigation is straightforwardly wrong, morally wrong... there is nothing distinctively epistemic going on here" (2014, 153). My objection to epistemic purism is that it makes the domain of the "epistemic" uninteresting. We should care about how we should epistemically evaluate our belief because these evaluations set the standard for whether or not we may *act on* our beliefs. If knowing X was no guide to whether we could assert that X, or act as if X, then it's unclear why we should fuss over figuring out what "knowledge" is.

There are two main kinds of epistemic purism. The first is evidentialism, according to which justified or reasonable epistemic stances depend only upon the evidence available to an agent at a time, and the degree to which an agent's beliefs conform to that evidence.[6] The trouble with this position is, as I've argued elsewhere (Case 2019, 552–557), that the notion of "availability" of evidence is itself prudentially and morally entangled. Whether evidence is available to you depends in part on how much effort it takes to use it in your reasoning (hence, deeply buried memories might not count as *available* evidence). Richard Feldman (2004) denies this in order to remain a consistent epistemic purist—with the consequence that only evidence immediately present before the agent's mind counts as "possessed" by that agent! This creates a puzzle of explaining how it's possible for a belief not to fit evidence immediately before one's mind.

The other main kind of epistemic purism is *reliabilism*, a family of views that emphasizes the objective likelihood that an individual belief will be correct. The most common form of reliabilism is process reliabilism, according to which we should epistemically evaluate beliefs based upon whether or not they came about through belief-forming processes that generally produce true beliefs (for a seminal account, see Goldman 1979). There's an extensive literature on reliabilism that I can hardly hope to do justice to here. Suffice it to say that I think process reliabilists will have a difficult time answering the standard objections without introducing features that leave room for moral entanglement. Reliabilists generally want to provide accounts of knowledge and justification. Just how reliable must a process be before it produces beliefs that are justified and candidates for knowledge if true? A natural thought is that human needs and interests bear on this question: a belief mechanism isn't sufficiently reliable if in practice, we'd be ill-advised to rely on beliefs produced by that mechanism. Accepting this idea opens the door for prudential and moral entanglement.

A standard objection to reliabilism is that reliabilists have difficulty individuating processes in such a way that not every successful guess counts as a reliable process. Concern over this and other issues leads John Greco (2007) away from process reliabilism to

---

6 Arch-evidentialists Earl Conee and Richard Feldman define evidentialism "in its fundamental form" as "a supervenience thesis according to which facts about whether or not a person is justified in believing a proposition supervene on facts describing the evidence that the person has" at a time (2011, 1).

agent reliabilism, according to which the reliability of an agent's dispositions or states of character determine the epistemic status of beliefs. Greco's efforts to capture "subjective justification" then lead him to introduce moralistic features into his epistemology: a belief is justified for a person if and only if it's grounded in dispositions that the agent manifests when thinking *conscientiously*. Clarifying this, he adds: "One might say "thinking honestly" instead, and this is intended to oppose such modes as trying to comfort oneself, trying to get attention, or being pigheaded" (ibid., 191). Whether someone's thought pattern is *conscientious* depends on how thoroughly it's reasonable to expect that person to reflect in the circumstances. So we're back to moral entanglement.

Before I proceed, I want to reply to one further objection I've heard to this idea of epistemic-moral entanglement, which I call the "easy knowledge" objection: Plenty of examples of knowledge don't involve any sort of diligence whatsoever. I can just open my eyes and see that something is the case. Diligence only comes into the picture when we're talking about ethical issues—i.e., how to act on the knowledge you have—and not proper epistemic ones. Hence, there's no real argument for entanglement here.

I have two replies available. I could say that diligence is required for justification when the investigation is important and sufficient evidence isn't immediately presented to the investigator. Clifford's shipowner might be justified in concluding that he was looking at a ship right in front of him without satisfying any diligence constraint; he wouldn't yet be justified in concluding that the ship is seaworthy because that belief *does* require a diligent investigation. But I'm inclined to say that even easy knowledge requires diligence—*easy* diligence. Sometimes opening your eyes is diligence enough. Some of the bars we must clear are low. Prudentially, you shouldn't hold your breath until you pass out. Morally, you shouldn't stab passersby in the eye with your sharpened pencil just for the thrill of doing so. Don't expect high praise for satisfying these duties. Some of our epistemic duties are just as easily satisfied, though failure to satisfy them probably isn't *impossible*: an extremist might refuse to believe his own eyes when he's confronted with unwelcome evidence, or even have difficulty seeing unwelcome evidence. The rest of us will have done our due diligence by being in touch enough with reality that we don't doubt our senses for ideological reasons.

Epistemic evaluations of beliefs depend in part on facts about the inquirer's investigative practices, and moral qualities. Thus, moral considerations are relevant to epistemic considerations. Moral anti-realists who want to embrace epistemic realism might try to avoid realism by embracing the view that epistemic reasons are all hypothetical, or by embracing epistemic purism. But if I'm right, neither of those moves will work.

5.4   The Normative Workshop Argument

In §4.1, I briefly described Reid's "workshop" argument against skepticism. Here's the critical passage of Reid:

> Sceptic: Reason is the only judge of truth, and you ought to rid yourself of every opinion and every belief that isn't based on reason.
>   Reply: Why, sir, should I trust the faculty of reason more than that of perception? They came out of the same workshop and were made by the same craftsman; and if he puts one piece of false ware into my hands, what's to stop him from putting another?
>
> (Reid, *Inquiry*, 6.20)

Some interpreters (Magnus 2008; McAllister 2016) take Reid's argument to be a trilemma between the following:

- *Credulity*: Trust all of our natural faculties (e.g., memory, the senses, and reason) as sources of *prima facie* epistemic justification.
- *Skepticism*: Distrust all of our natural faculties, so that we don't see any of them as sources of *prima facie* epistemic justification.
- *Quasi-skepticism*: Trust some of our natural faculties but not others.

We cannot accept *skepticism* and Reid says we must reject *quasi-skepticism* because there are no non-arbitrary grounds for trusting some of our faculties and not others (e.g., accepting reason but not accepting memory or the senses). That leaves *credulity*: we should trust all of our natural faculties as sources of *prima facie* justification. We should believe them unless and until something casts doubt on them. This suggests a parallel argument against moral skepticism:

Normative "workshop" argument

1   We have normative intuitions about epistemic reasons, prudential reasons, and moral reasons. With regard to these intuitions, we have three, and only three, choices:

- *Normative credulity*: Trust all of these categories of normative intuitions.
- *Normative skepticism*: Trust no normative intuitions of any of these categories.
- *Normative quasi-skepticism*: Trust normative intuitions of some of these categories, but not others (e.g., intuitions about prudential and epistemic normativity, but not moral normativity).

2   We must reject normative skepticism.
3   We must reject normative quasi-skepticism.
4   Therefore, we must accept *normative credulity*, meaning that we should trust all categories of normative intuition, including moral intuition, as sources of *prima facie* epistemic justification.

I've already railed against *normative skepticism*; anyway, moral skeptics who aren't normative skeptics are on board here. The argument against *normative quasi-skepticism* is the same as the argument against *quasi-skepticism* in the original workshop argument. If anything, this argument should be more persuasive than Reid's since it doesn't require us to posit natural faculties, only intuitions with similar content. Indeed, there seems to be a greater degree of similarity between intuitions about prudential and moral normativity than there is between logic, memories, and sense perceptions, which seem quite different from one another. Intuitively, the workshop argument is stronger when the things being compared are more similar. It's very plausible that if we trust sight, touch, taste, and smell, then out of consistency, we should also trust hearing and proprioception (the "sixth sense" of knowing our bodily position). Therefore, we should find the normative workshop argument at least as compelling as Reid's original argument, and probably more so.

To be clear, even if this argument is sound, the conclusion is that we should accept moral intuition as a source of *prima facie* justification, not that realism is true. In order to arrive at that conclusion, we'd need responses to all the reasons that might be given for thinking that moral intuition is untrustworthy. I've already addressed some of these, and I'll have more to say in the replies. We'd also need to supplement it with arguments against sundry forms of anti-realism, such as error theory. But if my responses to the usual skeptical maneuvers seem persuasive enough, and the alternatives don't seem appealing, then the normative workshop argument should increase our confidence that moral realism is true.

> This section pressed a new argument against moral error theory and skepticism. It proceeds from the thought that if we have evidence for the existence of epistemic and prudential reasons—as we seem to, in the form of normative intuitions—then our moral intuitions must also be evidence for realism.

5.5 Moral Explanation

Can moral facts explain events? Soft realists say "no" and hard realists say "yes" (Zhong 2019). Soft realists include David Enoch (2011, ch. 9.1), Derek Parfit (2011), and Tim Scanlon (2014). Hard realists include Sturgeon (1988), Geoffrey Sayre-McCord (1988), Peter Railton (1986), Michael Polanyi (1969), and Graham Oddie (2005, ch. 7). This question matters because of two related arguments against moral realism and non-skepticism, respectively. Here's the first:

Metaphysical idleness argument

1 For any type of entity, if that entity exists, then it's causally networked with other existing things.
2 Moral facts aren't causally networked with other existing things.
3 Therefore, moral facts don't exist.

(1) asserts the so-called "Eleatic Principle," which is named after the Eleatic stranger in Plato's *Sophist*. It says that everything that

exists is causally networked: "Respectable entities work for a living" is how Oddie (1982, 285) puts it. Not all philosophers accept it, however; some, Oddie included (ibid.), think that causally idle entities exist and so, to continue with Oddie's analogy, the universe has a social safety net of sorts.[7] (2) is also contentious, but it's harder to reject than (1).

The epistemic argument, which Harman (1988) pressed, is a tougher nut to crack. Lei Zhong writes:

> If moral facts are *explanatorily isolated* from moral beliefs, then it is mysterious how we can have *epistemic access* to moral facts. Such a requirement also applies to other domains of knowledge, such as physics, biology, economics, and even mathematics. According to many philosophers, for a person to know about a domain of facts, those facts must figure in the etiology of her corresponding beliefs. If the real explanations of a domain of beliefs are "debunking" ones—namely, explanations that do not appeal to the relevant facts—then the beliefs are not knowledge.
>
> (Zhong 2019, 558)

The argument can be stated as follows:

Explanation argument

1 We can have moral knowledge only if moral facts play explanatory roles in non-moral domains (such as the role of explaining moral beliefs).
2 Moral facts can't play explanatory roles in non-moral domains.
3 Therefore, we can't have moral knowledge.

This is the objection that should worry realists. Indeed, I think many of the most well-known arguments against realism—including Mackie's "queerness" argument and Street's evolutionary debunking argument—are getting at some version of

---

7 We can quibble about (1), since the issue is whether moral facts are causally active *outside of the moral domain.* We might reformulate (1) to say that there are no types of entity, all of whose instantiated particulars are causally isolated from particulars of all other entity types.

this concern. Soft realists reject (1), but I'm convinced that this is a bullet train to skepticism. If I discovered that my perception of a tree ten feet in front of me could be fully explained without mention of any tree, then my sensory evidence would be undermined. Similarly, if I discovered that my belief that the trans-Atlantic slave trade was evil could be *fully* explained by cultural and evolutionary influences, then I'd have reason to doubt this belief and the intuitions that gave rise to it. And that doubt would be exacerbated by the thought that the moral facts *couldn't* have any role in explaining my belief.

The realist doesn't have the usual companion-in-innocence here because mathematical facts arguably do explain events. Consider the so-called "hairy ball theorem" in topology. This states that, to put it colloquially, "you can't comb the hair on a coconut"; there must be a cowlick somewhere on it. Less colloquially: there can't be a continuous vector field tangent to a sphere without there being at least one zero-vector point. One consequence of this is that there must always be at least one place on the Earth where the wind isn't blowing (the cowlick on the coconut we'd be trying futilely to comb) (Richeson 2008, 5–6). So mathematical facts explain meteorological facts. Cicadas, insects recognizable for their shrill chirping, provide another example. Periodic cicadas emerge from the ground every 13 or 17 years. Some scientists believe that their life cycles take place over a prime number of years because this helps them evade predators and avoid interbreeding with other cicada species. Alan Baker (2005) argues that an adequate explanation of this phenomenon must refer to facts about prime numbers. So there's no special difficulty in mathematical facts explaining our thoughts about them.

So it seems to me that if we want to avoid skepticism, then we must embrace "hard" realism: moral facts must be able to explain our thoughts about them. Others have arrived at the same conclusion. Nicholas Sturgeon, in his decades-long debate with Harman (e.g., Harman 1988; Sturgeon 1980), argued that any explanation of the success of the abolitionist movement in the nineteenth century that makes no reference to the fact that chattel slavery is evil is incomplete. In a neglected essay, Michael Polanyi argued that the motives to the Hungarian revolutionaries of 1956, who revolted against Soviet domination, can only be understood fully understood in light of the fact that the rebels were resisting real, and not merely perceived, injustices:

The awareness of moral truth is founded on the recognition of a valid claim, which can be reasonably argued for and supported by evidence; moral illusion, in contrast, is compulsive, like a sensory illusion. Thus once we admit … that true human values exist and that people can be motivated by their knowledge of them, we have implicitly denied the claim that all human actions can be explained without any reference to the exercise of moral judgment … If true human values exist, the Hungarians may not have been driven by economic necessity, propaganda, or any other compulsion; they may have been rebelling against a real evil, and may have done so because they knew it to be evil. But this cannot be decided without first establishing whether faked trials are in fact evil or not. Therefore … This value judgment proves indispensable to the political scientist's explanation of their behaviour.

(Polanyi 1969, 33–34)

We must be careful to distinguish metaphysical and epistemic commitments. Hard realism requires that moral facts play explanatory roles in non-moral domains, not that we come to know about moral facts through their explanatory footprints. To say that awareness of moral truths should influence our understanding of history isn't to say that we can infer the existence of moral truths by attentively observing historical developments. I don't think we can do this. A cynic could explain them in terms of power dynamics, false consciousness, and sublimated impulses (Huemer 2000). Because I find the case for non-skeptical realism more compelling than the cases for anti-realism and skepticism, I don't think that the cynic's explanation of these events is the best explanation. It's important to be clear about the order of explanation on this point, though: I'm skeptical of these explanations *because I accept realism*; I don't accept realism because I reject cynical interpretations of history, and I don't think, as Polanyi seems to have thought, that we can establish realism by tracing the historical consequences of moral truth.

Doesn't this entail that we should *in principle* be able to detect the causal influence of moral facts? Not if moral causation is causally redundant, i.e., that it always overlaps with non-moral causation, as Shafer-Landau once argued (2003, 106–107). If we reject explanatory redundancy, then the answer will be "yes" in principle and "no" in practice. By the same token, we could in *principle* establish the truth of the hairy ball theorem by exhaustively observing the Earth's weather patterns and making inferences about the formal structures that govern meteorological events. But no mathematicians think this is how topological theorems should be established. I think something similar is true of moral truths: it would be practically impossible to come to know moral truths by observing the events they help explain. However, once we accept that there are moral facts, we can put them to explanatory work.

We should expect Harman's sympathizers to object that the realist *owes us an explanation* about how moral facts could explain events, meaning that we should reject realism unless such a convincing account can be provided. I don't think that's right. Presumably, we can make justified inferences about the objects in our environments without having a story in hand about how physical objects can explain our mental states. If we're allowed to punt on questions like that when we're challenged by non-moral skeptics, then the realist should be able to punt on some metaphysical and epistemic questions, too. The further objection that moral causation is especially mysterious doesn't advance the dialectic since the word "mysterious" is effectively a term of abuse like "spooky." Moral causation is no more mysterious than moral facts, so I think this adds nothing to the standard queerness objection.

Still, the realist would be on stronger footing if he could give a more complete story. Realists, as we've seen, often respond to skeptical challenges by challenging the skeptic's presuppositions rather than by offering a positive account (the details of which would surely be controversial). I think that habit, and the desire to be ecumenical, explains why so many realists are tempted to reject the first premise of the explanation argument. However, it seems to me that the only way forward is for the realist to develop a positive account of moral explanation, which will inevitably mean taking controversial positions in epistemology, metaphysics, and maybe normative ethics. That's no easy task, and to be honest, I'm not sure about what the details of the final account will be. Nonetheless, realists have offered some intriguing thoughts about moral explanation.

The most straightforward solution is for the hard realist to embrace some form of naturalism. In my view, the strongest form of naturalism is Rawlette's view that "good" simply *means* pleasure, and "evil" *means* pain (2020, ch. 4). Since goodness and badness are mental states, these notions can of course explain the mental states of inquirers, as well as whatever events are causally down-stream of these mental states. One downside to Rawlette's solution to the moral explanation puzzle is that it commits us to a specific normative moral theory: hedonistic utilitarianism, according to which the best actions are those that maximize the balance of pleasure over pain in the world. This theory has its defenders, but it has some counterintuitive conclusions (e.g., if you could kill every person in the world and replace each with a happier person, you should do so). Realists might be reluctant to embrace these commitments.

Oddie (2005, ch. 7), who speaks in terms of "value" rather than "moral facts," develops an account of value explanation, and even causation, that's consistent with moral non-naturalism. His account proceeds from general considerations of explanatory adequacy. Romeo's gift of a crimson rose arouses Juliet; a red rose of any specific shade would have aroused her; a rose of any other color wouldn't have. The best explanation for Juliet's arousal is that Romeo gave her a red rose, not a colored rose (that's too general), nor a crimson one (that's too specific). The explanation for the effect needs the cause to be at the right level of specificity (i.e., *commensurate* with the cause).

Value explanations are in some cases most commensurate with the events that need to be explained. Consider Harman's original case: you see teenagers dousing a cat with gasoline and lighting it on fire for amusement, and you're filled with moral revulsion. Harman thinks that non-moral properties are doing all the explaining here: we can scientifically explain your revulsion without mentioning the fact that an act is wrong. Oddie responds that explaining your revulsion through the specific physical realizers would be like explaining Juliet's arousal through the crimsonness, not the redness, of the rose. The cause is too specific, and thus isn't "commensurate" with the effect. What *is* commensurate with the effect is the *cruelty* of the act—or more, generally, its wrongness—which can be realized in many different ways (e.g., you'd still feel moral revulsion if the teenagers were torturing the cat by beating it, rather than burning it). Thus, for Oddie value-laden properties can't be eliminated from the *best* explanation of your reaction, after all.

A third kind of response is to reject the idea that moral facts or values *cause* our mental states, but to maintain that there's some other kind of relationship that obtains between our mental states and moral facts (or value) that allows moral facts to explain our mental states about them. John Bengson explores a theory of this kind. On Bengson's (2015a) account, we may grasp abstract truths because such truths *constitute* the mental states about them. This is analogous to "direct realist" accounts of perception, according to which perceived objects, and mental states, are the direct objects of perception. Bengson's account of the constitution relation is more elaborate than I can hope to do justice to here. Both Oddie's account and Bengson's are metaphysically robust, but it seems to me that those who already accept objective moral facts shouldn't see accepting these accounts as much of an additional burden.

I'm not sure whether or not any of these accounts is true, but there's one feature common to all of them that I think the true account must have. All of these philosophers see moral intuition as something that is integrated with experience in such a way that a complete account of the metaphysics and epistemology of sensory perception would go a long way to explaining how moral intuition works, and how moral facts explain our mental states about them.

> Realists disagree about whether moral facts explain events. Hard realists answer "yes"; soft realists answer "no." I've argued that we ought to accept hard realism because soft realism makes moral skepticism difficult to avoid (and we've got good reason to reject skepticism). After all, it's hard to see how we can have any knowledge about some domain if nothing in that domain can exert any influence over the beliefs that we have.

5.6 Conclusion

To recap, in this chapter, I've defended the following argument:

Foothold argument

1 There are knowable normative truths.
2 If (1), then it's reasonable to think that there are some knowable truths about non-hypothetical normativity.
3 If (consequent of 2), then it's reasonable to believe that there are some knowable truths about moral normativity.

4   If (consequent of 3), then it's reasonable to believe that some of those moral truths are objective (i.e., that moral realism is true).

5   Therefore, it's reasonable to believe that moral realism is true.

I've argued, in brief, that (1) is difficult to avoid and the center will not hold: once we acknowledge there are knowable normative truths of some kind, then the realist has a good case that moderate moral error theory and skepticism—i.e., moral error theory and skepticism that doesn't extend to all normativity—seems like an untenable halfway house. And if we must choose between being all one thing or all the other, then surely it's most reasonable to be on the realist side of that divide. So what kind of realism should we adopt?

I've argued that we must accept hard realism, meaning that moral facts, or moral value, must play some role in explaining events, and in particular our mental states when we arrive at correct moral judgments. By the definition of naturalism that Matt and I laid out in Chapter 3, this straightforwardly makes me a naturalist. But not everyone accepts that definition. Oddie rejects naturalism, which he defines as the view "the value realm reduces to the natural realm." That's because he thinks this implies that "the value realm" is second-rate:

> The term reduction is more than a little suggestive of diminished ontological status. A complete but succinct inventory of the universe need not make reference to them at all. Reduced entities lack ontological independence ... Reduction is the débutante's ball for aspiring entities, allowing them an entrée into respectable society. Reduced entities are genuine entities all right—their reduction gives them a pass into the realm of the real—but something is lost. Like the débutante who makes a successful match, they forfeit their names, they have an adjunct status, their identity is absorbed, and thereafter they are rendered virtually invisible.
>
> (Oddie 2005, 17)

If *that's* what moral naturalism amounts to, then I reject it. If naturalism is the view that moral properties can be referred to using terms that have a descriptive "feel" to them, then it's no slight to the normative features of the universe. I don't think that moral normativity, or normativity generally, can be fully explained in descriptive terms, though I'm open to persuasion on this point. That doesn't seem like naturalism to me. Ultimately, though, what positions we should adopt is more important than how they should be classified.

Admittedly, what I've said in this chapter and the previous one leaves many loose threads untied. I haven't argued that any particular normative theory is true, and I don't know which normative theory is true. That's OK: what I think I've established is significant enough. The upside to a defense of realism that's detached from controversies in normative ethics is that it's ecumenical. The downside is that it doesn't provide us with many clues about how to proceed in normative ethics. Contrast Rawlette's defense of realism, which is inseparable from her defense of utilitarianism. If she succeeds, she solves normative ethics and metaethics in one fell swoop. The downside is that this is a *very* heavy lift. For present purposes, I think that the ecumenical approach is the wisest one.

I noted earlier that one point of dissatisfaction with Moorean responses to skepticism is that they don't tell us where skeptical arguments go wrong. You might have the same objection to my case for realism thus far. Before I can critique the arguments for moral skepticism and anti-realism, we'll need to see them presented in a sympathetic way. And so I yield the floor to Matt.

B. For Anti-realism

Chapter 6

The Case for Error Theory

Matt Lutz

Contents

Moral realism has always seemed incredible to me. When, as a beginning philosophy student, I discovered that many philosophers defend moral realism, that was shocking, like entering a biology classroom and learning that many biologists believe in unicorns. Why would it be surprising if biologists did believe in unicorns? The claim that unicorns exist is not self-contradictory, so it cannot be ruled out on logical grounds. Nor do we have conclusive evidence that unicorns don't exist—"You can't prove a negative," as the saying goes. But it would be strange if unicorns existed, because they don't fit well with the naturalistic picture of the way the world works that is revealed to us by contemporary science. And we have no evidence that they exist. Therefore, we shouldn't think that they do. I'll argue that much the same is true of moral facts. Moral facts are strange and hard to square with a naturalistic picture of reality. And we have no evidence that moral facts exist. So we should not believe that they do (compare Joyce 2019).

DOI: 10.4324/9781003183174-10

My argument for moral anti-realism will be in three parts. In this chapter, I'll explain why the existence of moral facts would be strange. In Chapter 7, I'll argue that we have no evidence that moral facts exist. And in Chapter 8, I'll argue that these are conclusions we can live with.

6.1   Queerness and Categorical Normativity

In Chapter 2, we saw that Mackie argued that moral facts are queer, or strange, in four ways. The most popular of those four "queerness" arguments is the categorical normativity argument. According to the categorical normativity argument, morality is categorically normative, which means that the normativity of morality is independent of our desires. We ought to act morally not because acting morally would satisfy any of our desires. Instead, we ought to act morally *just because*. The idea that we ought to do anything *just because* is one that many philosophers have found strange. These philosophers say that all normativity is hypothetical (desire-dependent). "Desire" should be understood in a broad sense to include values, cares, commitments, etc. And the things that you value needn't be things for yourself; hypothetical normativity isn't selfish. So if you care deeply about making your friends happy, then making your friends happy is hypothetically valuable. Let's call the theory that all normativity is hypothetical the **Humean theory of normativity**.

The most well-known version of the Humean theory of normativity is the Humean theory of reasons, which says that if an agent has a *reason* to do something, it's because doing that thing will tend to bring about the satisfaction of one of the agent's desires. Proponents of the Humean theory of reasons focus on reasons because they also tend to believe that the concept of a reason is the most fundamental normative concept, such that all of normativity should be explained in terms of what reasons there are (Schroeder 2007). I'm neutral on whether the concept of a reason is the most fundamental normative concept, which is why I'll talk about the Humean theory of normativity rather than the more specific Humean theory of reasons (Joyce 2019). But because the concept of a normative reason is important whether or not it's the most fundamental normative concept, and the Humean theory of normativity entails the Humean theory of reasons, I'll often talk about the reasons that people have.

Normativity depends on our desires, but we can have conflicting desires. If you enjoy the buzz you get from smoking a cigarette, but also want to live a long and healthy life, then smoking will be good for you in some ways (you get your buzz), and bad in others (it'll kill you, eventually). There might be other relevant considerations. Perhaps your friends want to share a cigarette with you (and you want to humor them), but your spouse will get mad if they find out you've been smoking (and you don't want to anger them). It's a further question how this all adds up to determine what you ought to do. (I'll look at this question in more detail in §6.5, below.)

If you morally ought to do X, then you ought to do X no matter what you desire; moral normativity is categorical. So there's a conflict between the Humean theory of normativity (henceforth: "Humeanism"[1]) and morality.[2] Kant thought that this meant we had to reject Humeanism. Many error theorists think we should reason the other way, and reject morality because the existence of moral facts doesn't fit with Humeanism (Mackie 1977; Joyce 2001).

We should accept Humeanism for three reasons. First, it does a good job of making sense of our intuitions about cases. Consider Jane, who wants coffee, and who is walking past a good coffee shop. We can say about Jane that it would be (at least somewhat) *good* for her to go into the coffee shop, that she has a *reason* to go into the coffee shop, and that, all else equal, she *should* go into the coffee shop. We can say all of these things about her because she wants coffee, and because going into the coffee shop is an efficient means of getting what she wants. If Jane didn't want coffee, then she wouldn't have a reason to go into the coffee shop. In general, if there's something that an agent wants, values, or cares about, then that agent will have a reason to do what it takes to get that thing.

Second, Humeanism only appeals to naturalistically respectable entities that we should already believe in. Hypothetical normativity depends on an agent's desires, the general causal processes that will lead to the satisfaction of those desires, and an agent's ability to recognize those causal processes and use that recognition to guide

---

1   There are lots of other theses that are called "Humeanism," but the Humean theory of normativity is the only one that will concern us in this book.

2   Not everyone agrees. See Foot (1972), Williams (1993), and Schroeder (2007).

deliberation. None of these elements are mysterious; all can be, and have been, studied by scientific methods.

Third, Humeanism does a good job of explaining what normativity is all about. As we noted in Chapter 1, normativity is a rather elusive concept, since it's close to a conceptual bedrock. But we can say some significant things about normativity. For one thing, it's *action-guiding*. If it's a fact that you ought to do X, then that fact, in some sense, guides you to do X. This isn't to say that the fact that you ought to do X will *make* you do X. It's possible to fail to do things that you ought to do. Normative guidance is guidance in a normative sense, not a causal sense. You *can* fail to do X, but if you fail to do X when you ought to do X, then you are making a *mistake* of some kind. An account of normativity, then, should tell us what it means for your actions to be guided such that you make a mistake if you don't act a certain way. Desires are well-suited to explain this feature of normativity. If I value something, then my valuing gives me a goal. And, unless I am lucky, I won't achieve my goal by sitting motionless and waiting for it to fall into my lap. I have to take action. If I fail to do so, I'm making a mistake by my own lights (Smith 1994, ch. 5). In this way, my actions are guided by my goals.

To reject Humeanism is to say that there's a kind of normativity—categorical normativity—that *cannot* be explained in these terms. Categorical normativity is a kind of action-guiding-ness that cannot be explained by appeal to an agent's desires. So what explains the action-guiding-ness of categorical normativity? Nothing! Categorical normativity *is* action-guiding-ness. And what explains why it's a mistake not to act how you categorically ought to? Again: nothing! Categorical normativity *is you're-making-a-mistake-if-you-don't-act-how-you-ought-to-ness*. If you have a categorical obligation to do X, then X is to-be-done, and this to-be-done-ness can't be explained in terms of your goals or desires. It's *simply to-be-done*. That's weird.

The point here is similar to the one about unicorns. Science gives us a simple, naturalistic framework for understanding the way animal biology works. Positing an animal with magic powers will force us to discard that framework, together with the general model of causation given to us by the natural sciences. We need to add a new kind of inexplicable causal power: *magical* powers. This is reason enough not to posit an animal with magic powers, unless we have damn good reason to do so. Similarly, Humeanism gives us a simple, naturalistic framework for understanding normativity. Positing categorical normativity will force us to discard that framework; this is reason enough not to posit categorical normativity unless we have damn good reason to do so. Categorical normativity is the magic of metaethics.

Because moral facts imply the existence of categorical normativity, positing moral facts would force us to give up a simple, intuitive, naturalistic, and constructive account of normativity. For that reason, we shouldn't believe in morality. This argument for error theory is so common and popular that it has some claim to be *the* argument for error theory (Joyce 2001; 2019). Let's call the package of views consisting of error theory, Humeanism, and the argument from Humeanism to error theory **Humean error theory**. I am a Humean error theorist, and you should be one, too.

6.2 Projection

According to Humean error theory, categorical normativity is the error in our moral thought and language. Moral judgments are untrue because they erroneously ascribe categorically normative properties. Why would we make such an error? Hume said that our tastes are a "productive faculty, and gilding or staining all natural objects with the colours, borrowed from internal sentiment, raises, in a manner, a new creation" (Hume, *ECPM*, Appendix 1). That is, when we have an "internal sentiment" of like or dislike, we have a tendency to *project* that sentiment onto the world (Blackburn 1993). This gives rise to a "new creation"—the concept of categorical value.

To understand how projection works, consider what it's like to enjoy a certain kind of food. Take kimchi. I enjoy the taste of kimchi; when I think about kimchi, it seems appealing to me. I might even say "kimchi is delicious," a statement which conveys the idea that this appeal isn't a fact about my psychology, but instead about kimchi itself. I might unreflectively say that kimchi has a property of *to-be-savored-ness*. But a moment's reflection dispels the illusion. The sharp, funky flavor of kimchi isn't for everyone. If you don't like kimchi, that's fine. You're not making a mistake; it's just that Korean fermented cabbage isn't for you. So while the experience of eating kimchi inclines me to think that kimchi is to-be-savored, I can resist the tendency to judge that kimchi has any such property. Kimchi's just something that I like to eat.

Other kinds of food are enjoyed much more universally. Pizza and chocolate ice cream, for instance, are widely enjoyed. But these don't have an objective quality of to-be-savored-ness in them either. These foods simply contain large amounts of fat or sugar, which are excellent sources of energy for human bodies, and so we have a stronger evolved tendency to enjoy these foods than we do to enjoy fermented cabbage. Culture matters, too. Pizza lovers are more common in America than in Korea, and kimchi lovers are more common in Korea than America. This is a product of different culinary traditions.

The tendency to project our appetites isn't restricted to our culinary tastes. This is a general phenomenon that obtains for any of our desires. If we desire something, then the thing itself, or particular features of that thing, attract us to it. Part of how this works is that our minds represent the thing that we are attracted to as being *worthy* of that attraction. This tendency is mirrored in our language. For most (all?) of the words that we have for our desire-like attitudes, there's a corresponding normative word that means something like "deserving of that attitude." When we're attracted to something we call it "attractive." When we love something we call it "lovely." When we like something we call it "likable," when we desire something we call it "desirable," etc.

As the examples of pizza and kimchi show, what we desire/value/enjoy/etc. is partly a matter of biology, and partly a matter of culture. We tend to view the objects of these attitudes as deserving of those attitudes, and this tendency is stronger the stronger the attitude is and the more prevalent it is in society. For more selective tastes, we can easily recognize that our desires are idiosyncratic features of our own mental life and resist the tendency to judge that the thing we desire is *desirable*. But for attitudes that are deeply felt and widely shared, this tendency is harder to resist.

This applies to our moral attitudes. As we said in Chapter 1, moral attitudes are different from moral beliefs. The outrage that we experience when we see someone being discriminated against is different from the belief that this discrimination is unjust. Yet the two tend to come together. Projection explains why. We project our attitude of outrage just as much as we project our taste for chocolate ice cream. Projecting outrage inclines us to judge that the thing we're outraged about has the property of being to-be-outraged-about, i.e., the property of being unjust. Generally, our moral beliefs are beliefs that things have properties that justify our moral attitudes towards them (McHugh and Way 2016). We abhor murder, and thus judge it to be abhorrent. We value friendship, and thus judge it to be valuable. In general, we project our moral attitudes onto their objects, and this inclines us to judge that those attitudes are *fitting for* those objects. This is the source of our categorical normative concepts.

The tendency to judge that moral values are objective is strong. Moral attitudes are different from other desire-like attitudes in part because they're more deeply felt (Horgan and Timmons 2017). I care passionately about freedom, equality, and truthfulness in a way that I just don't care about kimchi, or even chocolate ice cream. Abuse, oppression, and dishonesty create feelings of revulsion and outrage that even lima beans never could. This isn't happenstance; it's a product of evolution. The parts of our brains that are responsible for formulating moral emotions are different from the parts of our brains that give rise to the enjoyment of food (Sinnott-Armstrong 2008c). Moral attitudes have a particularly demanding phenomenology because it was beneficial for our ancestors to have demanding moral attitudes. Moral attitudes are also often widely shared within a society. Societies that tolerated murder would tend to kill themselves off while those that abhor, condemn, and sanction murder survive (Joyce 2006, ch. 1–4). Because abhorrence of murder is a deeply felt and widely shared attitude, we are strongly disposed to project it. Thus, we judge that murder is abhorrent, and, accordingly, not-to-be-done.

6.3   End-Relational Normative Semantics

It's now time to say a bit about what normative terms mean. While it's tempting to dive right into the ways that normative terms like 'good' are used in moral contexts, this is not the only way that normative terms can be used. As we saw in §3.1.1, it's intelligible to talk about a "good toaster," and in doing so we aren't saying anything about morality. A good toaster is just one that toasts bread or bagels efficiently (Thomson 2008, ch. 1). Indeed, we can use the word 'good' to talk about things that are (purportedly) immoral. An efficient, stealthy killer is a good assassin, but isn't morally good (Harman 1975). We can say similar things about other normative terminology. We talk about the right road to take, or say that the chess player ought to castle early in order to develop her rook and protect her king, and nothing moral is thereby intended by the use

of the words 'right' or 'ought.' Non-moral uses of normative terminology are widespread.

What are we to make of this? Wittgenstein claimed that normative terminology can be used in two senses. The sense in which a
toaster can be good or a road can be the right one are what he
called the "relative sense." In ethics, however, we use moral terms
in an "absolute sense." And Wittgenstein claims that these senses
are quite different. We can analyze normative terminology used in
its relative sense as making straightforward statements of natural
fact. "The word 'good' in the relative sense simply means coming
up to a certain predetermined standard" (1965, 5). When normative terminology is used in its absolute sense, however, it resists
analysis or understanding:

> In ethical ... language we seem constantly to be using similes.
> But a simile must be the simile for something. And if I can
> describe a fact by means of a simile I must also be able to drop
> the simile and to describe the facts without it. Now in our case
> as soon as we try to drop the simile and simply to state the facts
> which stand behind it, we find that there are no such facts. And
> so, what at first appeared to be simile now seems to be mere
> nonsense.
>
> (Wittgenstein 1965, 10)

Wittgenstein concludes, with characteristic bombast, that he can
"see clearly, as it were in a flash of light, not only that no description that I can think of would do to describe what I mean by
absolute value, but that I would reject every significant description that anybody could possibly suggest, *ab initio*, on the ground
of its significance" (ibid).

I agree with Wittgenstein about most of this, but his suggestion
that there are two distinct "senses" in which we can use normative
language is somewhat misleading. As Mackie points out, "it would
be most implausible to give the word 'good' in moral uses a sense
unconnected with its sense or senses in other contexts" (Mackie
1977, 51). Mackie held that all uses of normative terminology
should be understood in a relative sense. To say that something is
good is always to say that it tends to satisfy certain standards or
goals. Moral uses of normative terminology are distinguished from
other uses by what the standards in question are. In non-moral contexts, the standards are typically determined by the function of the

thing being called 'good' or by the interests of the speakers. But in moral contexts, the standards are the standards of objective morality. Mackie approvingly cites Sidgwick, who equates moral goodness with what is good "from the point of view (if I may put it like this) of the universe" (Sidgwick 1907/1981, III.13.3).

Sidgwick's "if I may put it like this" aside shows the aptness of Wittgenstein's observation that descriptions of absolute (moral) value always seems to involve simile or metaphor. The moral standards are the standards that matter from the point of view of the universe. But the universe doesn't have a point of view. This is metaphor. Yet it's a natural metaphor to use to describe categorical normativity: if you have a categorical obligation to do X, then some rule applies to you that doesn't have its source inside of you. A rule applying to you from outside, and yet there's no one formulating the rule and applying it to you? Why, it's almost as though the universe itself were commanding you to do X! This pattern of metaphor crops up all the time in discussions of categorical normativity, although it's typically hidden in a shift to the passive voice. It's embarrassing to say that the universe literally calls on us to show kindness to strangers. We can avoid this embarrassment by saying that showing kindness to strangers "is called for." But this metaphor, even in the passive voice, still carries the lingering feel of absurdity, since it implicitly invokes the notion of an authority who is doing the calling. (Voluntarists will say this authority is God. But as the Euthyphro dilemma shows, God's calling is arbitrary unless the thing that God calls for us to do has the property of to-be-called-for-ness.) There's also the sense that it's not *the universe as a whole* that is calling on you to perform the required action. The demand is much more local; it's as though the action itself is calling on you to do it. This is how projected desires work. It's not the universe as a whole that is calling on you to savor chocolate ice cream, it's the ice cream itself that calls for you to savor it. Categorical normativity is a command expressed in the passive voice and then ascribed as an intrinsic property of the action that is commanded. Again: this is weird.

The meaning of normative terminology should always be analyzed in terms of ends or goals, but the ends or goals in question change depending on context (Finlay 2014). The fact that the meaning of normative terminology is always relative to contextually determined ends or goals means that normative terminology is incredibly flexible. But there are (at least) three identifiable patterns of use of normative terminology that correspond to three different kinds of ends. First is the moral end of "what matters from the standpoint of the universe." These claims are always untrue, since nothing matters from the point of view of the universe. We think that things can matter in this way only if we're deceived by our tendency to project our moral attitudes. Second, the ends in question could be commonly understood standards. When we call a toaster "good," this will usually be because the toaster satisfies commonly understood standards for toasters, i.e. efficiently and reliably making golden-brown toast. Call this the *standard-relative use* of normative terminology. Third, the ends in question could be the desires of some agent. We say that Jane has a reason to go into the coffee shop because doing so will satisfy her desire for coffee. Call this the *desire-relative use* of normative terminology. Only the desire-relative use of normative terminology refers to considerations that are normative in the action-guiding sense.

A particular use of normative terminology can be both desire-relative and standard-relative when there's a commonly understood standard that we care about satisfying. Indeed, this is the usual case, since we typically only use normative terminology to talk about what will satisfy a commonly understood standard if that standard is one that we care about. But, in principle, these two usages of normative terminology can come apart if there's a common standard that we don't care about. Similarly, a particular use of normative terminology can also be both desire-relative and moral, when there's something that we care about that we also take to matter from the standpoint of the universe. Indeed, this is typical, since we project our attitudes and are thus inclined to judge that something matters from the standpoint of the universe if we desire it. But again, in principle these uses of normative terminology can come apart.

Moral claims imply the existence of categorical normativity. Accepting the existence of categorical normativity means rejecting Humeanism, which makes sense of the central features of normativity in an intuitively compelling way. Categorical normative concepts are illusory projections of our attitudes. When we use normative terminology to refer to what satisfies certain standards or what will satisfy our desires, we can speak truly and coherently. But when we use normative terminology to refer to categorical normativity, our assertions are untrue.

6.4   Hampton's Objection

Thus far, I've laid out the basic case for Humean error theory. Humean error theory is a popular enough view that many objections have been leveled against it over the years. In the rest of the chapter, I'll respond to the five objections that I think are most pressing. Along the way, I'll develop the case for Humean error theory by giving a more robust account of hypothetical normativity.

The first major objection comes from Jean Hampton. Hampton (1998) objects that there's no way to avoid the existence of categorical normativity. Everyone agrees that we have reason to pursue the objects or actions that we value. But this is itself a normative fact: that agents must pursue the objects of their desires. This isn't a hypothetical norm; we shouldn't pursue the objects of our desires because we desire to pursue the objects of our desires. It's a categorical norm: we ought to pursue the objects of our desires, period. Therefore, if you believe in *any* normativity, you have to believe in categorical normativity. So Humean error theory is wrong. Call this **Hampton's objection**.

To see where Hampton's objection goes wrong, we need to slow down a bit to understand exactly how it works. Consider the following claim:

> **The hypothetical principle:** An agent has a reason to perform an action if and only if that action will promote one of that agent's desires.

Humeanism entails the hypothetical principle, but you don't need to be a Humean to accept the hypothetical principle. Even a non-naturalist realist could accept it. If non-naturalism is true, then there are some things that just are to-be-done, and the property of to-be-done-ness is not identical to any natural property, like the property of satisfying one's desires. It's its own thing. Still, we might ask what actions have that property. Can we make a list of them? Perhaps, if we do, we will find that all and only the actions that have that property are actions that satisfy our desires. Then the hypothetical principle would be true, for it would tell us what kinds of things we have categorical reasons to do. In this way, a non-naturalist realist could accept the hypothetical principle as stating an accurate first-order normative theory about what sorts of things we have reasons to do (Moore 1903, §9; Scanlon 2014, 47–50). Call this the categorical reading of the hypothetical principle because it interprets the hypothetical principle as stating a rule that has categorical action-guiding force.

It's common for metaethicists to understand a "reason" as a state of affairs that *favors* or *counts-in-favor-of* some action. The categorical reading of the hypothetical principle interprets reasons in this way: that an action will satisfy an agent's desires *counts in favor of* doing that action (Bedke 2010). But "favoring" or "counting in favor of" aren't part of the concept of a *reason*. They're part of the concept of a *categorical reason*. Indeed, we can see the same metaphorical pattern of projecting commands in the passive voice in this notion of "favoring." To favor something, or to count something in favor, isn't something that states of affairs do. It's something that *we* do in the course of deliberation, as when we make lists of pros and cons. The common notion that reasons are considerations that "count in favor" is another metaphorical command expressed in the passive voice and attributed as an intrinsic property of the fact in question. Humean error theorists reject this sort of metaphor as incoherent, and so they reject the categorical reading of the hypothetical principle.

How, then, does the Humean error theorist understand the hypothetical principle? First and foremost, they understand it as providing an *analysis* of the notion of a hypothetical normative reason. Call this the analytic reading of the hypothetical principle. The hypothetical principle doesn't state a norm, it states a definition. Specifically, it's a definition of what it means for an agent to have a hypothetical reason to do something.

Once we understand that the Humean anti-realist accepts the hypothetical principle as a definition, not as a norm, an obvious objection presents itself: that the definition is a bad one. Recall G. E. Moore's open-question argument: Any question of the form "X has natural property N, but is X good?" is bound to feel open; therefore, we cannot define goodness in natural terms. Moore argues that we cannot give a definition of *goodness*, but he focuses on goodness because he takes goodness to be the most fundamental normative concept. The point is supposed to generalize to all other normative concepts; we cannot define *any* normative concepts in natural terms. The analytic reading of the hypothetical principle provides a definition of a normative concept in natural terms. Therefore, it's false.

My response to this objection is to reject the open-question argument, at least as it applies to *hypothetical* normativity. "Doing X will satisfy one of my desires, but do I have some reason to do X?" isn't a question with an open feel, at least not for me (Rosen 2020). That an action will satisfy one of my desires is *precisely* what I mean when I say that I have a hypothetical normative reason to do it. Moorean questions will feel open when normative terminology is used in the *moral* sense. But this isn't the case when normative terminology is used in the desire-relative or standard-relative sense. The analytic reading of the hypothetical principle is just a definition of what I have called the desire-relative use of normative-reasons terminology.

But is that really *normativity*? Indulge me for a moment, and imagine that the universe makes no demands of any kind, that there truly are no categorical reasons, and no standards, other than your own, for what kinds of actions to pursue. If the world were that way, what would you do? How would you act? The problem of practical deliberation, of how to live your life, does not arise from the fact that objective facts about how we ought to live our lives exist. It arises from the fact that we are agents with a particular kind of ability: the ability to deliberate, and to act in the way that we choose as the result of that deliberation. If there were no fact of the matter about how you *really ought to* act, what would you do? Would you slump down in despair, sinking into the couch never to arise again? I hope not; yet even if you did, this would be an action, in a broad sense. You'd be choosing to sink into the couch. The neurological systems that control how you move your body are wired through the neurological systems that deliberate. Those connections can be weakened or destroyed by deep depression or developmental defects, but most of us aren't thus afflicted. Deliberative action is inescapable for agents who aren't dead, depressed, or disabled. That being the case, and imagining that you know full well that there's nothing that you really ought to do, the deliberative question remains. What shall you do? How shall you act? How shall you live your life? Shall you do things that you don't want to do? Or shall you do things that you do want to do, things that bring you happiness, satisfaction, and a sense of meaning? It makes no sense to pursue what you dislike at the expense of what you like. You wouldn't be able to justify your actions to yourself if you act in a way that doesn't cohere with the standards that you have for yourself (Williams 1981).

This thought experiment—and of course it's not merely a thought experiment, since this is an accurate description of reality and of the actual conditions of our deliberation—shows that deliberation and rational action are possible in the absence of categorical reasons. As agents, we have to act in one way or another, and we have to find some way of rationalizing our actions. We can do so by showing that those actions are in accord with the things that matter most to us.

Things appear to us as goals from our own deliberative perspective, and we reason about how to obtain those goals from that same deliberative perspective. That's all. The universe makes no demands on our actions, not even a demand to follow our own desires. Rather, we make demands of ourselves in the form of desires, and normativity is a matter of living up to those demands. Nothing more.

6.5 Korsgaard's Objection

The second major objection to Humeanism is that it makes irrational action impossible. If the thing that we have most reason to do is just what we most want to do, then we'll always end up doing the thing that we have most reason to do, since our desires are what cause us to act the way that we do. Yet surely it's possible to do something that you shouldn't have done; irrational action is possible. As Christine Korsgaard writes, "Suppose, as Hume sometimes seemed to think, that the authority of our reasons for action must be derived from the strength of our desires. Then you will always do what you have reason to do, and you can do no wrong" (Korsgaard 1996, 30). Call this **Korsgaard's objection**. I agree that it would be quite bad if our Humean account of reasons implied that it was always impossible to act irrationally. But the Humean theory of reasons doesn't have this implication.[3]

To understand why it doesn't, we need to distinguish between two questions that are, at first blush, easy to confuse. First, what makes it the case that an agent *has* a reason? Second, what determines the *strength*, or *weight*, of that reason? The thing that an agent *ought* to do is determined by what that agent has *most reason* to do. This idea of "most reason" is typically explained in terms of

---

3 I talk about the Humean theory of *reasons* rather than the more general Humean theory of *normativity*.

the weights of an agent's reasons on a metaphorical balance scale. Individual reasons have weights. We take all the reasons to do an action and add up their weights, then take all the reasons to not do that action and add up those weights. Whichever side has more weight is what you should do. This is reflected in how we make "pro" and "con" lists. If we want to make a list of pros and cons to decide what to do, we don't just count up the pros and the cons and pick whichever action has more pros or cons. Some of the items on the list might be very important, and others less important. The importance or weight of various reasons is what concerns us here.

What determines the weights of reasons? If we accept the Humean theory of reasons, a natural thesis suggests itself which Mark Schroeder, the foremost contemporary defender of the Humean theory of reasons, has called **proportionalism**. "Proportionalism is the thesis that when a reason is explained by a desire ... its weight varies in proportion to the strength of that desire, and to how well the action promotes that desire" (2007, 98). Schroeder notes that proportionalism is a natural idea, which is why it's accepted by most Humeans. But it's not entailed by the Humean theory of reasons. It's coherent to say that an agent *has* a reason only if that reason is part of what explains why an agent desires an action, but that the *weight* of that reason has nothing to do with the strength of the desire. So it's possible to accept the Humean theory of reasons while rejecting proportionalism. (That's what Schroeder does.)

Proportionalism is what gives rise to Korsgaard's objection. Let's grant, as seems plausible, that what an agent does depends on the strength of the agent's desires. An agent *will* do what she *most strongly desires* to do. And if proportionalism is true, then what the agent has most reason to do will be the thing that she most strongly desires to do. Thus, agents will always do what they ought to do; that was the problem.

One way to solve this problem is to point out that deliberation isn't just a matter of the strength of our desires, but our ability to reason and figure out what will satisfy those desires. We desire ends, not actions. (We may have the performance of actions as one of our ends, but that's certainly not always the case.) Thus, we might not always do what we ought to do, since we might reason poorly about how to get what we want, and so act in ways that will frustrate our desires.

This helps, but the view that what an agent ought to do is what they most strongly desire to do still has bad implications regarding impulses or pathological desires. To illustrate with an example from Gibbard (1993, 56): suppose you have a taste for nuts and find yourself seated at a party next to a dish of nuts. If your desire to eat nuts is strong enough, you might find yourself stuffing yourself with nuts all evening long even if it ruins your diet, deprives the other guests the opportunity to eat nuts, and makes you look a bit of a slob. In such a case, your strongest desire is to eat the nuts, and you're not making any mistakes in reasoning about how to achieve that desire. But you should still stop eating the nuts. We can't account for this if we accept proportionalism.

But rejecting proportionalism brings its own problems. Proportionalism is often conflated with the Humean theory of reasons because it's a natural view about the weight of hypothetical reasons. I've argued that the Humean theory of reasons gives a natural explanation of why our desires can guide and rationalize our actions. We're guided by our desires, and guided most strongly by our strongest desires. If we fail to successfully pursue our ends, we fail only ourselves. So the degree to which we fail ourselves seems like a product of how strongly we desire the goal that we fail in our pursuit of. In this way, proportionalism seems to fall out of the argument for the Humean theory (Rieder 2016).

So while Schroeder rejects proportionalism completely, I'm not so bold. Rather than reject proportionalism outright, we should refine it. Schroeder's proportionalism—call it *simple proportionalism*—says that the weight of a reason is proportional to two factors, the strength of the desire and the degree to which the action will promote the desire, where the strength of the desire is understood as simply the influence that desire has on an agent's motivations. I propose that the weight of a reason is proportional to *three* factors: the motivational strength of the desire, the degree to which the action will promote the desire, and how central the desire is to the agent's self-conception (Korsgaard 1996, lecture 3). Call this **reflective proportionalism**.

To see what this means in practice, let's consider a simple example.[4] A college student has a major exam the next day, and she hasn't finished studying. To get a good grade, she'll have to study more. But there's also a big party that night. It'll be a lot of fun;

---

4 Adapted from Huemer (2005, 164).

it's the social event of the semester. To enjoy herself and maintain her popularity, she'll have to go to the party. She cannot both go to the party and study. She both wants to get a good grade and to go to the party. And in the end, she more strongly desires to go to the party. So she does, enjoys herself immensely, makes some new friends... and bombs her test the next day. Did she make the right decision? According to simple proportionalism, she did. She most wanted to go to the party, and she did what she most wanted to do; thus she did what she had most reason to do. But according to reflective proportionalism, there's a further question we must ask: which of these desires is more central to our student's self-conception? We can imagine the story going either way. Perhaps our student is only at college at the urging of her parents, carried there by social inertia, but with no interest in academia. Nor is she attempting to get a job with the aid of a stellar transcript; she plans on going into a field where who you know is more important than what you know, and while employers might care whether or not she graduates, Cs get degrees. And at the same time, our student is a highly social person, and gets a deep sense of fulfillment from making connections with new people and having new experiences. In such a case, she might well have most reason to do what she was most strongly motivated to do. Alternatively, perhaps our student deeply cares about learning for its own sake. She's a lover of knowledge, considers herself to be a scholar, and sees her college education as an important step in her lifelong pursuit of learning. In that case, she'd have most reason to stay home and study. While the temptation of the party exerted a stronger pull on her at the moment, the desire to party was a mere temptation, while the desire to study is central to her self-conception.

One might ask at this point what, precisely, is meant by talking about how close a desire is to an agent's self-conception. I'm happy to leave this a little vague, since I see a few different accounts that could be offered and have no strong preference for any of them. But I'll offer two potential accounts here. One, more Humean in spirit, is that a desire is central to my self-conception if that desire is one that I desire to have. This account has some welcome implications. Higher-order desires give rise to reasons the same way that first-order desires do; I can have a reason not to have a desire if I desire not to have that desire. Thus, we can explain the fact that my reasons are weaker when they don't align with my self-conception by saying that I have higher-order reasons to reject my first-order desires.[5]

Another, more Kantian in spirit, is that centrality to self-conception is an unanalyzable feature of the structure of the self. This account has the benefit of being truer to the phenomenology of the self. When I reflect on the kinds of desires that I take to be closest to my self-conception, I don't think of these as desires that I *want* to have. I think of these desires as constituting *who I really am*. When I think of my desire to study and think about philosophy, this isn't (just) a desire that I desire to have. It's a desire that is constitutive of who I am, because I am a philosopher, and I couldn't imagine myself being the same person without that desire (Korsgaard 1996, lecture 3). I feel similarly about my love of my family. I can't imagine not loving my wife and son dearly, and if I try to conceive of myself as not loving my wife and son, it feels in some sense like I'm trying to imagine a different person. I don't feel the same way about my love of craft beer or my dislike of people who use the phrase "begs the question" to mean "raises the question."

Put a gun to my head and I'll pick the second account over the first, although I find the theoretical unity of the first account attractive. Perhaps these two accounts can be combined. At any rate, I remain pretty flexible about what to say about this notion of "centrality to the self." But hopefully you have a sense of what I'm trying to put my finger on. It's an important notion.

6.6 Cuneo's Objection

The next objection to Humean error theory that I'll consider is a companions-in-innocence objection. Companions-in-innocence objections, as we saw in §3.2, are objections to error theory that attempt to show that the supposedly problematic feature of morality is shared by some other subject matter. If that feature is enough to make us be error theorists about morality, then it should be enough to make us error theorists about this other subject matter. However, the objection continues, it's impossible or incoherent to be an error theorist about this other subject matter. Therefore, the supposedly problematic feature of morality can't really be that

---

5 Compare Schroeder (2007, chapters 7 and 10).

problematic to begin with. The Humean error theorist says that the problematic feature of morality is *categorical normativity*. So one prominent companions-in-innocence objection to Humean error theory maintains that morality isn't the only thing that's categorically normative: epistemic normativity is categorical as well. If a subject S's evidence strongly supports the proposition P, then S *ought to believe* P, no matter what S wants to believe. So if there's no such thing as categorical normativity, then there's no such thing as epistemic normativity. But if a Humean error theorist says that there's no such thing as epistemic normativity, then there's no (epistemic) reason to believe error theory about epistemic normativity; error theory about epistemic normativity is directly self-undermining. Therefore, epistemic normativity exists. Therefore, categorical normativity exists. Therefore, Humean error theory is wrong. This argument was forcefully and influentially developed in Terence Cuneo's *The Normative Web* (2007). Call it **Cuneo's objection**.

We already have the resources to answer Cuneo's objection. I noted earlier that there's a standard-relative use of normative terminology. This use of normative terminology doesn't imply the existence of normative reasons in the action-guiding sense, since the conventional standard in question might not be one that anyone desires. Yet in typical cases, the standard will be introduced because it's desired by the speaker (or the person they're speaking to, or about), and so it's often the case that agents will have a normative reason in the action-guiding sense to conform to the standard in question. This applies straightforwardly to epistemic reasons.

In epistemology, normative terminology is typically used in the standard-relative way. The broadest and most widely applicable standard is the standard of knowledge. That knowledge is the relevant standard is frequently implicit, and supplied by context. But we can make the standard explicit by saying that agents have an *epistemic* reason or that they *epistemically* ought to believe something; "epistemic" just means "relating to knowledge," after all. Thus, to say that someone epistemically ought to believe P is to say that believing P will tend to bring about knowledge of P. What it takes to know P, and what will bring about knowing P, doesn't depend on anyone's desires. So when we talk about epistemic normativity in the standard-relative sense, we're talking about something categorical. Cuneo is right to say that what our evidence supports doesn't depend on what we want.

But this does not mean that epistemic normativity in the action-guiding (or, in this case, belief-guiding) sense is normative. We need not say that P has any property of to-be-believed-ness if P is supported by your evidence. Rather, you ought to believe P *insofar as you care to know whether P*. To illustrate: suppose that vaccines don't cause autism, there's a huge body of scientific evidence demonstrating this, this evidence is readily available to me, and I care to know whether or not vaccines cause autism. In that case, I can know whether vaccines cause autism. The most efficient way for me to obtain this knowledge is by consulting the scientific evidence and, on the basis of this evidence, drawing the conclusion that vaccines don't cause autism. Thus, because I desire to know whether vaccines cause autism, I ought to believe that they don't on the basis of the available evidence that demonstrates this. This is hypothetical normativity (compare Olson 2014, ch. 8; Cowie 2014).

Most people are fairly curious. Aristotle famously begins the *Metaphysics* with the claim that "all people, by nature, desire to know." But our curiosity isn't unlimited; there are some things that we really don't care to know. Suppose you're presented with a large jar of marbles, and asked whether the number of marbles in the jar is or isn't prime. Perhaps this question piques your curiosity. But for me, and probably for you as well, it's uninteresting. You don't care how many marbles are in the jar, much less whether the number of marbles in the jar is prime. But now suppose that you're presented with overwhelming evidence that the number of marbles in the jar isn't prime. Should you now believe that the number of marbles in the jar isn't prime? How we answer the question depends on how we understand the use of the normative term 'should.' That term could be used in either its standard-relative or desire-relative sense. Usually, those two standards coincide. But this is one of the atypical cases where we don't care about the standard in question. So you should believe that the number of marbles in the jar isn't prime (in the standard-relative sense of 'should'). That's what it would take to get knowledge of whether the number of marbles is prime. But it's not the case that you should believe that the number of marbles in the jar is prime (in the desire-relative sense of 'should'). You have no desire that would be satisfied by believing that the number of marbles isn't prime, and so you would make no mistake in failing to form that belief. So while Cuneo is correct to say that there is a sense in which epistemic normativity is categorical (viz., the standard-relative sense), this doesn't substantiate the existence of categorical normativity in the guiding sense, which is what he needs for his companions-in-innocence argument to succeed.

6.7 Tiefensee's Objection

The next objection to error theory holds that error theory is logically incoherent. This objection was introduced by error theorists trying to figure out the best way to formulate their own view (Pigden 2007), but in recent years it's increasingly been seen as an important challenge to error theory, as critics, most notably Christine Tiefensee, have argued that there is no coherent formulation of the error theory. We'll call it **Tiefensee's objection.**

Tiefensee's objection has two versions, a simple version and a sophisticated version. According to the simple version, error theory says that all moral claims are false. But 'killing is wrong' and 'it's not the case that killing is wrong' are both moral claims. Yet it's incoherent to say that both of those claims could be false, since they're logical contradictories. So error theory is incoherent (Tiefensee and Wheeler 2022, 3–4). This objection rests on a misunderstanding of error theory. Error theory isn't the view that all moral claims are false; it's the conjunction of cognitivism with non-negotiable error: moral predicates are about moral properties, but there are no moral properties for them to successfully refer to. That means that simple, atomic moral sentences like 'killing is wrong' are guaranteed to be untrue. But complex moral sentences, particularly those that contain negations, may well be true. The simple version of Tiefensee's objection is a bit like saying that atheism is incoherent because the atheist believes that all religious sentences are false, which means the atheist thinks that 'God exists' and 'God doesn't exist' are both false, and that's incoherent. But of course the atheist thinks that 'God doesn't exist' is true. Similarly, the error theorist thinks that some "moral" sentences—to wit, the sentences that say that moral properties don't exist—are true.

The sophisticated version of Tiefensee's objection begins from the observation that everything is either permissible or forbidden. It's both common sense and a theorem of deontic logic that if an action isn't forbidden, it's permissible, and if it isn't permissible, it's forbidden. But both permissibility and forbiddenness are moral properties. So it's a theorem of deontic logic that everything has a moral property. Therefore, it is incoherent to deny the existence of moral properties, as error theory does (Tiefensee 2020).

This objection can be answered by distinguishing between two senses of 'permissible.' In the *normatively committed sense*, something is permissible if and only if *it is appropriate to permit it*, where permitting some action means (something like) being cool with it and not giving anyone a hard time if they do it. In the *minimal sense*, something is permissible if and only if it's not forbidden. Deontic logic only shows that every action is either forbidden or minimally permissible. But that is consistent with error theory; minimal permissibility isn't a moral property, it's just the absence of the property of forbiddenness. Normative permissibility is a moral property, but it's not a theorem of deontic logic that everything that is not forbidden is normatively permissible. That is, it's not a theorem of deontic logic that everything is either to-be-forbidden or to-be-permitted. So it is not incoherent for error theorists to say that nothing is forbidden and nothing is normatively permissible, and it is not inconsistent with error theory to say that everything is minimally permissible.

6.8   Finlay's Objection

The last objection to error theory questions whether or not we're really committed to morality being categorically normative. Humean error theorists claim that it's a conceptual truth about morality that moral facts (if they exist) are categorically normative, then argue that there's no such thing as categorical normativity. Most objections to Humean error theory—particularly Hampton's objection and Cuneo's objection—challenge the claim that there's no such thing as categorical normativity. But Stephen Finlay (2008) has called the conceptual claim that morality is categorically normative "the error in the error theory". So we'll call this concern **Finlay's objection**.

There are two versions of Finlay's objection. The weak version holds that categoricity is part of our concept of morality, but this conceptual commitment is "negotiable" and so doesn't threaten the truth of any of our moral judgments. A concept of morality-minus-categoricity is close enough to our original concept to count as the concept of morality. The strong version holds that categoricity was never part of our concept of morality at all.[6] Finlay illustrates the point with an

---

6   Finlay uses the term "absolutism" rather than "categoricity," where "absolutism" is supposed to capture both categoricity and anti-relativism.

analogy. It's common sense (for most of us) that space and time are absolute, and that certain spatiotemporal properties, like the property of being in motion, are equally absolute. Something is either in motion or it's not, period. But then Einstein's theory of relativity comes along, thereby substantiating the Leibnizian hypothesis that all motion is relative to a frame of reference. Did we come to believe that *motion doesn't exist* as a result? Of course not. We just learned something new about motion. The weak version of the objection says that non-relativism is part of a naive concept of motion, but it's a negotiable part. The concept of relative motion is different from our naive concept of absolute motion, but it's close enough to count; the theory of relativity didn't, and shouldn't have, made us error theorists about motion. The strong version of the objection says that the ease with which we made the transition to a relativistic conception of motion shows that our naive concept of motion wasn't absolute to begin with. Absolutism about motion was an esoteric hypothesis that was disproved by subsequent investigation. Similarly, when we reflect on Mackie's arguments, realize how weird categoricity is, and come to believe that nothing is categorically normative, we shouldn't stop believing in morality. We've just learned something new about morality: that it's not categorically normative. This shows that categoricity is a negotiable part of our concept of morality, or else that it was never part of our concept of morality at all. Finlay, ambitiously, wants to push the strong version of the objection and say that categoricity was never part of our concept of morality.

Not only is categoricity part of our concept of morality, but there is no different concept, morality-minus-categoricity, that is close enough to our original moral concept to count as morality. So both versions of Finlay's objection fail. This is a hard point to argue because the point of contention is so abstract. There's no agreed-on method for establishing what makes something a non-negotiable conceptual commitment.[7] Philosophers just rely on our intuitions here: I have the intuition that categoricity is non-negotiable and there's no morality-minus that's close enough. Finlay lacks that intuition. We're at an impasse.[8]

---

7 Although see Prinzing (2017).
8 Steve was my dissertation advisor. Surprisingly, we rarely debated this point at length; I suspect this is because neither of us knew how we could make progress on the debate.

I think I can provide some support for my intuition. What would morality-minus look like? Perhaps it would look something like a set of rules of conduct or standards of evaluation, any or all of which you *may* care about (and many of which you *do* care about) but none of which are *to-be-cared-about*. We've already talked about what rules like that are: they're what we called "descriptive morality" in Chapter 1. There we said that descriptive morality is different from normative morality, and that normative morality is our subject in this book, not descriptive morality. I hope everyone nodded along when they read that: yes, right, of course. But suppose you were told that normative morality, in the sense we described it there, doesn't quite exist, and the only morality that exists is descriptive morality. But that's not a really big deal, since descriptive morality is close enough to normative morality to count. So really normative morality *does* exist, it just exists *as* descriptive morality. Looks like moral theory just got a lot easier! Philosophy departments should start hiring empirical anthropologists or psychologists to help them work out the answers to moral problems. I find that suggestion bizarre.

Learning that descriptive morality is the only kind of morality that there is would amount to learning that there's no morality of the kind that moral philosophers care about. This was a big part of our objections to relativism and moral naturalism in §2.2 and §3.1.2: that relativists and naturalists looked for a naturalistically respectable subject matter for morality, found one in descriptive morality, and said "good enough." But descriptive morality obviously isn't good enough; it's a different thing.

This response to Finlay's objection assumes that morality-minus is descriptive morality. Finlay doesn't endorse that assumption, but this is what morality-minus always seems to amount to.[9] Still, there's room for an opponent of error theory to give a different account of

---

9   Finlay's own account is more complicated than this simple presentation suggests; the view I'm targeting in the main text is closer to the view of Peter Railton (2017) than Finlay's. In "The Error in the Error Theory," Finlay (2008) argues for a kind of relativism where the meaning of our moral terminology is determined by shared moral standards. In later work (particularly Finlay 2014), he argues for a looser contextualist semantics for normative terminology. I'm actually quite sympathetic to his contextualist semantics, and endorsed the essence of it in §6.3. But I think that there is a distinctive moral use of normative terminology, and Finlay denies this. I think we sometimes talk about what *really* matters, "from the point of view of the universe." Finlay thinks moral discussion is pragmatic negotiation over what ends to desire and pursue.

morality-minus. We'd need an account of morality-minus that both emphatically rejects categorical normativity while also offering up a picture of what morality consists in that is substantially different from descriptive morality and thus more plausible as an account of what morality really consists in. I'm aware of no account that's up to this task.

Hampton's objection fails because the hypothetical principle isn't a categorical imperative, it's the analysis of what I called in §6.3 the desire-relative use of normative terminology. Korsgaard's objection fails because people can reason poorly and because the weight of a reason is not proportional to the motivational strength of the desire on which it's based. Cuneo's objection fails because the epistemic use of normative terminology is always standard-relative and frequently desire-relative, but neither of those uses of normative terminology imply the existence of categorical normativity. Tiefensee's objection equivocates on two distinct senses of 'permissible.' And Finlay's objection is just mistaken; categoricity is a non-negotiable part of our concept of morality.

Chapter 7

The Case for Skepticism

Matt Lutz

Contents

In Chapter 6, I argued that we can make sense of hypothetical normativity in a way that we just can't make sense of categorical normativity. This is a reason to not believe in categorical normativity or in morality, but it's not a conclusive reason. As weird as categorical normativity is, it might be rational to believe in morality if we have strong evidence for it. However, I'll argue in this section that we have *no* evidence for the truth of any moral claim.

7.1 The Explanationist Argument for Skepticism

My argument takes off from a famous argument by Gilbert Harman. Harman asks us to imagine a case of "moral observation," where you encounter a group of hoodlums who douse a cat with gasoline and light it on fire. If you were to observe this, you'd

DOI: 10.4324/9781003183174-11

have an immediate feeling of shock and horror and form a judgment about what you just witnessed: "That's wrong!" But why would you form that judgment? Why would you have that feeling of horror? There's an explanation for why you made the judgment that you made, but that explanation doesn't seem to involve the fact that it was wrong to light the cat on fire. We can fully explain your judgment by appeal to non-moral facts about your environment, cats, and fire, and psychological facts about you and how you are disposed to react when you see something so sadistic. You don't believe that it was wrong because it's wrong (Harman 1977, ch. 1).

If you know that it's wrong to light the cat on fire, then presumably you have some evidence that it's wrong. So what's the evidence? Presumably, it's something about the nature of the action that you're observing and your experiences of that action; perhaps it also includes the feeling of shock and horror that attends that observation. You think that it's wrong to burn the cat because it just feels so wrong! But now the question is: what explains that supposed evidence? Why do you have the visual experience of burning the cat; why do you feel horror at the sight? The fact that it's wrong to burn the cat isn't part of that explanation. Physical and psychological facts are sufficient to explain your evidence. This means that your (supposed) evidence doesn't really support your moral belief. If there's no connection between your evidence and the fact that your evidence is supposed to be evidence for, then that evidence isn't an indicator of that fact, and so not evidence for that fact.

Harman's argument is one of the most important arguments for moral skepticism. Other popular arguments include evolutionary debunking arguments and arguments from disagreement. These arguments make the same point in slightly different ways. Arguments from disagreement begin from the observation that not only is there widespread moral disagreement, but that moral disagreement typically breaks down along social and cultural lines. This implies that our moral intuitions, and thus beliefs, are explained by a variety of cultural factors. Similarly, evolutionary debunking arguments begin from the observation that humans are the product of evolution, and thus our tendency to form moral judgments is likely a product of evolution as well. And, indeed, agents who live in groups that exhibit altruistic behavior towards other members of their group will have a survival advantage over agents who don't (Joyce 2016, ch. 1; Christakis 2019). So our moral intuitions and thus beliefs are explained by evolution. All of these arguments make the same point as Harman: our moral intuitions, and thus moral beliefs, aren't explained by moral facts. They're explained by something else (Lutz 2018).

But what are they explained by? Evolution, culture, or personal psychological factors? The answer, of course, is all three. Full explanations are complex; they include both ultimate and proximate causal factors. Evolution, culture, and personal psychology are all different parts of one complex explanation. Evolution explains why we're the kind of creatures with the capacity to make moral judgments in the first place (Joyce 2006). It also explains some of our most basic, universal dispositions: to help those who have helped us (Joyce 2006, ch. 1), to give particular attention to those that we are genetically related to (Street 2006), to distinguish between "ingroups" with whom mutual cooperation is expected and "outgroups" who are objects of suspicion and potential competition (Zimmerman 2017), and to punish members of the ingroup who don't help us as they're expected to do. These basic tendencies to form moral judgments are flexible, and different cultures enact these basic moral dispositions in different ways. Primitive societies will be more likely to draw the ingroup/ outgroup distinction along kinship lines, more advanced societies will draw the distinction along religious lines, and the most advanced civilizations draw the line between those who do and those who don't support Donald Trump. And finally, these various social pressures will come to shape the intuitions and dispositions of particular agents, whose psychology is subject to a host of other dispositions and biases (Sinnott-Armstrong 2006, ch. 9). These forces all shape our moral attitudes, which we then project when we form moral judgments. This is just a sketch of a vastly more complex story. But this is, in outline, the best scientific account of why people form the moral judgments that they form, according to the psychologists and sociologists who study this sort of thing (Sinnott-Armstrong 2008a, 2008b; Joyce 2006, ch. 1–4). Because it includes evolutionary, cultural, and psychological (ECP) factors, I call it the **ECP story**.

For some, simply reflecting on ECP's ability to explain our moral judgments is enough to convince them that those judgments are unreliable or unjustified. Others will point out that the ECP story doesn't *entail* that there are no moral facts or that our moral beliefs are unsupported. Some further argument is needed to show that our moral beliefs are in trouble. I think that the best way to flesh out the idea that ECP causes trouble for our moral beliefs is the following argument:

Explanationist argument for skepticism

1   A belief in a proposition P is supported by evidence for a subject S just in case P fits with the well-confirmed elements of S's explanatory map.
2   Beliefs in moral propositions don't fit with the well-confirmed elements of anyone's explanatory map.
3   Therefore, no one's moral beliefs are supported by evidence.
4   Therefore, no one's moral beliefs amount to knowledge.

In this chapter, I'll explain and defend this argument. The key premise is the first one. That's the epistemological premise that says what evidence is and what it takes for a claim to be supported by evidence. Everything turns on this premise, so it requires some rather extensive elaboration and defense. Moral epistemology is a species of applied epistemology; as such, you can't productively evaluate arguments for or against moral skepticism without taking on substantive epistemic commitments about the nature of evidence or knowledge. So let's set ethics aside briefly and turn our attention to epistemology.

7.2   The Epistemic Premise

Premise 1 is a bit complicated, so I'll first introduce the basic ideas and then gradually add on some complications. Premise 1 is an instance of an **explanationist** account of evidential support. According to explanationism, a proposition is supported by evidence for a subject if and only if the truth of that proposition is part of the best explanation of why the subject has that evidence (McCain 2014, 63). The idea that we know about the world by "inference to the best explanation" (a phrase actually coined by Harman 1965) is popular, but the idea that we can know about a claim if it's "part of the best explanation" of why you have your evidence is more of a slogan than a worked-out view. This is because the idea of "best explanation" is a bit vague. What's an explanation? And what makes an explanation the "best?"

7.2.1   Best Explanations: Explanatory Maps

The word 'explanation' has two meanings. One is verbal. An explanation in the verbal sense is the sort of thing that you provide when you're trying to get someone to understand something. Right now, I'm trying to get you, dear reader, to understand my account of evidence. This text is an explanation. The second definition is metaphysical. An explanation is a *cause* or *reason why* something is the case. Metaphysical explanations are generally causes, but there are relations other than causation that have been described as metaphysical explanations. We'll look at some of these in due course. For now, it's simplest to think of metaphysical explanations as causes. That the vase fell off the table explains why it broke; the vase's falling is the explanation of the breaking.

Both of these definitions are relevant to understanding the idea of the "best explanation." The best explanation is the best verbal account of metaphysical explanations. Verbal accounts of metaphysical explanations attempt to provide understanding by answering a "why?" question. We see the vase broken on the floor. Why is it broken? We can offer a number of different hypotheses about the causes of the breaking. Each of these is an explanation of why the vase broke.

Verbal accounts of causes are important in epistemology because we posit hypotheses about causes in order to explain our evidence. So what's "evidence"? Primarily, our evidence is our experiences. We can understand "experience" quite broadly, to include not only sensory experiences but also intuitions, memories, feelings, reflections on our own mental states, and possibly other mental states as well. So suppose I see a table. That visual experience of a table is part of my evidence. Why do I have that visual experience? We can consider a number of different explanatory hypotheses. One possible explanation of my experience is that it's the product of a VR simulation. Another possible explanation is that I'm really seeing a table. Which of these two hypotheses is supported by my evidence? That depends on which explanation is best. If the table hypothesis is the best explanation of my evidence, then that visual experience supports the claim that there's a table. If the VR hypothesis is the best, then my visual experience supports the claim that I'm observing a VR simulation.

So what makes an explanation the best? This depends on your background beliefs. To a first approximation, the best explanation is the one that fits best with your background beliefs. If you have just put on a VR headset (and are aware that you have done so), then you should take your visual experiences to be evidence for how things are in the VR simulation. If you haven't put on a VR headset and are in normal circumstances, you should take your visual experiences to be evidence for how things are in reality because in normal circumstances you believe that your visual experiences are caused by the real world. If you're wearing a particularly advanced and realistic VR headset, you might have exactly the same visual experiences as you do when you're experiencing the real world. But because you have different background beliefs about the causes of your visual experiences, your evidence will support different things in the different cases.

A basic causal explanation will have different parts. We can cite a *particular fact* which is the (purported) cause of your experience. The existence of the table is such a particular fact: you have that visual experience because a table exists. We can also cite a *particular explanatory relation* that holds between the particular explanans and particular explanandum: *that* table causes *this* experience. And particular explanatory relations can be generalized. It's not just that table which causes this table-like visual experience; in general, tables cause table-like visual experiences in agents with functioning eyesight who are appropriately situated. And that follows from an even more general principle: that agents with functioning eyesight will have visual experiences that are caused by objects in their environment. So we also have beliefs in *general explanatory principles*.

Beliefs in general explanatory principles are extremely important for determining which explanation is best. The "best explanation" isn't just one that fits your beliefs about particular causes and particular explanatory relations; if they were, any explanation could count as "best" if you were willing to add *ad hoc* beliefs about causes to your background beliefs. The particular explanatory relations that feature in an explanation of our experiences must be instances of general explanatory beliefs. This is how things work for normal human agents. We have a variety of beliefs about particular facts; we have beliefs about the particular explanatory relations that hold between those particular facts; and we have beliefs about general explanatory relations of which those particular explanatory relations are instances. Taken together, these beliefs form a general model of the way the world is and the way the world works. I call this model an **explanatory map** of the world. Because explanatory maps contain a wide variety of beliefs in particular facts and general explanatory principles, they can be called on to explain *all* of our experiences. The better our explanatory map fits our experiences, the better it is.

As an indication that we're on the right track, this is an (approximate) account of how scientific investigation works. Scientists collect data through experiments. They then attempt to construct causal models of the world that fit their data. Good scientific theories are theories that explain the data.

We've been diving into epistemology, although still remaining in the shallows. Let's come up for air and see what this means from the perspective of the argument for moral skepticism. We're trying to figure out whether moral beliefs are supported by evidence. In the context of our moral beliefs, our evidence for moral claims is often supposed to bottom out in our moral intuitions or emotions, like the feeling of shock and horror that we'd feel if we saw some hoodlums light a cat on fire. Those intuitions and emotions are experiences, so they're part of our evidence. We can now ask what explains that evidence. Fortunately, this is a question that has been scientifically investigated. The result of that investigation is the ECP story. Not only is the ECP story *an* explanation of why we have our moral evidence, it's the consensus view among scientists. So it's a pretty good explanation, arguably the best (Sinnott-Armstrong 2008a, 2008b, 2008c). The ECP story is supported by a variety of evidence. But what of moral beliefs? To answer that, we need to dive a bit deeper into epistemology. Take a deep breath.

7.2.2   Best Explanations: Confirmation

A major worry for the account I've been developing so far is that it makes evidential support arbitrary. If whether a belief is supported by evidence for a subject depends on the background beliefs of that subject, it seems that we could make any of our beliefs supported by making suitable *ad hoc* modifications to our background beliefs. (This is what conspiracy theorists do. Give a conspiracy theorist any observation, and they'll construct some story that fits that observation into their conspiratorial model of the way the world works.) I've partly addressed this worry by saying that evidential support requires not just beliefs about the particular causes of particular pieces of evidence, but also integration into an explanatory map that is structured by general explanatory beliefs. But even such a map could be gerrymandered in various ways to accommodate any evidence. The worry remains.

To solve the problem, we need to replace our simple synchronic account of evidential support with a diachronic account. Having a belief that is supported by the evidence is like buttered toast. If you want to understand what buttered toast is, I could try to tell you by describing the physical structure of buttered toast in detail. But such an account would be missing something important: that buttered toast is the outcome of a process of toasting and buttering. Similarly, having a belief that's supported by evidence is the outcome of a process of *confirmation*.

Explanatory maps *generate predictions:* beliefs about the way the world is and the way the world works have implications for how the world will be in the future. Furthermore, we all have beliefs in our explanatory maps about the way that the world causes us to have experiences (e.g., tables cause table-like visual experiences). Thus, explanatory maps generate predictions not just about what the world will be like, but about what our experiences will be. In this way, explanatory maps make predictions about evidence that we haven't collected yet. We might have the experiences that the map predicts, but we might not. Accepting an explanatory map is *epistemically risky.*

If we have the experiences that the map predicts, that's an indication that the map is accurately reflecting reality, at least in part. Successful predictions (somewhat) confirm all of the elements of the map that were instrumental to making that successful prediction. On the other hand, if we don't have the experiences that the map predicts, that's an indication that something has gone wrong. This serves to (somewhat) disconfirm all of the elements of the map that were instrumental to making the unsuccessful prediction. Beliefs that make many successful predictions while making relatively few unsuccessful predictions are *well-confirmed.*

We can make *ad hoc* modifications to our explanatory maps to fit any arbitrary set of beliefs to any set of experiences. But a map full of *ad hoc* modifications probably doesn't accurately represent the causal structure of the world, and so will not end up being well-confirmed over time (Lipton 2004, ch. 9–10). So a belief isn't supported by evidence for a subject if it merely fits well with that subject's explanatory map at a given point in time. Beliefs gain support by evidence *over time* as they become well-confirmed by facilitating successful predictions. A belief is supported by evidence for a subject if and only if it fits with the beliefs in that subject's explanatory map *that are well-confirmed.*

Well-confirmed beliefs in general explanatory principles can extend our model beyond the scope of the immediate causes of my experiences. Once some beliefs are well-confirmed, any new belief that fits the well-confirmed beliefs is also supported by evidence. Primarily, it's supported by the experiences that have confirmed the map, and secondarily it's supported by the well-confirmed beliefs from which these further beliefs can be derived.

For instance, when I take a pen in my hand and toss it up, I believe that it will soon begin to fall. This belief is supported by evidence. I see and feel the pen in my hand, and see and feel the upward motion as I toss it. These sensory experiences are my evidence of what's happening. The following general principle is very well-confirmed: that if I have sensory experiences like these, then I really am throwing a pen in the air. So the claim that I am throwing a pen in the air is supported by the evidence of my sensory experiences, together with the evidence that confirmed that general principle. My map contains another principle: that things that I throw in the air will soon begin to fall back down. That general principle is also well confirmed, by my myriad experiences of tossing things in the air. So I believe that the pen will soon fall, and that belief is also supported by evidence. What evidence? All of the evidence that supports my belief that I'm throwing the pen, together with the evidence that confirmed the general principle that what goes up comes down.

Claims are supported by evidence only if they can be linked to that evidence via well-confirmed principles as part of a general explanatory model of the way the world works. So if a belief isn't well-confirmed, nor linked to well-confirmed elements of the map via well-confirmed explanatory principles, then that belief isn't supported by evidence. To illustrate, consider Zuzu. Zuzu has all of the beliefs about bells and what makes them ring and what it sounds like when they ring (and so on) as you do. These beliefs are all typical and well-confirmed. However, Zuzu also believes that whenever a bell rings, an angel gets its wings. (And this is grounded in a further belief about explanatory structure: that angels get their wings *because* bells ring).[1] Both Zuzu's particular beliefs about angels and

---

her general belief about explanatory structure are not supported by the evidence of experience (unless she's been granted some rather extraordinary visions). Her angel beliefs have facilitated no successful predictions, and so are not well-confirmed. So even though Zuzu's angel beliefs fit with her explanatory map, the pathways through her explanatory map that connect her angel beliefs to her experiences aren't well-confirmed. That's why Zuzu's beliefs, while cute and uplifting, aren't supported by evidence, and so don't amount to knowledge.

In sum: A belief in a proposition P is supported by evidence for a subject S just in case P fits with the well-confirmed elements of S's explanatory map. That's the epistemic premise.

7.3   The Vacuity of Moral Explanations

The other premise of the explanationist argument for skepticism states that beliefs in moral propositions don't fit with the well-confirmed elements of anyone's explanatory map. The ECP story is supported by evidence because its various elements have been well-confirmed by scientific experiments. The ECP story is purely descriptive: it contains no moral facts. So moral facts aren't part of the best explanation of our evidence.

We could attempt to remedy this by adding moral facts to the ECP story. The ECP story tells us that part of why we have a feeling of horror when we see kids lighting the cat on fire is that this causes a cute little critter pain for no other reason than taking pleasure in its suffering. And we might add: causing cute little critters pain for no other reason than to take pleasure in its suffering is wrong! But in appending this claim to the ECP story, we're adding a belief that isn't well-confirmed and indeed isn't confirmable. A belief can only be confirmed if it facilitates successful predictions of our future experiences. But moral beliefs don't facilitate any predictions about our experiences; that's not the role that moral beliefs play in our psychology.

---

that Zuzu believes that bells are caused to ring by angels getting their wings, and not the other way around. But this would be to saddle Zuzu with some rather implausible beliefs about the causes of bell-ringing.

The point here is precisely analogous to the one about Zuzu's belief that angels get their wings when a bell rings. Her angel-beliefs are coherent, but lack predictive power. Accordingly, if we compare Zuzu's explanatory map to one that is exactly similar, except all beliefs about angels are removed, we find that the former makes all the same predictions as the latter. This means that Zuzu's angel beliefs aren't well-confirmed and so not supported by evidence. Similarly, if we compare a typical person's total explanatory map to one that's exactly similar except that all moral beliefs are removed, we find that the former makes all the same predictions as the latter. That means that moral beliefs aren't well-confirmed and so not supported by evidence. That's the explanationist argument for skepticism.

> Moral knowledge requires that our beliefs be supported by evidence. A belief is supported by evidence only if the truth of that belief is the best explanation of that evidence. "Best explanation" should be understood primarily in terms of the explanatory power of that explanation and, in particular, the capacity of the claims that compose that explanation to facilitate successful predictions. A claim that facilitates no successful predictions cannot be supported by evidence. Moral claims facilitate no successful predictions, and thus aren't supported by evidence.

7.4   Objections to the Explanationist Argument for Skepticism

The explanationist argument for skepticism holds that moral beliefs can't be confirmed by evidence because moral facts can't explain our experiences. But moral naturalists hold that our moral beliefs *can* explain our experiences and be confirmed in this way—that's the naturalist's main commitment, as we saw in Chapter 3. So the naturalist will reject premise 2 of the argument, which says that adding moral facts to the ECP story adds nothing to the explanatory power of that story. The non-naturalist, on the other hand, will reject premise 1, and say that explanatory connections aren't a necessary condition on evidential support. Let's look at how those objections play out.

7.4.1   The Naturalist's Objection

There are two ways that a naturalist might go about objecting to premise 2. One strategy, the *identity strategy*, says that moral facts are identical to some of the facts that feature in the ECP story. Thus, the ECP story has just as much explanatory power as a story that includes moral facts, because the ECP story *is* a story that includes moral facts. A second strategy, the *higher-order properties strategy*, says that moral properties are higher-order properties that add to the explanatory power of the ECP story by providing explanations at the right level of generality.

We'll look at the higher-order properties strategy first. According to the higher-order properties strategy, moral properties are higher-order properties that are multiply realizable in underlying natural properties. Thus, for instance, the state of injustice could be realized in a myriad number of different social/political circumstances (Sturgeon 1988). Suppose a particular unjust society undergoes a revolution. What explains the revolution? It could either be the higher-order property of injustice or the more fundamental facts about the particular social/political circumstances. But explanations at the more fundamental level are often worse explanations than explanations at the higher level (Yablo 1992). If any unjust society is more prone to revolution, then the revolution isn't best explained by the particular configuration of social facts. If the society had slightly different social circumstances, it would still be unjust and thus the revolution still would have happened. But if it weren't unjust, the revolution wouldn't have happened. Thus, the explanation that appeals to injustice is the best explanation, because it explains at the right level of generality (Oddie 2005, ch. 7; Majors 2007).

The problem with the higher-order properties strategy is that the ECP story doesn't exclude higher-order properties. That higher-order properties will be part of the ECP story was already implicit in the fact that the ECP story is a story about evolutionary, cultural, and psychological factors, not a story about the interaction of fundamental physical properties. All ECP explanations will be explanations in terms of higher-order properties, and the best version of the ECP story will be one that appeals to the appropriate higher-order properties that explain at the right level of generality. So if all and only those societies with higher-order property X are strongly disposed toward revolution, then the ECP story will include property X as part of the explanation of why revolutions occur. Including beliefs about property X in your explanatory map will facilitate reliable predictive success about what societies will undergo revolutions.

This shows that the higher-order properties strategy is an instance of the identity strategy. The higher-order property X explains a society's tendency toward revolution (and thus our experiences of the revolution), and so injustice explains the society's tendency toward revolution because injustice is identical to property X. In general:

Natural Identity: Moral facts are identical to some of the natural facts that explain our experiences.

The problem with this response is that it's not enough to assert that Natural Identity is true. We need some evidence that it's true (Huemer 2005, ch. 4). This is a reasonable demand. We can get evidence that identity claims are true because claims about identity can have explanatory power. The claim that the morning star and the evening star are the same celestial body explains why astronomers make certain astrological observations. The claim that water is H_2O explains why we can separate water into two different gasses through electrolysis. These claims can be supported by evidence because they make predictions about our experiences, and those predictions are successful, so those claims are well-confirmed. But the claim that goodness is identical to some natural property doesn't explain anything, and thus is unsupported by evidence.

Here's another way to put the problem. Consider unicorns again. Suppose I argue that we shouldn't believe in unicorns because we have no evidence that unicorns exist, and a unicorn-believer responds by saying that we do have evidence that unicorns exist, because facts about unicorns are identical to some of the natural facts that explain our experiences. This is the sort of the thing that a unicorn-believer (who accepts the key epistemic premise of my argument) will have to say, but it's absurd: which facts that are part of the explanatory history of my experiences are the unicorn facts, exactly? What reason do we have to think that any of those facts are unicorn facts? This question cannot be waved away—"Call whichever natural facts you like the unicorn facts!"—because unicorns are a particular kind of creature. The unicorn facts need to be facts about magical horse-like creatures with a single horn. Similarly, moral facts are (putatively) a particular kind of fact. Moral facts must be facts about what gives us categorical normative reasons. Why think that any of the natural facts that explain our experiences are categorically normative? Property X might be (part of) the best explanation of why a society undergoes a revolution. But unless property X is a source of categorically normative reasons, property X isn't injustice. So what evidence do we have that property X is injustice? We have none, because the claim that a property is a source of categorically normative reasons adds nothing to the explanatory power of any theory that includes that property. Categorical normativity is always an unnecessary addition to our picture of the world.

One way that naturalists have tried to solve this problem is by accepting causal reference theory: 'Good' refers to whatever causally regulates our use of the term 'good.' This provides us with a way of locating goodness within the mess of natural facts that explains our various experiences. We're not just looking for *any* natural fact, we're looking for the fact that makes us say things like "That's good." There's surely *something* that causes us to say "that's good;" the word 'good' refers to that something; thus, there's something which is goodness.

But as we saw in §3.1.2, causal reference theory lands the naturalist with the causal relativism problem. If different properties cause different people to say things like "that's good," then the word 'good' means different things for those people. Thus, causal reference theory implies that people with different moral systems are talking past each other, when in fact they're disagreeing with each other. The deeper problem for the naturalist who relies on the causal reference theory involves the distinction between normative and descriptive morality. Descriptive morality consists in actual moral attitudes and practices; it's what anthropologists investigate. Ethics is the study of *normative* morality, i.e., what our moral attitudes and practices *ought to be*. If naturalists attempt to substantiate Natural Identity by identifying goodness with whatever *does* regulate our use of moral language, they're giving an account of descriptive morality, not normative morality. It's no surprise that naturalists encounter the causal reference problem: anthropologists studying different cultures have different subject matters.

Some naturalists have responded to this problem by denying that moral facts are categorically normative. David Brink accepts Humeanism, and argues that normal people with normal desires will have reason to act morally, but people with different desires will not (Brink 1989; see also Boyd 1988; Railton 1986). But as we saw in §6.8 with our discussion of Finlay's objection, categorical normativity is a non-negotiable aspect of our concept of morality. To give up on categoricity is to give up on morality.

7.4.2   The Non-naturalist's Objection

These considerations about whether moral facts can be located within the ECP story don't arise for the non-naturalist. For the non-naturalist, moral facts don't have the kind of explanatory power that would make them part of the ECP story. But that just shows that we're justified in believing in more than just the ECP story. The non-naturalist will reject premise 1 of the explanationist argument for skepticism, and hold that our moral beliefs can be supported by evidence even though moral facts lack explanatory power. The non-naturalist might pursue this objection in one of four ways. The *no connections strategy* says that evidence for a fact needn't be connected to the fact for which it's evidence in any way (Huemer 2005). The *non-explanatory connections strategy* says that there must be a connection between evidence and fact, but that connection needn't be an explanatory connection (Clark-Doane 2012). The *third factor strategy* says that explanatory connections are needed, but these explanatory connections can proceed through some third factor which is a common cause of both evidence and fact (Enoch 2011, ch. 7; Wielenberg 2014). And the *companions-in-innocence* strategy argues that we can have knowledge of other kinds of facts that lack explanatory power, and thus that explanationism must go wrong somewhere (although it might be hard to say more than this) (Pust 2001; Koons 2000).

The no connections strategy looks like a non-starter. Evidence must be connected *in some way* to the fact for which it's evidence, or else it's not evidence. The connection between evidence and the fact for which it's evidence is what makes that evidence an indication of the fact in question. That's just part of our concept of evidence. Advocates of the no connections strategy are likely to say that what matters isn't a connection between evidence and fact, but instead similarity in *content* between evidence and fact. If you have an intuition *that P*, then this is evidence for the belief *that P* because both the intuition and the belief have the same content: P. But why should similar content make for evidential support? Wishing that P or dreaming that P aren't evidence that P because there's no connection between wishing that P and P's being the case.

Better, then, to opt for the non-explanatory connections strategy. There must be a connection between evidence and fact, but that evidence needn't be an explanatory one. A probabilistic or counterfactual connection between belief and fact will suffice. On a probabilistic account, smoke is evidence for fire because the presence of smoke makes the presence of fire more probable, i.e., there's a strong statistical correlation between smoke and fire. And, as statisticians will eagerly point out, *correlation isn't causation*. So a probabilistic account would be a genuine alternative to an explanationist account. However, the statistician's warning that correlation isn't causation is a warning not to take correlations too seriously, since it's causation (or, more generally, explanation) that is our ultimate concern. If there's a correlation between two different kinds of facts, but we can identify no plausible causal mechanism linking those two kinds of facts, this immediately casts doubt on the correlation. We consider it a "spurious correlation," a mere coincidence. Concluding that a correlation is coincidental is a strong reason to discount it in reasoning; although coincidental correlations have obtained in the past, we have no reason to think they'll obtain in the future. Statisticians and scientists care about correlations because we can (sometimes) come to know that two things stand in a causal relation by establishing that there's a statistical correlation between those things. We care about statistical correlations because we care about causation, not the other way around.

The suggestion that counterfactual connections are what matter for evidence has the same problems as the probabilistic account. First, these counterfactual connections often are accompanied by causal connections, and it's the causal connections that explain why there's a counterfactual connection. "If there were fire, then there would be smoke" is true because fire causes smoke. Second, counterfactual connections can be used to establish the existence of causal connections. Experimentally manipulating fire and observing that smoke comes and goes as fire comes and goes indicates that there's a causal relation between fire and smoke. And third, it's sometimes possible to devise cases where two things are counterfactually related even though there's no causal relation between them. For instance, if two facts are necessary, then there will be counterfactual connections between them because one will be true whenever the other is. It's necessary that water is H_2O, and it's necessary that $2 + 2 = 4$, so water is H_2O whenever $2 + 2 = 4$. But in cases like this, where there's a counterfactual connection without an explanatory connection, there's no evidence. The fact that $2 + 2 = 4$ isn't evidence that water is H_2O. From these three observations, we draw the same conclusion that we did in the case of statistical correlations: We care about counterfactual connections because we care about explanations, not the other way around (Faraci 2019; Lutz 2020; Korman and Locke 2023).

This takes us to the third factor strategy. Third factor theorists accept that an explanatory connection between E and P is required for E to be evidence for P, but hold that those explanatory connections can proceed from a common cause (i.e., some third factor which explains both P and E). For instance, the fact that a situation is painful might explain why we have the intuition that it's morally bad; at the same time, that the situation is painful might explain why it's bad. Thus, the pain would be a common cause of both our intuition that the situation is bad and the fact that it's bad. And so the intuition of badness would be evidence of badness because of the common-cause explanatory connection linking the intuition of badness and the fact of badness.

We've already seen the problem with this strategy: unless both of the explanatory pathways that proceed out from the common cause are well-confirmed, the belief isn't supported by evidence. Zuzu holds that there's a common cause of her belief that the angel gets its wings and the angel's getting its wings: the ringing bell. But Zuzu's hearing the bell isn't evidence that an angel got its wings because her general explanatory belief that bells cause angels to get their wings isn't well-confirmed. Similarly, an intuition that a painful situation is bad isn't evidence that the situation really is bad, because the general explanatory belief that some things are bad because they are painful isn't well-confirmed for any agent.

Finally, let's look at the companions-in-innocence strategy. Explanationist arguments for skepticism seem to be self-undermining: what explanatory evidence do we have for explanationism? If we have none, then either explanationism is false or else beliefs in explanationism are unsupported. Either way, explanationism is in trouble (Pust 2001; Koons 2000).

Similar worries have been raised about mathematics. We know that $2 + 2 = 4$, but mathematical facts are abstract and thus can't explain any of our evidence (Clarke-Doane 2020). So explanationism fails as an account of mathematical knowledge. The mathematics analogy doesn't show that explanationism is self-undermining, but it does show that explanationism struggles to account for how evidential support could work in a variety of cases. In general, *a priori* knowledge presents a challenge to the explanationist account of evidence and knowledge I've outlined here. Perhaps *a priori* knowledge requires no evidence. Or, if it does require evidence, it requires a different kind of evidence—a kind that can't be accounted for in explanationist terms.

In light of this challenge, the explanationist might retreat to the claim that explanationism is only appropriate for *a posteriori* knowledge; we don't need explanatory connections to know about math or about explanationism itself. But saying this would give away the whole game. Some moral knowledge is *a priori*, so that retreat would undermine the explanationist argument for skepticism. So how can the explanationist account for *a priori* knowledge?

7.5 *A Priori* Knowledge

Here's the answer in outline: We can have *a priori* knowledge of conceptual truths, i.e., knowledge of propositions that are guaranteed to be true by the nature of the concepts that proposition is composed of. We can come to know such a claim is true simply by reflecting on those concepts. Concepts are mental states. Thus, if a truth is a conceptual truth, it's a truth about an agent's mental states, not about some abstract Platonic realm containing concepts. Mental states are individuated in part by their functional profile. Thus, concepts are individuated in part by their functional profiles. For instance, I'll deploy the concept "two" in different circumstances than I'll deploy the concept "fish." This difference in my dispositions to deploy these concepts is explained by differences in the functional profiles of those two distinct mental states. I can therefore use abstract reasoning to test the limits of my concepts, as my intuitions in abstract reasoning will be explained by the functional profiles of the concepts involved. In this way, the facts in question—i.e., facts concerning relations between our concepts—can explain our intuitions. This means that our intuitions can be evidence for conceptual truths.

One might wonder *how*, precisely, intuitions are explained by conceptual truths. Do these facts about our concepts *cause* our intuitions? It's hard to say; this will depend on what we say about the nature of mental states in general, and their relation to their functional profiles. It might be that possessing certain intuitions is *constitutive of* having certain concepts, not *caused by* having those concepts. But this is no problem. As I said in §7.2.1, explanatory connections are *almost always* causal. But constitutive connections are also a species of explanatory connection (Setiya 2012, ch. 3). Most of the time, that fact is irrelevant. But it becomes relevant in the case of *a priori* knowledge. *A posteriori* knowledge is knowledge from the evidence of our senses, where our sensory experiences are causally connected to the fact in question. *A priori* knowledge is knowledge from the evidence of our intuitions, where those intuitions are either caused by or constitutive of the functional profile of the concepts that make up the *a priori* conceptual truth.

This account of *a priori* knowledge is consistent with the explanationist principles I've defended in this chapter. We have *a priori* knowledge on the basis of evidence (intuition), that evidence is a kind of experience, and our intuitions are explained by the facts (facts about the relations between our concepts) that they're evidence for. These explanations can generate predictions about what our intuitions will be in a variety of circumstances, so we can test those explanations (e.g., through thought experiments) to see if we have the intuitions that our account predicts.

One common objection to this view is that it gives our *a priori* knowledge the wrong object. We have *a priori* knowledge of facts in the world, not just facts about our own mental states. To know *a priori* that all squares are four-sided is to know something about squares, not (just) about our concept of a square. But this objection is mistaken; we can have knowledge of the world via knowledge of our concepts, and there's nothing particularly odd in our ability to do so. Allow me to illustrate. We can gain trivial conceptual knowledge by introducing a new concept with an explicit verbal definition. So let me do so: I hereby introduce the concept of a "blook," which is the conjunction of being blue and being a book. For all *x*, *x* is a blook if and only if *x* is blue and *x* is a book. But this entails a fact about the world: that all blooks are blue. That's not a fact *about my concept*. That's a fact *about blooks*. So purely conceptual knowledge can give us knowledge of the way the world is.

How'd that work? It works because propositional knowledge is knowledge *of propositions*. Propositions represent the world as being certain ways, which is why propositional knowledge is knowledge about the way the world is. But whether or not a proposition is true also depends on the manner in which the proposition represents the world as being. And some propositions—the *a priori* knowable propositions—cannot help but represent the world truly, in virtue of the nature of their constituent concepts. To represent something as a blook is to represent it as blue. So everything that we correctly represent as a blook is something that we *ipso facto* already correctly represent as blue. This redundant representation of blueness is how we can know *a priori* that all blooks are blue. Similarly, to represent something as a square is *ipso facto* to represent it as having four sides. And that this is redundant *representation* means that this *a priori* knowledge yields knowledge of the world. Anything that we correctly represent with the concept "square," i.e., squares, is also something that is correctly represented with the concept "four-sided," i.e., four-sided figures. That's how we know *a priori* that all squares are four-sided.

Moral knowledge is thus knowable *a priori* if moral truths are conceptual truths. But the open-question argument prevents us from saying that they are. If any substantive moral claims were conceptual truths, questions about those conceptual truths would have a closed feel. This closed feeling of a question serves as evidence that we've lighted on a conceptual truth. For instance, it's a conceptual truth that all vixens are foxes, which is why "That animal is a vixen, but is it a fox?" has a closed feel. The closed feel is a product of redundant representation; to represent something as a vixen is *ipso facto* to represent it as a fox. But to represent something as killing is not *ipso facto* to represent it as wrong. That is why moral questions are open, which is why we cannot have conceptual knowledge of substantive moral claims.

The kind of view I'm presenting here is hardly unprecedented. In a recent book on the *a priori*, Paul Boghossian argues that our understanding of concepts, which takes the form of dispositions to assent to various claims, can be the basis of *a priori* knowledge. However, he ultimately rejects this account of conceptual *a priori* knowledge as at least incomplete, since he maintains that there's non-conceptual *a priori* knowledge which comes from a "faculty of intuition." He admits that this faculty of intuition can seem mysterious, but nonetheless maintains that we are stuck with it, since we have no other way to account for non-conceptual *a priori* knowledge. Yet Boghossian offers only one example of non-conceptual *a priori* knowledge: our knowledge of substantive moral propositions. That substantive moral propositions aren't conceptual is, according to Boghossian, established by (a version of) the open-question argument (Boghossian and Williamson 2020, ch. 13). So whereas Boghossian thinks that conceptual understanding is a generally adequate account of *a priori* knowledge but our account of the *a priori* must be expanded into the mysterious in order to account for moral knowledge, I hold that we should stick with a simpler, comprehensible account of the *a priori* that fits with a larger explanationist account of evidence and knowledge. But such an account leaves no room for moral knowledge.

Another recent attempt to explain *a priori* moral knowledge comes from Cuneo and Shafer-Landau. Cuneo and Shafer-Landau have argued that some very widely accepted claims, which they call the "moral fixed points," are, indeed, conceptual truths. They avoid the open-question argument by defending a different view of concepts. Rather than say that concepts are mental states that we can test by reflection on our dispositions to deploy them (as Boghossian and I both claim), Cuneo and Shafer-Landau assume that concepts are abstract entities. The moral fixed points are "conceptual truths" because they concern the relations between Platonic abstract concepts. We have knowledge of them not by reflecting on our own mental states but by performing the intellectual activity of "grasping" these concepts (Cuneo and Shafer-Landau 2014). The problem with this view is that it's unclear how we can understand this talk of "grasping" abstract concepts with our minds given a naturalistic account of the mind as realized in the brain. Abstract objects are inert; they can't causally impact our brains in any way, and so they can't cause us to have intuitions or beliefs or anything else that might count as evidence. So we could have no evidence about how things stand with abstracta. This view of *a priori* knowledge just pushes the bump under the rug. You can't explain the possibility of knowledge of non-natural moral facts by saying that it's conceptual *a priori* knowledge if your account of concepts raises all the same epistemic problems that confront the moral non-naturalist to begin with (Copp 2017).

A priori knowledge of conceptual truths is possible, and the nature of *a priori* knowledge fits with the account of evidence and knowledge defended in §7.2. So the existence of *a priori* knowledge is no counterexample to explanationism. Because no substantive moral claims are conceptual truths, we cannot have *a priori* knowledge of any substantive moral claim. So the companions-in-innocence strategy fails.

The naturalist will object that moral facts are part of the best explanation of our evidence. But adding categorical normativity to the ECP story does not add to its explanatory power, so there's no evidence in favor of the naturalist's position. The non-naturalist will object that explanatory connections are not needed for evidential support, but every other proposed account of evidential support has serious problems. The biggest objection is that the explanationist cannot explain how we can have *a priori* knowledge, but *a priori* knowledge is possible for the explanationist if all *a priori* knowledge is conceptual.

Chapter 8

The Life of an Anti-realist

Matt Lutz

Contents

> You must do what you feel is right, of course.
>
> —Obi-wan Kenobi

I hope that you're somewhat persuaded by the arguments I've given for skepticism and error theory. Yet anti-realism might still seem unappealing. In Chapter 1, we saw that there are two main reasons why people care about the realism/anti-realism debate: a practical reason, and one coming from "philosophical angst." So perhaps you're wondering what changes you'd have to make to your life, practically, if you became an error theorist. Or perhaps you're overcome with angst at the thought of losing out on the guiding light of objective morality, and perhaps these doubts are keeping you from accepting anti-realism. In this chapter, I'll try to assuage those worries. Against the practical concerns, I'll offer arguments for how you ought to structure your life if what I've argued here is true. Against the angst, I'll offer therapy.

8.1 The "Now What" Problem

Let's turn to the practical worries first. If I become an error theorist, what should I believe? How should I feel? How should I act? What should I say? This cluster of practical problems is known as the **"now what" problem** for error theory, as in: I'm an error theorist;

DOI: 10.4324/9781003183174-12

now what? (Lutz 2014a). The answer follows from the account of normativity I defended in Chapter 6: you should do what you have most reason to do, and you have most reason to do whatever is most efficient in promoting the satisfaction of the desires that are closest to your self-conception. One upshot of this is that different error theorists ought to respond to the "now what" problem in different ways, depending on their different desires. However, there are a few general things we can say by looking at certain strong and widely shared desires.

People generally don't want to believe false or unsupported things. I've argued that substantive moral claims are false and unsupported by evidence. If either of those arguments persuades you, and if you have the corresponding desire, then you should abandon your moral beliefs. For this reason, most error theorists abandon their moral beliefs, and they're rational in doing so.

Our moral beliefs are, mostly, the product of our projections of our moral attitudes. You have good reason to abandon your moral beliefs. But the arguments I've advanced here give *no reason whatsoever* to abandon those moral attitudes. The belief that killing is wrong is a belief that attributes a non-existent moral property to killing, and thus is false. But the horror and disgust that you feel when you think of killing isn't a belief, and isn't false, so you have no reason to abandon that attitude. Furthermore, it's not clear that it's even possible to rid yourself of that attitude of disgust. Humans are endowed with a remarkable and powerful faculty of empathy (Hume, *An Enquiry Concerning the Principles of Morals*, §2). Others' joy makes us joyful; others' sadness makes us sad. This is part of our makeup as social creatures. The ancient Chinese philosopher Mengzi (usually Latinized as "Mencius") writes:

> The reason why I say that all humans have hearts that are not unfeeling toward others is this. Suppose someone suddenly saw a child about to fall into a well: anyone in such a situation would have a feeling of alarm and compassion—not because one sought to get in good with the child's parents, not because one wanted fame among one's neighbors and friends, and not because one would dislike the sound of the child's cries. From this we can see that if one is without the feeling of compassion, one is not human.
>
> (Mengzi 2A6; Van Norden 2008, 46)

Unless we have some mental defect or put ourselves through radical mental reconditioning, we'll desire to help others. Few people are defective in this way, and we have no desire—and thus no reason—to put ourselves through any de-moralizing mental reconditioning. So I assume that almost all error theorists won't abandon their moral attitudes. We might worry about error theorists who, through cognitive defect or mental reconditioning, have weak moral attitudes and so would be led to act "wrongly" by accepting error theory. But we already have the solution to this problem: as a society, we punish those who break the laws, thus providing an external motivation to follow the rules where an internal motivation is lacking. That will do for the remaining cases (Mill, *Utilitarianism*, ch. 3). If you worry about how an error theorist can justify enacting laws that restrict others' behavior, remember that being an anti-realist doesn't mean that you have to be tolerant (see §1.4). You should follow your desires, and most of us share a strong desire to see society protected and killers punished. There's no reason why learning that killing isn't objectively wrong should remove that desire.

If two of our desires conflict, then each desire will give us a reason to abandon one or another of the conflicting desires, since the conflict is preventing the efficient satisfaction of both desires. But if there's no conflict between our desires, then there's no reason to abandon a desire. Coming to believe in error theory means changing my beliefs, but it doesn't involve adopting attitudes that would conflict with my moral attitudes. So accepting moral error theory gives us no reason to change our moral attitudes. These attitudes remain a source of strong reasons.

This point is, I think, under-appreciated in discussions of the "now what" problem. One of the central questions in this debate is whether or not error theorists should act in conventionally moral ways. The dominant approach to that question is to ask whether a group of self-interested error theorists would have reason to form a society that enforces moral rules (Joyce 2001, 177). This has allowed error theorists to draw on some influential work in political theory in answering this question (Kalf 2018). But this approach is too removed from actual human concerns. The practical question that a potential error theorist confronts is not how to draw up a social contract from behind a Rawlsian veil of ignorance, but rather the question of how to live her life. The answer to that pressing practical question isn't one that can or should be answered by abstracting away from a person's moral commitments since the answer follows from that person's moral commitments. Most agents' moral attitudes are strong in multiple senses. They're strong in a motivational sense: the horror at the thought of actually killing someone else is enough to dissuade most of us from doing it. And they're strong in the sense that they're central to our conceptions of ourselves. Even if it would be tempting to kill an enemy of mine, I would reject that temptation, channeling *Fiddler on the Roof*'s Tevye: "If I try to bend that far, I will break ... No!" I imagine that my own experience isn't unique in this respect. The fact that our moral desires are both motivationally strong and central to our conceptions of ourselves means that we'll have very strong reasons to act in accordance with our moral attitudes. Similarly, I have a strong moral attitude to see those who do things that I morally approve of be rewarded, and those who do things that I morally disapprove of be blamed and punished. So I have a very strong reason to hold others to account for their actions in accordance with the moral standards that I accept.

How should an error theorist change their use of moral language? Should they refrain from calling anything "wrong" or "unjust" because they have ceased to believe in any properties of wrongness or injustice? That depends. If I assert "killing is morally wrong," people will generally take me to believe that killing is morally wrong. But I don't believe that killing is morally wrong. Thus, by asserting "killing is morally wrong," I will be saying something misleading. I don't like to mislead others; disapproval of lying is one of my strong moral attitudes. So I have a strong reason not to use moral language, and any error theorist who is also opposed to misleading others will have similarly strong reasons to cease or modify their use of moral language. But moral language also has its uses. Moral language is well-suited to signal your affiliation with a community of individuals with similar moral commitments, or to persuade others to act in ways that you approve of and dissuade others from acting in ways that you find abhorrent. This gives error theorists reasons to use moral language, and potentially quite strong reasons. How those reasons balance out will depend on how strongly you care about the various costs and benefits you can obtain by using moral language, and how central those concerns are to your self-conception. But I think it's fair to say that most moral error theorists will be rational in continuing to use moral language at least some of the time.

In sum, people ought to do what they have most reason to do, and what they have most reason to do will almost always be the thing that they were doing before: acting the way that their moral attitudes prompt them, and, potentially, using moral language to describe the objects of their moral attitudes. For this reason, moral error theory has no real practical upshot. As Sharon Street puts it: "Nothing 'really' matters, but that's not what matters" (Street 2017). Error theorists are afflicted with a more well-organized and reflective cognitive life. That's all.

8.2 Therapy

Despite my reassurances, many will still feel like they'd have to abandon their moral attitudes if they abandoned their moral beliefs. I've argued that this needn't happen as a matter of logical necessity: there's no rational rule that would force us to abandon our moral attitudes once we accept error theory. But some might worry that this would follow as a matter of *psychological necessity*: that if we came to believe in error theory, our moral attitudes would become hollowed out and we ourselves would become cynical. This worry is so common that the view that we have been discussing in this book under the label of 'error theory' is more commonly known as 'nihilism.' The term 'nihilism' carries all of these implications: a nihilist is despairing, egotistical, ironic, and cynical. This is a reflection of the fact that pessimistic assumptions about the psychological impact of being an error theorist are widespread. But these assumptions are false. Alex Rosenberg (2011) tries to dispel the idea that "nihilists" must be despairing; he refers to himself as a "nice nihilist." I think the little shock that you get when you hear the phrase "nice nihilism" is a good indication that this is a bad label: I'm an error theorist, but I'm no *nihilist*. I'm much too earnest. So count me, at least, as one counterexample to the idea that the sun shines a little duller on the worlds of anti-realists. I don't consider myself exceptional in this. The obituary of J.L. Mackie, the popularizer of error theory, described him as "courteous, genial, modest, and unpretentious." I'm fortunate enough to have met many error theorists during my philosophical career, and have found them all to be friendly, decent people.

It's easy to maintain your good humor as an error theorist. Coming to believe error theory might be a big shift in your cognitive life if you're currently a realist. But it's not a change in the world. Becoming an error theorist wouldn't drain the world of its beauty. The world is as beautiful as it ever has been, though it has never contained anything with a property of to-be-admired-ness. If your life has been happy and meaningful to this point, it has been happy and meaningful despite the absence of any moral goodness in it. Clearly, then, a world without goodness is no barrier to happiness and meaning. If your life has been unhappy and meaningless, you have my sympathy. But I venture that your life wouldn't be more happy and meaningful if there were moral values in the world for you to live up to.

Of course, it's possible that some people are psychologically constituted in such a way that becoming error theorists will lead them to become full-blown nihilists. There's no rational reason why this must happen, but perhaps it will happen for some for irrational reasons. This response would be an overreaction by someone with an excessively gloomy and anxious disposition. If you have this sort of disposition, then, once again, you have my sympathies. Hume recognized that philosophical arguments can invoke this sort of skeptical gloom; his entirely appropriate recommendation was for philosophers to leave their gloomy studies, have a good meal with friends, and play a game with them. There's much to enjoy in life, and there's no reason to divorce yourself from it because nothing has the property of to-be-enjoyed-ness.

This encouragement to find meaning in life where you have always found it—in family and friends, in simple pleasures and honest dealing—might seem to point back towards an image of the error theorist as an egoist employed in the enjoyment of their own life, unwilling to give to others or sacrifice for them. I can only repeat that this is a misapprehension. Living up to our own moral values is a huge source of meaning in the lives of most people. I've always found the following quote from Philippa Foot inspiring:

> It is interesting that the people of Leningrad were not similarly struck by the thought that only the contingent fact that other citizens shared their loyalty and devotion to the city stood between them and the Germans during the terrible years of the siege. Perhaps we should be less troubled than we are by fear of defection from the moral cause; perhaps we should even have less reason to fear it if people thought of themselves as volunteers banded together to fight for liberty and justice and against inhumanity and oppression.

(Foot 1972, 316)

What kind of person would only fight for liberty and justice and against inhumanity and oppression because they have a property of to-be-fought-for-ness? We fight for these things because they *matter* ... to *us*.

> Moral facts don't exist. But that doesn't mean we should abandon our moral attitudes. Those moral attitudes can still provide a rational basis for action (and occasionally speech) in accordance with our moral commitments. Nothing "really" matters, but that doesn't matter. Don't worry; be happy.

Part III

Disagreements

Chapter 9

Humeanism

Matt Lutz and Spencer Case

Contents

We've now each made the case for our respective views. We don't disagree about everything—we agree that moral facts must play an explanatory role, for instance—but the differences between our views are substantial. In the rest of the book, we're going to take a closer look at some fundamental disagreements. Most of our other disagreements stem from our disagreements about these issues. If we could be persuaded to adopt the other's position on these points of controversy, we'd be much more inclined to accept the other's views as a whole. These disagreements concern our differing accounts of the nature of *a priori* knowledge, the relative quality of the realist's and anti-realist's explanations of our moral beliefs, and whether our concept of epistemic justification is entangled with moral considerations. But first, let's look at what is perhaps our most fundamental disagreement: the adequacy of Humeanism.

9.1 Against Humeanism

Spencer Case

Humeans believe that all an agent's normative reasons derive from her desires. This leaves no room for categorical reasons which are independent of desires. Since Matt thinks Humeanism is all that and a

DOI: 10.4324/9781003183174-14

bag of chips—find someone to love you the way that Matt loves Humeanism—he rejects categoricity. My reasoning goes the other way: I accept categoricity and reject Humeanism. Matt mentions three advantages of Humeanism: it's intuitive, it's compatible with naturalism, and it provides a constructive explanation of the sense in which normativity is action-guiding. Here I'll attack Humeanism on intuitive grounds, though I think this critique will also show that the theory doesn't do a very good job of accounting for the sense in which morality is "action-guiding."

Let's revisit Jane and her noble quest for a cup of coffee. It's intuitive that she has a reason to get some coffee given that she wants some. But Matt is committed to saying that *all* her reasons to get a cup of coffee, or do anything else, can only be desire-satisfaction reasons. Intuitively, reasons arise not only because we have desires, but also because certain things promote our well-being, help us develop as people, give us knowledge, or are morally good to have. Humeanism says that *only* desires are reason-generating. So if Jane only wanted coffee to relieve her caffeine withdrawal headache, and not because she'd enjoy the coffee or the ambiance of the cafe, then, according to Humeanism, the fact that she'd enjoy these things wouldn't add to her reasons for acting. Moreover, Humeanism notoriously says that *all* desires are reason-generating; if a man wants to beat his wife, and doing this doesn't interfere with satisfying any of his other desires, then he has a reason to beat his wife and no reason to stop. Likewise, someone who didn't value his own future well-being wouldn't have any reason to promote it. The Humean might retort that everyone prefers his own well-being to misery, but I see no reason to think it's *impossible* to prefer one's own misery. People are weird. There's no telling how strange some people's desires could possibly be.

Even if some perverse preferences are psychologically impossible for humans—and, importantly, all other rational creatures that possibly could exist—there's still an objection to Humeanism here. Recall the objection to voluntarism in Chapter 3 that, intuitively, God couldn't make some awful things good or right by commanding them. Some voluntarists reply that it's impossible for God to command evil deeds because of His eternal character. Morriston (2009, 253) counters that the voluntarist is still committed to saying, "*if* God commanded [horrible], *then* [horrible] would be good." The antecedent doesn't need to be possible for this objection to bite. Cicero, the Roman statesman and philosopher, made a similar point. He noted that some philosophers in his day, the Epicureans, were committed to saying that a person who knew he could evade punishment by turning invisible would have no justice-related reasons not to behave reprehensibly. Some Epicureans dismissed this objection because it depended on an impossible counterfactual. Cicero was having none of it:

> The condition, they say, is impossible. Of course it is. But my question is, if that were possible which they declare to be impossible, what, pray, would one do? They press their point with right boorish obstinacy: they assert that it is impossible and insist upon it; they refuse to see the meaning of my words, "if possible."
>
> (Cicero, *De Officiis*, 3.39)

Similarly, I'd say, *if it were possible* for someone to be motivated to promote his own misery, for its own sake, that person would have no reason to satisfy this aim. Certainly, he wouldn't have the same sort he'd have if he desired his own happiness. That's a sensible desire. The Humean can't distinguish between sensible and insensible desires except in reference to other desires the agent has. I think that an agent's whole set of desires could be insensible, just as a consistent set of beliefs could be irrational. The Humean might reply that it's psychologically impossible to desire one's own misery, or to desire it to the exclusion of all other aims. I'm not so sure. Again, we can find sundry examples of people having desires that seem repugnant and incomprehensible to others, so it's hard to say for sure that there are any desires that are so strange that no one could possibly have them. Moreover, if Cicero and Morriston are right, we could still reflect on what would be true *if it were possible* for people to have such desires. I want to say that if people had such desires, they'd have no good reason to act on them.

Matt can try to control the damage as follows. Admittedly, the wife-beater has some reason to beat his wife, and the self-hater has some reason to make himself miserable, though given the way humans are psychologically constituted in the real world, these reasons are bound to be vastly outweighed by other reasons. Decide for yourself how much better this makes things. In any event, this raises the question of how the Humean should compare the relative "weights" of reasons. On the standard view called *Proportionalism*, it's more-or-less a matter of which desires are stronger. This is too simple, as Matt realizes, and so he modifies proportionalism in an interesting way.

On Matt's account, three factors determine the comparative strength of a reason: the strength of an agent's desire for an end, the likelihood that the action would promote the desired end, and the centrality of the end to the agent's self-conception. That last factor allows Matt to identify some desires as temptations that should be given less weight. So if Jane's committed to kicking her caffeine addiction, then her desire to go into the coffee shop has less weight in virtue of that commitment. That's plausible. Other consequences of Matt's view are more dubious. For instance, an abuser who conceives of himself as a wife-beater has extra reason to beat his wife in virtue of this self-conception. Likewise, the person who conceives of himself as self-loathing has extra reason to hate himself.

Here's a final point about how Matt understands hypothetical normativity. I've assumed this throughout my constructive essays that hypothetical reasons, no less than categorical reasons, *count in favor* of the things that they're reasons for. Matt sees things differently. He thinks that the property of "to-be-done-ness" or "counting-in-favor-of-ness" is a relic of categorical normativity. And so while it's consistent for a Humean to say that hypothetical reasons have this property, it would be better to reject it entirely. But it seems to me that once we jettison "to-be-done-ness", we've jettisoned normativity altogether. Try to imagine having a reason to buy a bus ticket to Omaha, Nebraska while recognizing that nothing counts in favor of doing that. I can't make sense of that. It's like trying to imagine something's having economic value although no one would exchange anything for it.

Note that the normative error theorist, who rejects even hypothetical reasons, agrees that our actions can either satisfy our desires or not. So it seems as though Matt's disagreement with the normative error theorist is semantic, about the meanings of terms such as 'rational', 'reasonable', and 'hypothetical reason'. Desire-fulfilling actions are supposed to be rational *as a matter of definition*. Matt is standing on his own linguistic intuition when he makes these claims. That's trouble. Even if Matt were correct about the semantics, his case against normative error theory would be confined to the English language. It's not clear how this would generalize to metaethical research being conducted in other languages, whose key terms might not align perfectly with English words. I'm not interested in the word 'reasons'; I'm interested in *reasons*. I think the same is true of Matt; however, since he rejects synthetic *a priori* knowledge, he's forced to interpret his intuitions as semantic intuitions.

9.2   In Defense of Humeanism

Matt Lutz

Among error theorists, there's a divide between moral error theorists and normative error theorists. All error theorists think that there's something weird about morality, but there's disagreement about what the weird thing is. Humean error theorists like me are moral error theorists. We think that *categorical* normativity is weird, but hypothetical normativity is fine. Normative error theorists think that *normativity as such* is weird. Spencer agrees with the normative error theorist; as he puts it in §5.2, "all normativity is a *bit* mysterious." This is the main idea behind his Foothold Argument: Moral error theorists admit that hypothetical normativity exists, so they admit that something mysterious exists, so they can't consistently reject moral normativity for being mysterious. But hypothetical normativity isn't mysterious. After all, hypothetical normativity is simply a matter of what desires an agent has, causal facts about what will promote the satisfaction of those desires, and psychological facts about the agent's ability to recognize those causal facts and act to satisfy their desires on that basis. None of this is mysterious. Indeed, as I argued in §6.1, the fact that Humeanism removes the last bit of mysteriousness from normativity is a good reason to accept it.

The suspicion that a bit of strangeness lingers even in hypothetical normativity is the basis of Hampton's Objection. Hampton's Objection presumes that, even if Humeanism is correct, the act of pursuing one's desires is *to-be-done*, or that a fact's explaining why an action would promote one of those desires makes that fact *count-in-favor-of* doing the action, and this to-be-done-ness or counts-in-favor-of-ness is a residual mystery. This presumption is mistaken. To-be-done-ness and counting-in-favor-of-ness are indeed mysterious. That's why the Humean doesn't understand normativity in these terms.

Spencer objects that without to-be-done-ness or counting-in-favor-of-ness, hypothetical reasons are "reasons" in name only, and cannot be an appropriate guide for rational action. Again, this is a mistake. In a world without to-be-done-ness or counting-in-favor-of-ness, agents would still be able to act in pursuit of their desires and do a better or worse job of satisfying their desires. Reasoning in such a way that your actions do a good job of satisfying your desires is all that rationality amounts to. So even in the absence of to-be-done-ness or counting-in-favor-of-ness, rational action is possible.

One of the oldest and most well-known objections to the Humean theory—an objection that Hume himself considered—is the "sensible knave" problem. If someone wants to do bad things and doesn't want to do good things (and doesn't want anything he could get by doing good things), the sensible thing for him to do is to be a knave. As Spencer points out, Humeanism implies that if someone really wants to abuse their wife, then this is what they'll have most reason to do. I accept this implication of Humeanism; sensible knaves are rare (thank God), but they exist. And if they strongly desire to prefer their own selfish ends at others' expense, and none of their other desires would be frustrated by doing so (say, because they'd lose valued friends), then they have most reason to act selfishly. But let's be careful about what exactly this means.

To say that the knave acts sensibly or rationally in following his knavish desires isn't to commend the knave in any way. It's not to say that he's doing the right thing. It's simply to say that he's successfully pursuing his desires. From the deliberative perspective of the knave, that's significant. From my perspective, it isn't. I don't care whether people satisfy their desires. All else equal, I want others to be happy. But if someone is made happy by harming others, I don't want him to be happy. I want him to be miserable. Indeed, I'd like to see him punished—with the full force of the law, if what he's done is illegal as well as harmful. This is why we have laws; it's why punishment exists. As a society, we work hard to make sure that it isn't sensible to be a knave. The sensible knave is a rarer figure than myth would have us believe and the mere possibility of a sensible knave isn't worrisome. Again, to call the knave "sensible" isn't to commend him. The sensible knave is a jerk (Street 2009).

9.3   Practical Implications of Humeanism

Spencer Case

Matt isn't worried about being unable to adequately criticize sensible knaves, and he labors to reassure us on this score in Chapter 8. To this end, he provides "therapy" for readers who worry that his position doesn't justify their sense that we have sufficient reason to behave morally. Matt presents these thoughts almost as though he's doing a victory lap, having already proven his case. But the therapy matters for two reasons. First, if Matt's conclusions were ones that we couldn't *live with* on a day-to-day basis—teaching them to our children, letting them inform our life decisions, and so forth—then we might conclude that Matt is leading us into a coal pit, and he must have gone wrong somewhere. Without the therapy, then, he's more vulnerable to a Moorean counterargument. Second, I think his therapy targets a major source of philosophical angst that provides much of the motivation for resisting his views. So let's see whether this therapy is worth the going rate.

Matt reassures us that "accepting moral error theory gives us no reason to change our moral attitudes" and "moral error theory has no real practical upshot." Apparently, the same goes for moral skepticism, though he's not explicit about this. The reason that these metaethical views are supposedly practically neutral is that Matt assigns moral beliefs a diminutive practical role. Moral beliefs on his view turn out to be decorative false columns while attitudes bear the real weight of our moral practices. Views like this aren't uncommon among error theorists. Bart Streumer once told me that at a philosophy conference dinner, he found himself seated at a table with other self-proclaimed error theorists, all of whom ordered vegan meals apparently on ethical grounds.[2] I sometimes think I detect subtle moral boasting from error theorists, who insist they don't *need* to believe in queer moral facts in order to behave themselves. That always strikes me as strange, as though the moral facts that I and other realists believe in were Santa Claus particles that spy to catch you in the act of being naughty.

Assigning such significance to moral attitudes, to the detriment of beliefs, implies a chasm between theory and practice in mortality that doesn't obtain in other domains. Imagine a self-proclaimed skeptic about the external world, other minds, and time, who manages to avoid walking into things, communicate with others, and keep his appointments. In fact, he's a successful manager of a construction team that builds skyscrapers.[3] I'd doubt that he really

2 Thanks to Streumer for allowing me to use this example.
3 Thanks to Tim Perrine for this example.

holds these commitments. Or imagine a self-proclaimed atheist who acts like a practicing Catholic in all contexts outside of philosophical debate: he goes to mass and all the rest. I'd doubt that this person is an atheist, notwithstanding his protestations. I wouldn't be persuaded by his insistence that he simply finds the practice of Catholicism aesthetically pleasing or whatever. We should draw similar conclusions about the error theorist who talks and acts like a realist most of the time. His behavior betrays his true beliefs. Economists talk about "revealed preference"; I think there's also revealed *philosophy*. What morally decent error theorists reveal through their behavior is that they don't accept the theory *deep down*.

Let's for the sake of argument concede that error theorists like Matt really lack moral beliefs, or at least that whatever vestigial moral beliefs they do have play no important behavioral role for them. Moral beliefs and attitudes seem thoroughly intertwined for the rest of us. Significant revisions of moral beliefs generally impact an agent's attitudes and behavior in the long run, idiosyncratic error theorists notwithstanding. I've been a vegan for several years, and a vegetarian for longer, but I'd help myself to a steak if I thought that there was nothing wrong with doing so, even if my other beliefs, including about the environmental impact of meat eating, were unaltered. I also doubt I'd continue giving to charity at the rate I do if I didn't think I morally ought to, even if none of my beliefs about the efficacy of donating changed.

True, I wouldn't become a serial killer if I adopted Matt's metaethical views. My position isn't that we'd become psychopaths if we abandoned the One True Metaethics, only that adopting error theory or skepticism—and not just in seminar rooms—must have practical ramifications. It's often hard to keep our promises, own up to our mistakes, and be compassionate. It's with regard to these things that we might slacken if we disavowed morality. True, attitudes and beliefs can come apart. A philosophy student might be intellectually convinced that she ought to give a huge proportion of her money to aid distant victims of famine, and yet not feel guilty for falling short. A former conservative Christian who became a liberal might continue to feel that homosexuality is wrong despite no longer believing this on reflection. In both cases, though, we'd expect that the person's attitudes would eventually move toward her beliefs. If her attitudes presently seem unaffected, we should conclude that her new beliefs haven't "sunken in" yet. We'd say the same thing of someone in the denial stage of grief who says, "I can't believe my father is dead" when she must believe this.

The practical significance of error theory might even seem like good news at first. It means that we don't have obligations to provide famine relief to distant strangers. We don't have to worry about being vegans, stress about whether abortion is wrong, or fret about the environmental impact of our lifestyles. There's no reason not to forget about ethics altogether and enjoy our lives. Probably all of us have at times felt that morality is onerous. On the other hand, we might find it unsettling to think that there's no reason not to renegotiate our most fundamental values whenever that's expedient.

Consider again Foot's example of the Soviet troops in Leningrad. State coercion certainly motivated them, but probably many also believed that their cause was just, and that they were duty-bound to protect the Motherland. Assuming that this is so, are we supposed to believe that they'd have fought with the same resolve without these beliefs? It must affect their motivation in some way. Suppose a soldier on the defensive side of a war is resolved to fight to the bitter end, while another surrenders at the earliest opportunity to trade intelligence for favorable treatment. Matt must say that the stalwart simply values what he values; he happens to disvalue oppression. Matt can say he shares his moral values, but not that he or anyone else has any reason to. Things just bottom out here, and searching for a foundation is like looking for the turtle that upholds the world.

Is that so? If the stalwart believes that his values are in the end mere preferences, then it's hard to see a compelling motive for him not to renegotiate them when the going gets tough, as we do with preferences that we don't take to be based on objective principles. Suppose I pair wines with every dinner, and I insist that nothing less than the best will do. If I can't afford to keep this up, it's reasonable for me to adjust my attitudes to fit the circumstances: maybe I can tolerate a ten-dollar bottle of wine, or just drink water. Moral beliefs seem not to be fungible in this way; indeed, it seems essential to their being *moral* beliefs that they aren't like this (compare the "stand your ground" argument in Enoch 2011, ch. 1). A similar point holds for skepticism. It's hard to see a compelling rationale for our soldier to hold out under rough interrogation either if he lacks any objective reason to hold his current set of preferences, or lacks epistemic justification for believing that objective reasons exist, and he knows this.

In short, I find it hard to avoid the conclusion that moral error theory and skepticism must have some practical implications, which even anti-realists and skeptics find very unappealing.

9.4   Acting on Humean Reasons

Matt Lutz

Spencer contends that moral beliefs are more intricately entangled with moral attitudes and action than I've claimed. Abandoning your moral beliefs has a practical upshot: we wouldn't give to charity or become vegans if we didn't believe that we were morally required to. He also argues that abandoning your moral beliefs would cause you to give up your moral attitudes; he even suggests that I myself have moral beliefs. I take it that this is because he knows I have moral attitudes, so he concludes that, deep down, I can't be an error theorist.

Let me assure you that I really am a moral error theorist and a moral skeptic, and I really do guide my actions by my attitudes. These attitudes are contingent, the product of my upbringing. But they're mine, I endorse them on reflection, and I act from them with confidence and, occasionally, with passion.

What does it mean to act from an attitude rather than acting from a moral belief? Let's look at the example of veganism. Why not eat animals? Because to eat an animal someone must first raise it and then kill it, and the conditions under which animals are raised and then killed exposes them to immense suffering. We could raise animals in happy conditions and kill them painlessly, but in fact we don't. To eat animals is to contribute to and incentivize their further suffering. But why does all of this add up to the practical conclusion that you shouldn't eat animals? Here's one story: it's a moral fact that it's wrong to participate in the suffering of animals. You can recognize this fact and, out of a sense of obligation, refrain from doing something wrong. Here's another story: You care about animals and can't stand the thought of contributing to their suffering, so you don't. The second story is just as intelligible as the first, perhaps more so. Indeed, I'd guess that the second story is more common than the first among vegans. To use a metaphor popularized by the psychologist Jonathan Haidt (2001): when it comes to morality, the emotional dog wags the rational tail. Our moral actions are determined by our attitudes, and rational moral deliberation primarily serves to provide *post hoc* rationalizations for what we're already emotionally inclined to do. Error theorists are abnormal only in that they decline to provide *post hoc* rationalizations of a certain kind.

This isn't to say that no one is motivated in accordance with the first story. There's actually one (and only one) group where moral reasoning plays a substantial role in determining moral judgments: professional philosophers (ibid.). Error theory is a remedy for the corrupting influence of a certain kind of realist moral philosophy.

Spencer and Matt disagree over whether Humeanism is worth its intuitive costs, as well as over its practical ramifications. Spencer presses the "sensible knave" objection: it seems repugnant that a person who doesn't desire to do good has no reason to do good. Matt emphasizes that we still have good reasons to condemn people like this given our own desires. The other main disagreement discussed in this chapter is whether Humean error theory has practical implications. Spencer thinks moral beliefs must have practical significance, but for Matt, it's moral attitudes alone that are load-bearing.

Chapter 10

Moral Explanations

Matt Lutz and Spencer Case

Contents

10.1   The Inadequacy of the "ECP Story"

Spencer Case

Matt's argument for moral skepticism is a version of Harman's explanation argument. Roughly, we can only know about entities that are part of our best explanations for our experiences, and that moral facts don't factor into these best explanations. Therefore, we can't know about them. His argument targets moral knowledge whereas I've focused on justified beliefs. This doesn't matter so much: I'd consider it bad news if I had to renounce moral knowledge; moreover, if Matt's argument against moral knowledge succeeds, similar reasoning could show that our moral beliefs are unjustified. (I'm eliding some details that make Matt's version of the explanation argument distinctive, but I'd like my response to potentially be effective against versions of it other than Matt's).

I think this is his best argument. There's no obvious flaw in it. Realists are divided about whether they should reject the explanation condition on knowledge, or defend the explanatory usefulness of moral facts. I accept the explanatory condition on knowledge, and not just *arguendo*: it seems to me that I can't know about moral facts if those facts play no role in explaining my beliefs about

DOI: 10.4324/9781003183174-15

them. Other realists wouldn't make this concession, but—what can I say?—I agree with Matt on this one. That means that in order to defend realism, I must show that moral facts factor into our best explanations of moral intuitions, or at least that they *could*. And that's what I think we should say. It would be ideal if I could also give a positive account of moral explanation, but that's a heavy lift. In Chapter 5, I considered some of the possibilities; here I'll take on the more modest task of making space for accepting one of these accounts, or possibly a different one.

Matt says the best explanation for our moral intuitions is the "ECP [evolutionary, cultural, and psychological] story." This is very broad. Indeed, the "ECP story" seems to be shorthand for all of the non-moral factors that influence our normative moral beliefs. This looks question-begging: our moral beliefs aren't explained by any moral truths because they're explained by things other than moral truths! Matt says: "Not only is the ECP story an explanation of why we have our moral evidence, it's the consensus view among scientists. So it's a pretty good explanation, arguably the best." We can surmise that scientists believe that ECP factors shape our moral responses, but what needs to be established is that *all* of our moral responses are best explained as *merely* products of these influences, so that moral truth *never* explains our moral judgments. We've no reason to believe that a consensus of scientists (in all areas of science?) accepts this. Given the philosophical contestability of many claims about the epistemology and metaphysics of causation, the ECP story is partly a philosophical position, and not a purely scientific one. Even if all scientists did accept the ECP story, that might be because many of them presuppose *philosophical* naturalism without recognizing that this takes them beyond their areas of expertise.

Let's consider evolutionary debunking more closely. Evolution explains some of our moral intuitions very well—for instance, the special sense of obligation parents feel toward their children. Perhaps that's a good reason to doubt whether special parental obligations are a foundational part of morality. But that would fall far short of a general debunking of moral intuition. Our moral intuitions don't seem tailor-made to promote evolutionary fitness: we lack moral intuitions that seem like they'd be fitness-promoting, and we have intuitions that have no clear Darwinian upshots. The intuition that it's morally required to have children would be damn handy from an evolutionary perspective, but many regard reproduction as a lifestyle choice, and "anti-natalists" such as David Benatar (2008) even think it's wrong to create new lives. Apparently, the imperative to reproduce isn't enshrined among our most deep-seated and universal moral convictions. And nobody thinks that a man who spends his life donating as much of his semen as he can to sperm banks is thereby living a saintly life, though this might be the best strategy for replicating his genes.

Some people adopt vegan diets because they believe that animal suffering makes the world worse, and not because of any imperative to replicate their genes. A lot of science fiction shows that the moral circle could be expanded to include sentient extraterrestrials who share none of our genetic material. Orson Scott Card's (1991) novel *Ender's Game* explores the idea that it'd be terrible to annihilate a sapient alien race even in a war that threatened the survival of humanity. Such qualms make little sense from an evolutionary-fitness-promoting perspective. This isn't to say that no one could come up with a sophisticated evolutionary explanation for these intuitions (e.g., empathy aids human survival and incidentally enables compassion toward extraterrestrials). But coming up with sophisticated evolutionary explanations is too easy. We can explain practically anything this way. If we had the intuition that rape and genocide were morally good, it'd be trivially easy to explain those intuitions in terms of evolutionary pressures. Explanations that can accommodate any conceivable data aren't good explanations.

Matt could enlist the "C" and "P" as part of his sophisticated explanation, but the same issues arise with these. Moral reasoning *sometimes* transcends deep-seated cultural and psychological biases. When it does, it can be reasonable to conclude that our minds are snagging on protruding shards of reality. This doesn't always happen. We're deceived by all sorts of biases. Occasionally, though, what explains our judgments that some things are right is apprehension of the fact that they're right. To deny this is to assume, not to prove, moral skepticism.

10.2   ECP is as Good as it Gets

Matt Lutz

Spencer worries that evolutionary explanations of our moral beliefs are woefully incomplete. Of course evolutionary explanations are incomplete. Evolution doesn't fully determine our moral beliefs, it simply supplies us with some basic capacities and dispositions. Human beings have a capacity for moral emotions and attitudes that (most) other kinds of animals don't have; mollusks can't feel righteous fury. Evolution also provided us with the rough contours of our moral system. We evolved from social apes. If we had evolved from ants or lions—which are also social animals, but have a different social way of life than apes—our moral attitudes would be different (Street 2006). Beyond that, evolution doesn't do much to explain our moral beliefs. The bulk of the work is done by cultural and personal factors. C and P are more important than E in the ECP story. A useful analogy: many features of human sexuality are explained by evolutionary forces. That doesn't mean that we can derive every feature of your date last night from Darwinian first principles.

Spencer anticipates that I'll respond this way, but still complains that the ECP story, as a whole, is too schematic. It's schematic, but that's for two good reasons. First, a full accounting of moral psychology falls outside the scope of my argument here. (Those who are interested in more details should check out Walter Sinnott-Armstrong's four-volume collection, *Moral Psychology*.) Second, any particular moral belief is going to have a complicated explanation, and different moral beliefs will have different explanations. So generality is only possible by being schematic. By analogy: If we wanted to take the time, we could go through the vast mess of evolutionary, cultural, and personal factors that together explain why your date last night went the way it did. But that wouldn't explain every date. If we want to give a *complete* explanation of *every* date, we'd have to give an insane amount of detail about billions of distinct interactions. Alternatively, we could give a schematic explanation in very general terms: evolution explains why dating is the kind of thing people might want to do, cultural expectations for how a date should go explain the general outlines of the date, and the psychology and other contingent circumstances of you and your crush explain the more particular details. Similarly for explaining moral beliefs. There's a huge variety of moral beliefs, and everyone's beliefs are formed and maintained in different ways. A general explanation of a varied phenomenon is guaranteed to be schematic. For more detailed mid-level explanations, see Sinnott-Armstrong's marvelous collection.

Even if the lack of detail in the ECP story is a vice, it still has an excellent claim to being the best explanation of our moral practices. Spencer's preferred explanation is that "our minds are snagging on protruding shards of reality." That's a lovely metaphor but a terrible explanation. The ECP story is the best explanation of our moral beliefs not because it's so phenomenally good but because other explanations are so tragically bad.

To be fair, Spencer offers a bit more than this metaphor. He also suggests that moral explanations can be modeled on mathematical explanations. But this isn't promising; there are no genuine mathematical explanations of natural facts. To see why not, recall the account of *a priori* knowledge I defended in §7.5. All *a priori* knowledge is conceptual knowledge. And conceptual knowledge is knowledge of relations between our concepts. Mathematical knowledge is *a priori*, so (pure) mathematical facts are also facts about the relations between our concepts. Conceptual truths are knowable *a priori* because they involve a sort of *redundant representation*. To conceive of a figure as being a square is *ipso facto* to conceive of it as being four-sided, in precisely the same way that if you've conceived of John as being a bachelor, you have *ipso facto* conceived of him as being unmarried. This is why it's a conceptual truth that all squares are four-sided and that all bachelors are unmarried.

Let's consider our bachelor, John. Why is he unmarried? The answer is a long, sad story of unrequited love. It wouldn't be accurate to say that he's unmarried because he's a bachelor. (If anything, it's the other way around.) If we want to know what makes it the case that John is unmarried, the answer is that his love is unrequited, not that he's a bachelor. There are more bachelors than just John, though. There are also Jim, Joe, and Jack. Why are these bachelors unmarried? Each will have a story of their own. We can generalize and ask why *all* bachelors are unmarried. And again, each unmarried man will have his own story of frustrated romance.

But why *must* all bachelors be unmarried? That's a different question. Now we're not asking about any particular bachelor or class of bachelors; this question asks for an explanation of a modal claim. Modal terms, like 'must,' are contextually variable. To say that something is x-ly necessary is to say that it's entailed by the x constraints. For instance, to say that something is logically necessary is to say that it's entailed by the constraints of first-order logic. Similarly, to say that something is conceptually necessary is to say that it's entailed by conceptual constraints. Thus, to explain why a claim is conceptually necessary means showing how that claim is entailed by the concepts that constitute that claim. This isn't hard to do in the case of "all bachelors must be unmarried," because this is a case of redundant representation. The conceptual necessity "must" is explained by the nature of the concepts involved in the necessary claim.

With this in mind, let's look at mathematical explanations. Spencer's preferred example is the hairy ball theorem so—if we absolutely must—let's talk about hairy balls. The hairy ball theorem says "you can't comb the hair on a coconut;" there must be a cowlick somewhere. This implies that there must be at least one place on earth where the wind isn't blowing. This is pretty cool! But it's not an example of a mathematical explanation of a natural fact.

Consider the place on the earth where the wind isn't blowing. Why isn't the wind blowing there? We can give some explanation in terms of a variety of meteorological factors (temperature, air pressure, etc.). Over time, there will be many different places where the wind isn't blowing. At any given time, for a given place where the wind isn't blowing, why isn't it? Each instance of windlessness will have its own complex meteorological explanation. But why *must it be the case* that there's a place where the wind isn't blowing? Now we're being asked to explain a modal. And because the hairy ball theorem is a conceptual truth (as all pure mathematical truths are), we explain this by showing how the hairy ball theorem follows from the concepts that compose the claim that "there must be at least one point on the earth where the wind isn't blowing." This is not an *obvious* conceptual truth, but it's a conceptual truth. You *can't imagine* a spheroid where wind is blowing at every location! You might think that you can—just have the wind be blowing in the same direction everywhere that it is here, say west to east. But if wind is always blowing west to east, it's not blowing anywhere on the poles; there are your cowlicks. Try to imagine wind blowing on the poles, and now you'll find that you can't have the same wind patterns near the poles, and so you've just moved the cowlick to some point on the border between the old global west-to-east wind flow and the new air currents you're attempting to imagine existing over the poles. Hopefully, you're now starting to see the difficulties involved in trying to imagine a planet with wind everywhere, or with trying to imagine a combed coconut. If you still think that this is something you might be able to conceive of if you were sufficiently clever, consult the hairy ball theorem for conclusive proof that you're wrong. The hairy ball theorem is a rigorous and general explication of what it means to have a combed coconut which shows why such a thing is, perhaps surprisingly, inconceivable. It isn't an answer to any "Why?" question concerning meteorological facts. Similarly with other purported mathematical explanations of natural facts. They're all merely tautological transformations of concepts which reveal non-obvious inconsistencies in various formulas. Because there are no genuine mathematical explanations of natural facts, this isn't a good model to use when trying to give an account of moral explanations.

Although Spencer doesn't consider himself a naturalist, he meets the criteria for naturalism that we laid out in Chapter 3.[4] That is, he claims that moral facts must enter into the explanation of our moral beliefs at some point, or else a skeptical conclusion is bound to follow. Spencer might prefer to define naturalism in other terms which would make him not count as a naturalist. But it's useful for us to think of Spencer as a naturalist because he faces the core problem that all naturalists face: the problem of locating the moral facts in the etiology of our moral beliefs. Where are they? The answer can't be "wherever you like!" For moral facts are a source of categorical normativity, and so the naturalist must locate the moral facts in a way that substantiates their categorical normativity. As I argued in §7.4.1, that's a hard task for the naturalist to undertake, and no existing proposal looks promising.

Spencer admits that he doesn't have all the answers, nor could he hope to provide them in a small book like ours. Fair enough! But the core challenge remains; the central questions have been unanswered. Realists have proven quite skilled at showing what it would mean for moral realism to be true. They have yet to provide a single piece of evidence that it is.

10.3   Final Thoughts on ECP

Spencer Case

Matt insists that we can put more meat on the bones of the ECP story to make it more compelling. But at some point, he's going to have to make a contentious inference to the best explanation

---

4   I confess this is my preferred account of naturalism, which I was able to persuade Spencer to adopt.

to the effect that the non-normative explanatory factors he mentions fully account for *all* of our moral judgments. The realist is going to deny that this explanation is satisfactory. Name all of the non-normative cultural and psychological influences that push me toward thinking that rape is bad and I'm going to think something vital has been left out if the story doesn't include any mention of the fact that it's wrong. The anti-realist will disagree, of course. Which explanations seem best to you will be determined in part by your metaethical commitments. So it seems to me that the dialectic over explanations is going to terminate in a standoff. Since I'm just trying to defend against the skeptic here, a stalemate is a win for me.

Matt's discussion of the hairy ball theorem illustrates that we can be mistaken about what's conceivable, a valuable philosophical lesson! You might think you can conceive of a combed coconut, but if you think again, you'll realize that you're only conceiving of one side of it being combed. Matt also observes that this seems to make the hairy ball theorem analytic. If all mathematical truths are analytic, which is a contentious view in the philosophy of mathematics, then the kind of moral realist who accepts synthetic *a priori* knowledge can't appeal to mathematical knowledge as a companion-in-innocence. That would make things more difficult for the realist; however, there are accounts of moral explanation, such as Rawlette's, that don't use mathematical knowledge as a companion-in-innocence. My main purpose in bringing up the hairy ball theorem wasn't to help us understand the metaphysical nature of moral explanation, however. It was to illustrate that we can know *a priori* truths that must have causal or empirical implications. I think that's true of moral facts, too: moral facts must explain some of our thoughts about them, but trying to learn about them by detecting their explanatory footprint is an unpromising way of investigating moral truth. So I don't think I've dropped the (hairy) ball here.

One of our most striking areas of agreement concerns the need for moral realists to locate moral facts within the explanatory etiology of our moral beliefs. If the fact that killing is wrong isn't part of the (best) explanation of why we believe that killing is wrong, the realist is in trouble. Spencer thinks that the ECP story is inadequate, and that mathematical explanations provide a possible analogy for how we can know *a priori* about things that help to explain events in the world. Matt thinks that moral facts play no role in the explanatory etiology of our moral beliefs, and that the non-moral "ECP story" provides the best explanation of why we have the moral beliefs that we do.

Chapter 11

Mooreanism and the *A Priori*

Matt Lutz and Spencer Case

Contents

11.1 From Mooreanism to Intuitionism

Matt Lutz

Spencer's first argument for realism is a Moorean argument. Moorean arguments come in two flavors. According to one flavor of Mooreanism, *dogmatic Mooreanism*, some claims—"Moorean claims"—are so certain that any argument against them must be wrong. Dogmatic Mooreans hold that diagnosing where a skeptical argument goes wrong would be a nice bonus, but it's not really necessary for the skeptical project. The argument must go wrong *somewhere*; enough said. Accordingly, there's no real reason to take skeptical arguments seriously or even to hear them out. Dogmatic Mooreanism is the methodological equivalent of putting your fingers in your ears and shouting until the person you're debating gives up and walks away. It's not a particularly attractive position.

Spencer is a *modest Moorean*. The modest Moorean says that Moorean claims enjoy a strong presumption in their favor, but they're not immune to argument. A sufficiently good argument could be enough to overcome the presumption in favor of the Moorean claim, and so those arguments merit careful consideration. Modest Mooreanism looks more reasonable than dogmatic Mooreanism, but is it really? Even modest Mooreans don't claim

DOI: 10.4324/9781003183174-16

to be under any obligation to explain where skeptical arguments go wrong. As Spencer says, "Moorean arguments don't tell us what we really want to know: where skeptical arguments go wrong." Modest Mooreans hear out skeptical arguments, but you can't be convinced by a skeptical argument and still be a Moorean. So modest Mooreans consider counterarguments carefully (that's what makes them modest) but ultimately reject them without any explanation (that's what makes them Mooreans).

This is not to criticize Spencer for resisting my arguments—that would be hypocritical, since I resist his, and I trust that he's sufficiently open-minded. Nor is it to criticize him for failing to offer an explanation for where he thinks my arguments go wrong—he does offer explanations. The problem is that the dialectical trappings of Mooreanism—the talk of common sense and coal pits—aren't actually doing much work. Spencer is providing a substantive argument for his view (as he should). Let's draw that argument out.

The nugget of good sense hidden within Mooreanism is the observation that when a set of premises entails some conclusion, this is not, by itself, reason to accept that conclusion. It could just as easily be a reason to reject one of the premises. Whether to accept the conclusion or reject a premise depends on which claims are best supported. If the premises are very well supported, the conclusion should be accepted. But if the evidence supports the negation of the conclusion far more than it supports any of the premises of the argument, then one of the premises must go.

Spencer's argument is therefore that our moral beliefs are much better supported than the premises of any arguments which would imply skepticism or error theory. I've already denied that this is the case. My main argument in Chapter 7 was for the conclusion that our moral beliefs are not supported by any evidence whatsoever. We might be extremely confident that some of our moral beliefs are true, but extreme confidence is not the same thing as evidential support. People can be irrationally confident. Paranoiacs are absolutely convinced that someone is out to get them, even if there's no evidence for it. And we should not say that this extreme confidence is evidence for the truth of their beliefs. We get very attached to our world view and very resistant to revising it, despite what evidence we may receive. The best way—I think the only way—to cut through the bullshit is by evaluating the capacity of our beliefs to generate successful predictions. Predictive success is an indication that you understand the way the world works—not a flawless indication, but the only one worth anything. But moral beliefs don't facilitate predictive success, and so they're not supported by evidence.

Spencer rejects my account of evidential support. He doesn't have a full account of evidence to offer in its place, but he does give us enough to evaluate. He tells us that some moral claims attain the status of common sense because they're so overwhelmingly *plausible*. Plausibility is a phenomenological concept; *plausible* is a way that claims can *seem*. If you consider a claim and (upon serious consideration) it *just seems right*, then that claim is plausible. Spencer's view is that if it's plausible that P, then this is evidence that P is true. The more plausible a claim is, the more it's supported by evidence. And Spencer says that certain moral claims are extremely plausible, and thus extremely well-supported. That's what gives those claims their Moorean status.

This is a version of *intuitionism*. Indeed, Spencer refers to "intuition" some thirty times in his chapter on Moorean arguments. He approvingly cites Michael Huemer's moral intuitionism with its reliance on the Principle of Phenomenal Conservatism. And he gives us the Normative Workshop Argument, which concludes that we should trust all of our normative intuitions (at least initially). So this is what Spencer's Moorean argument amounts to: he has an intuition that certain moral claims are true, and that intuition provides incredibly strong evidence for moral claims.

I've already refuted intuitionism. Intuitionism is a version of what I called the "no connections strategy" in §7.4.2. According to intuitionism, an intuition *that* P is evidence *for* P, no matter what. In particular, intuitions are evidence no matter *why* we have that intuition. If an intuition is the result of being drugged or duped or just a bad case of motivated reasoning, it still counts as evidence. The paranoiac's intuition that someone is after him is evidence that someone is after him: the more paranoid he is, the stronger his intuition, the more well-justified his paranoia is. But that's absurd. Evidence that P is an indication that P is true, and evidence can only be an indication if that evidence is connected in some way to the fact that P is true. The paranoiac's intuitions are not evidence that someone is after him because he doesn't have those intuitions because someone really is after him. He has those intuitions because he's crazy.

One might say that intuitions do count as evidence, but the paranoiac's intuitions are defeated. There are three problems with this response. First, it's at least somewhat counterintuitive to say that a paranoiac's delusions are evidence for the truth of those deluded beliefs. That's a cactus that we should hesitate to embrace, to use Spencer's preferred metaphor. Second, even if we grant that the strong intuitions of the paranoiac provide evidence but are defeated, this substantially undercuts the Moorean pretensions of intuitionism. If the evidential support of even a very strong intuition can be easily defeated, strong intuitions don't grant beliefs anything like a Moorean status. And third, this shows that intuitionism itself provides a thin conception of what evidence could amount to. If intuitions provide evidential support only in the absence of defeaters, the question of whether there are defeaters for our beliefs is at least as important as the question of whether we have an intuition at all. And as I've argued—and I think Spencer grants this, given what he says about the Explanation Argument in §5.5—a lack of an explanatory connection between your evidence for a belief and the fact in question is a defeater for that belief. So even if intuitions provide justification in the absence of defeaters, they don't provide justification.

This is not to say that intuitions can never count as evidence. Our dispositions to deploy our concepts give rise to phenomenological seeming states that are evidence about the nature of those concepts. The fact that it just seems right that all bachelors are unmarried is evidence that all bachelors are unmarried. But this is because the claim that all bachelors are unmarried is a conceptual truth, and the intuition that it's correct is a manifestation of competence with the relevant concepts. In this way, intuitions can be a source of *analytic a priori* knowledge. But there are no substantive analytic moral truths. In particular, none of the moral claims that Spencer indicates as overwhelmingly plausible are analytic.

This, incidentally, is the problem with Spencer's Normative Workshop Argument. He argues that we shouldn't treat moral intuitions differently than we treat other kinds of normative intuitions and, since we should trust other normative intuitions, we should trust our moral intuitions. Spencer is correct to say that we should try to sort the intuitions that provide good evidence from the intuitions that don't provide good evidence, but the place to draw the line isn't between moral intuitions and other normative intuitions. The place to draw the line is between intuitions for analytic claims and intuitions for synthetic claims. Only the former are evidence.

In sum, Spencer is committed to intuitions as a source of synthetic *a priori* moral knowledge: some moral claims seem so obvious that we know that they accurately represent the world even if our having those intuitions is completely unconnected to the way things are in the world, morally speaking. This is a mysterious way of knowing, to say the least.

11.2   Trust Yourself

Spencer Case

I should probably plead guilty to the charge of being an intuitionist, though with a couple of caveats. First, I don't think that only internal mental states are evidence; physical objects such as a bloody knife at a crime scene also constitute evidence that matters, epistemically. Second, I sometimes think, along with Greco (2007) and Rawlette (2020), that realists should emphasize moral experience or perception rather than intuition. I think our moral assessments are often integrated with our perception in the way Harman describes, and that much, and possibly all, moral intuition derives from these perceptions. Nonetheless, these caveats don't derail Matt's line of attack. Whether we choose to talk about intuitions or perception, I'm taking the position that we should often trust our mental states as a guide to truth about morality.

   Matt thinks that my epistemology is too permissive, and I think Matt's isn't permissive enough. Matt thinks that moral intuitions (and, presumably, perceptions) constitute no evidence for moral realism because, he says, there's no causal connection between moral facts and moral intuitions. But I think sometimes we perceive or intuit that certain actions are wrong because they're wrong. I've remained stubbornly agnostic about the details of this story, but I maintain that moral facts do play some causal role in explaining veridical moral intuitions. Matt's view is that intuitions can't count as evidence for moral facts unless and until moral facts are shown to be a part of the best explanation for the fact that those intuitions (maybe we should say "intuitings") have occurred. He takes that explanation to be the ECP story, which I've attempted to cast doubt upon. Let me try to get us past this logjam by suggesting an epistemic principle that Matt, or someone with similar epistemic leanings, might find attractive:

Principle of explanationist conservatism: If it appears that P to S, then that the truth of P is by default the best explanation for S for that appearance. Thus, S epistemically ought to accept P unless and until a better explanation for the appearance that P is found.

Note that we could also entertain a weaker version of this principle, according to which believing P is epistemically permissible, though not required, on the basis of the appearance that P. We could also modify it to eliminate agent relativity, so that anyone's having the appearance that P is defeasible evidence for anyone to believe that P. But for now let's just consider this version.

The principle of explanationist conservatism (PEC) construes Huemer's principle of phenomenal conservatism, or what I'm calling "self-trust", as an explanationist principle. One upshot is that we should trust our moral intuitions as a guide to reality unless and until a better explanation for them is found. Matt thinks he's found one; I deny this. PEC also gets the right result in non-moral cases, it seems to me. Suppose that Matt is coming home from Devil's Brewery one night when he has a vivid experience of being abducted by aliens. This is a one-off experience that I assume can't easily be integrated with his explanatory web, and one that is so seemingly unlikely to be repeated that it might not offer Matt any predictive guidance. I don't think that Matt needs to have several such experiences, or to have an explanatory theory in hand, in order to know that he really did experience this. Now if a companion told him that someone had spiked his beer with a hallucinogen, then this would no longer be the default hypothesis. But I want to say that Matt would be being irrational if from the get-go, he refused to think this experience offered *any evidence whatsoever* for the phenomenon of alien abduction.

I want to say something similar about certain religious experiences, albeit of a very rare sort. Most of what people describe as religious experience appears to me to just be undisciplined pattern seeking (e.g., deciding to interpret some bit of good news as a sign of God's benevolence). Although I'm not religious myself, I'm disinclined to dismiss all non-sensory religious experience—say, a profound, overpowering sense of the unity of the universe, or the presence of some higher power—as having no epistemic value whatsoever, no matter how compelling it seems from the point of view of the person having it. I think an experience like that could justify some religious beliefs at least until one has some good evidence against them. Matt just disagrees with me here. But it seems to me that if the alien abduction experience has evidentiary value, then so could some religious experiences. I want to say that with moral intuitions and these singular experiences alike, we should trust ourselves until we have good reason not to.

Matt says that realists like me are mistaking psychological attachment for evidence when we rely on intuition, and even those putative "Moorean facts" that seem especially compelling. I don't deny that what Shafer-Landau calls "irresistibility" and I call "compellingness" is playing a role. I think it has epistemic significance for our other epistemic faculties as well. Sensory perceptions are compelling, or irresistible, in the same way. As Bengson puts it, intuition and sensory perception don't just *represent* states of affairs; they *present* certain things as being true (2015b, 719–725). If perceptions were representational without being presentational—if we didn't feel compelled to believe our sensory representations—we'd be much more susceptible to external world skepticism. Implicitly at least, we all, empiricists included, take compellingness to be more than psychological as we must if we're to take our own minds seriously and avoid skepticism.

Finally, Matt seems unable to live up to the demands of his own stringent empiricism. Recall that Matt wants to dispense with categorical normativity, but not with hypothetical normativity. He endorses the hypothetical principle: "An agent has a reason to perform an action if and only if that action will promote one of that agent's desires." However, he cautions us against the most natural way to read this principle: we're not to interpret it as the idea that an action's propensity to promote an agent's ends is a normative fact which *counts in favor* of that action. Rather, the statement that an agent has a hypothetical reason to do something *just means* that doing that thing would realize an aim that the agent has. This analytic interpretation of the hypothetical principle makes no metaphysical concessions of the sort that I want to use to press my "foothold" argument, but it generates an "open-question" challenge.

Consider an immoral action that would realize an agent's self-destructive aim. To me, it doesn't seem *contradictory* to say that the agent has no normative reason whatsoever to perform this action: "Doing X would promote my aims, but do I have any reason to do X?" sounds like an open question. Reflective proportionalism also looks like a substantive normative claim. It's hard to believe that it could be *what people mean* when they talk about some reasons being weightier than others. I suspect that Matt is equivocating: engaging in substantive normative reasoning, while claiming that he's just unpacking definitions. If we combine the hypothetical principle and reflective proportionalism, then we arrive at the following:

Hypothetical principle + reflective proportionalism: An agent, who has a reason to perform action X, and a reason to perform action Y, has more reason to perform X than Y if and only if:

1   X has a tendency to promote an end that the agent desires with S degree of intensity, the action has with N likelihood of bringing that end about, and that end has C degree of closeness to that agent's self-conception. ($S \times N \times C = T$, the agent's total normative reason to perform X.)

2   Y has a tendency to promote an end that the agent desires with R degree of intensity, the action has with M likelihood of bringing that end about, and that end has D degree of closeness to that agent's self-conception. ($R \times M \times D = T^i$, the agent's total normative reason to perform Y.).

3   $T > T^i$

If we can consistently deny this, then it isn't analytically true. And apparently, we can deny it consistently. Now maybe the appearances are deceiving: many truths of mathematics are highly non-obvious, though according to Humeans they're all analytic. For now we can set aside the controversies in the philosophy of mathematics. If reflective proportionalism is correct, then it's either a highly non-obvious analytic truth or a synthetic *a priori* truth. If it's a synthetic *a priori* truth, then there are such truths, and we must know them by intuition (what else?). That leaves the door open for synthetic *a priori* moral knowledge, i.e., the realist gains a companion-in-innocence. Alternatively, we could understand this to be a subtle analytic truth, as Matt does. This, too, is good for me. After all, if philosophically substantive theses about rationality like this are analytically true, then perhaps the same can be said for many moral claims. If important moral claims could be analytic, then the skeptical threat to realism dissolves.

Let's look at this objection in more detail. Matt thinks we can't trust our intuitions about what's right and wrong, no matter how compelling and widely shared, but he apparently feels comfortable relying upon linguistic intuitions that many of his peers, including me, don't share. That looks like special pleading. For the sake of argument, though, let's grant that hypothetical normativity some-how derives from an analytic truth. Why couldn't the same be true of categorical, and therefore moral, normativity? Why can't we say, for instance, that for something to be morally right is by defini-tion for it to optimize overall, long-run happiness? This is a version of analytic descriptivism. Recall that the main objection to that view is the open-question argument: denying that "right" means "happiness-maximizing" is apparently consistent. But Matt's ana-lytic interpretation of the hypothetical principle faces the same objection. If his position can withstand the objection, then per-haps analytic descriptivism can as well. Moreover, not only must Matt rule out analytic descriptivism, he must also insist that moral thought and language can't be revised to make any version of ana-lytic descriptivism true. Otherwise, he faces Finlay's objection.

Don't think that Matt can stipulate his way out of this mess. As we noted in Chapter 2, the moral error theorist accepts tautolo-gies such as "impermissible actions aren't permissible" and "what's morally right isn't morally wrong." Likewise, a normative error theorist can stipulate statements about hypothetical normativity that are trivially true. If Matt's endorsement of hypothetical reasons reduces to a stipulation, then it's unclear how his position is distinct from normative error theory, which he officially rejects.

11.3 Normative Proportionalism

Matt Lutz

My core concern about Spencer's intuitionism is that intuitionists claim that having an intuition that P can be sufficient for being jus-tified in believing P, yet Spencer concedes that justification requires an explanatory connection. There's at least a tension between those two commitments. Spencer does an admirable job of resolving that tension with his endorsement of PEC. This also simplifies my dis-agreement with Spencer on the subject of intuitionism: he accepts PEC and I reject it.

PEC says that if it appears that P, then the fact that P is, by default, part of the best explanation of that appearance. I disagree. If it appears that P, then perhaps P is a promising hypothesis that is worth trying to fit into a network of explanatory relations that can facilitate successful predictions. But until the hypothesis that P (or the explanatory principles that link P to the appearance that P) has proven its mettle by facilitating predictive success, P is nothing more than an interesting hypothesis.

Spencer thinks that I need to appeal to something like PEC in order to explain why I have evidence that I've been abducted by aliens in the alien abduction case. But this is not so. My most well-confirmed belief is that my sensory experiences are caused by a world which is largely the way that I experience it as being. So if I experience aliens (provided that those experiences are clear, consistent, stable over time, mutually confirmed by different sense modalities, etc.), then the hypothesis that I really have been abducted by aliens fits well-confirmed elements of my map, and so is supported by evidence. Of course, there are other elements of my map that the hypothesis that I've been abducted by aliens fits poorly with; I don't believe that aliens exist. And those elements are evidence that I haven't been abducted by aliens (and so my experiences must be the product of hallucination or something). What my evidence supports on balance is a complicated question that involves consideration of many contingent factors about the nature of my experiences, my evidence that aliens don't exist, and the availability of alternate hypotheses. At any rate, my experiences of aliens *are* evidence for the existence of aliens. But that's because that hypothesis fits with my experiences *and my most well-confirmed background belief*; the experience by itself isn't evidence.

Spencer's argument against reflective proportionalism, on the other hand, raises much larger problems for my view. My argument for reflective proportionalism is *a priori*, but Spencer argues it's not plausibly a conceptual truth. So I find myself hoisted by my own petard. Spencer hopes that this will cause me to abandon the claim that all *a priori* knowledge is conceptual, which would then open the door for the possibility of synthetic *a priori* knowledge via intuition. Instead, I'm going to take a half step back from reflective proportionalism. This is a minor setback, at most. I endorsed reflective proportionalism as a way of answering a version of Korsgaard's objection. But all that I needed to do in order to answer Korsgaard's objection was reject simple proportionalism. I'd hoped to replace it with something more constructive. If I can't, that's merely disappointing.

I don't want to entirely give up on reflective proportionalism. I still find it plausible, and not all conceptual truths are obviously conceptual truths. So let's walk through the reasoning behind

Reflective Proportionalism again and see if we can find out if I over-stepped and, if I did, where.

The question at hand is what the "weight" of a reason consists in. If you have a reason to do something just in case doing that thing will promote the satisfaction of one of your desires, then the weight of that reason is obviously proportional to *how much* that action will promote the satisfaction of your desire. I'm happy to call that a conceptual truth. But the weight of your reasons doesn't *only* depend on the degree of promotion. Consider a situation where there are two actions available, A and B. A is guaranteed to get you something that you *really really* want. B is guaranteed to get you something that you kinda want. There are no other relevant considerations. What should you do? Clearly, you should do action A; your reason to do action A is weightier than your reason to do action B. So the weight of your reasons is proportional to the degree of promotion and also *something else*. I'm happy to call this a conceptual truth as well.

Now: what is that something else? What does it mean to *really really* want something? Simple proportionalism says that this is the "strength" of the desire, where strength is the impact that desire has on your motivations. As I argued in §6.5, this means that *compulsive* desires are your strongest desires, and thus compulsive action is always rational. This seems wrong. So simple proportionalism has to go.

This is the point in the dialectic where, earlier, I boldly advanced reflective proportionalism. Here's a more cautious step: Let's define the *normative strength* of a desire as that factor, whatever it is, that determines how weighty a reason based on that desire is (together with degree of promotion). This is an ugly stipulative definition, but it makes the following a conceptual truth: The weight of a reason to do an action is proportional to the degree to which that action will promote the desire and the normative strength of that desire. Call that **normative proportionalism**. That's my considered view.

Can we give a more constructive characterization of normative strength? Perhaps. It's not motivational strength. It might be motivational strength combined with centrality to the self (that's reflective proportionalism, which I remain sympathetic to). It might be unanalyzable—when we say that we *really really* want something, we just mean that that desire has great normative strength, and that's the end of the analysis. But whatever normative strength is, it's something about the phenomenology or functional profile of the desire. Normative strength is not to-be-pursued-ness. There's no such thing.

A key part of Spencer's case for realism is an endorsement of Moorean arguments for realism, although his Mooreanism is, in effect, just a version of intuitionism: certain moral beliefs are justified by the fact that they seem overwhelmingly plausible. Matt points out that this commits Spencer to the possibility of synthetic *a priori* knowledge, which he rejects. But Spencer defends intuitionism, and points out that Matt hasn't stuck to his own scruples about the nature of *a priori* knowledge in his argument for reflective proportionalism. In response, Matt retreats to the more modest normative proportionalism.

Chapter 12

Entanglement

Matt Lutz and Spencer Case

Contents

12.1 There's No Epistemic Entanglement

Matt Lutz

In §6.6, we looked at Cuneo's objection, which argues that we can't reject categorical moral normativity since epistemic normativity is categorical as well. In this way, moral and epistemic normativity are entangled. I responded to Cuneo's objection by arguing that, while some epistemic facts are categorical, epistemic normativity is hypothetical. Spencer provides a new argument for the idea that epistemic and moral normativity are entangled. This argument raises issues that go beyond what Cuneo offers. Let's dig into the details.

He begins by considering a view that we might call "weak evidentialism":

> **Weak Evidentialism:** A subject S is justified in believing a proposition P just in case P is supported by the balance of S's evidence.

Weak Evidentialism has an obvious problem. There are some cases—let's call them *weak evidence cases*—where a subject has very weak, circumstantial evidence for P and no evidence against P. For example, perhaps the only evidence for P is the testimony

DOI: 10.4324/9781003183174-17

of someone who is an inveterate bullshitter and almost always speaks without any regard to the truth, but who is honest and forthright once in a blue moon. As a result, what they say ends up being true barely more than 50 percent of the time. In weak evidence cases like this, the balance of the subject's evidence supports P, but it supports P so weakly that it's counterintuitive to say that a belief in P would be justified. To solve this problem, Spencer proposes:

> **Investigation:** A subject S is justified in believing a proposition P just in case (a) P is supported by the balance of S's evidence and (b) S has diligently investigated whether P is true.

A subject has diligently investigated whether P is true if there's no new evidence to be gathered that passes a pragmatic/epistemic cost/benefit analysis. In this analysis, the benefits are epistemic (how good is the evidence I could get by doing this investigation) and the costs are, broadly, pragmatic (how much time and energy, pain and suffering, would it take to conduct the investigation)? P has been diligently investigated if and only if there are no further investigations that are worth doing according to the cost/benefit test. This helps with the problem of weak evidence cases. If the subject's evidence is weak, there's much room for epistemic improvement, and so further investigation will likely pass the cost/benefit analysis. Therefore, the matter hasn't been diligently investigated, and so the subject's belief is not justified.

Moral entanglement enters the picture when we look at the nature of this cost/benefit analysis. When we are adding up costs in our analysis, *whose* costs do we consider? Spencer contends that it's arbitrary to consider only the costs to yourself when deciding whether to investigate further; a subject is justified in believing only if the benefits of further investigation exceed the costs to *anyone*. Therefore, what it takes to have a justified belief is determined, in part, by what is in the interests of others. In this way, moral considerations determine whether a subject's belief is justified. So if facts about epistemic justification are categorical, then moral facts must also be categorical.

There's a lot that I take issue with here. For one thing, I think that my response to Cuneo's objection, suitably modified, applies here. Even if we assume that knowledge requires diligent investigation in the way that Spencer contends, we can give an account of diligent investigation in entirely non-normative terms that wouldn't imply the existence of categorical reasons of any kind. But I think there's an even bigger problem for this argument for the entanglement premise: Investigation is not well motivated since the move from Weak Evidentialism to Investigation doesn't actually solve the problem posed by weak evidence cases.

Suppose that we are in a weak evidence case, where S's only evidence in favor of P is weak and circumstantial. And suppose further that to get any additional evidence, we'd have to perform painful experiments on human subjects. Call cases like this *high cost weak evidence cases*. In high cost weak evidence cases, further investigation would not pass the cost/benefit test. So P has been diligently investigated. Therefore, according to Investigation, S's belief that P is justified. But beliefs are not justified in weak evidence cases. So Investigation doesn't solve the weak evidence cases problem.

The obvious fix to this problem is to replace investigation with robust investigation:

> **Robust Investigation:** A subject S is justified in believing a proposition P just in case (a) P is *robustly* supported by the balance of S's evidence and (b) S has diligently investigated whether P is true.

A belief is "robustly supported" just in case it is sufficiently likely given the evidence. (We can propose any number of accounts of what "sufficiently likely" means, but a belief supported only by the testimony of an inveterate bullshitter, e.g., wouldn't count). Robust Investigation has no problem with weak evidence cases, since the requirement of robust support entails that the subject is not in a weak evidence case. But if the requirement of robust support solves the weak evidence case problem, what need do we have for the requirement of diligent investigation? That is, why accept Robust Investigation rather than Robust Evidentialism?

> **Robust Evidentialism:** A subject S is justified in believing a proposition P just in case P is robustly supported by the balance of S's evidence.

We can put this in the form of a dilemma. Either justification requires robust evidential support, where "robust" is defined in terms that are independent of the diligence of investigation, or it does not. If justification *does* require robust evidential support, then the diligence requirement is unmotivated, since the diligence requirement was introduced to solve weak evidence cases but those cases are solved by the robustness requirement. And if justification *does not* require robust evidential support, then a diligence requirement will not explain the lack of justification in high stakes weak evidence cases. But the diligence requirement was introduced in order to explain the lack of justification in weak evidence cases, and so the diligence requirement is unmotivated. So either way, the diligence requirement is unmotivated. But if the diligence requirement is unmotivated, then so is the moral entanglement premise, since moral entanglement (supposedly) follows from the diligence requirement.

If a subject's evidence is weak, additional investigation will be required to attain robust support. And since robust support is required for knowledge, sometimes knowing requires additional investigation. And if additional investigation involves taking on costs—to yourself and others—that you would strongly prefer not to incur, then you shouldn't investigate further. This doesn't mean that your meager evidence becomes sufficient for knowing. It just means that sometimes the best thing to do, given your desires, is to give up on knowing.

12.2   Practical and Moral Availability

Spencer Case

Does epistemic justification require robust evidential support or not? My answer is: it depends. In low-stakes contexts where other information isn't available or isn't worth hunting down, you can be justified in believing on pretty weak evidence. Recall Clifford's ship owner. If one of the crew members tells Clifford that there are between 250 and 260 barnacles on his ship's hull, based on his guesstimate, and there's nothing important at stake here, then maybe the shipowner can believe this and be justified. On the other hand, if the estimated number is just below the threshold at which the barnacles begin to threaten the integrity of the ship, then he shouldn't believe this casual testimony. He has a duty to suspend judgment until he's investigated more thoroughly.

Matt seems to think that I accept practical-epistemic entanglement because it seems unacceptable to believe on weak evidence. As I see it, though, the issue is believing on *insufficient* evidence; the context determines what is sufficient. You might have very strong evidence that something is true and still not have sufficient evidence.

Suppose a cursory investigation of the ship suggests that the ship has a 99 percent chance of crossing the ocean without incident. Is the shipowner justified in believing that his ship is seaworthy, or even that it's 99 percent likely to be seaworthy, based on this evidence? Clearly not. He should suspend judgment until he has undertaken a more thorough investigation. In short, unpossessed evidence that an agent could come to possess at a certain cost seems epistemically relevant; in high stakes situations, it remains relevant even when the agent's starting evidence is quite robust.

This still leaves some puzzles. For instance, suppose a dictator gives me weak evidence for believing some very important proposition and threatens to punish me and other innocents if I seek any further evidence. Am I justified in believing what the weak evidence suggests is the case? I'm inclined to think probably not, though it might be prudent to act *as if* I believed it. What precisely is the line between believing and acting as if one believes? I'm not sure, but the two are related. If there were no foreseeable circumstances in which I would desist from acting as if I believed the evidence, then it seems to me that I really do believe it. Real belief doesn't stay in the believer's head. It's practically significant. A belief must exert some kind of influence on the agent's tendency to act, however subtle. That's why it can be practically and morally entangled. If beliefs weren't practically entangled, then knowledge would be a lot less important and epistemology would be a lot less interesting.

12.3 Pragmatic Encroachment

Matt Lutz

Spencer claims that Investigation is motivated not just by the existence of weak evidence cases, but also by the existence of high stakes cases: If the stakes regarding whether P are high enough, then extraordinary evidence is required to be justified in believing P. This is Spencer's analysis of Clifford's shipowner. Even if the shipowner could be 99 percent certain that his ship is seaworthy, that's not enough to be justified given the terrible consequences if he's wrong.

This puts us on familiar ground. There's a substantial literature on the idea that high practical stakes raise the bar for what is required for justified belief. I've argued against this idea elsewhere. In short, my view is that high stakes don't affect what it takes to *be* justified in believing that P, but rather that high stakes affect what it takes to be warranted in *asserting that* someone is justified in believing P. If someone believes P, they'll be disposed to treat P as true in practical reasoning. So in a situation where someone faces a practical decision where P is relevant to deciding what to do, to *say* that S is justified in believing that P *implies* that S is rational to treat P as true in practical reasoning. But that doesn't mean that S's *being* justified in believing P *entails* that S is rational to treat P as true in practical reasoning. The correct thing to say about Clifford's shipowner is that he is justified in believing that the ship is seaworthy, but, given the horrible consequences if he's wrong, he'd better double check just to be sure (Lutz 2014b).

We don't need to appeal to Investigation to explain why the shipowner's belief is unjustified. That's because the shipowner's belief *is* justified, even if his actions aren't (assuming he cares about the lives of the people onboard). So Investigation remains unsupported.

Matt contends that we can specify the conditions under which a belief is justified in entirely non-normative terms, and that Spencer's argument for moral encroachment is undermotivated. Spencer responds that practical stakes (to others as well as yourself) make a difference to whether or not your belief is *sufficiently* well-supported to count as being justified.

12.4   Fin

So we end where we began: we disagree on quite a bit, but still agree about a number of things. Does that mean we've made no progress? Hardly. Philosophers talk about *compelling* arguments that are supposed to *force* all reasonable interlocutors to accept their conclusions. Robert Nozick comments on the coercive model for philosophical arguments: "Perhaps philosophers need arguments so powerful they set up reverberations in the brain: if the person refuses to accept the conclusion, he *dies*. How's that for a powerful argument?" (1981, 4). Fortunately, (or unfortunately, depending on how you look at it), we haven't offered any arguments like that. But Nozick's joke contains a serious point: offering lethally compelling arguments isn't the measure of philosophical success or progress. There need be nothing wrong with an argument that can't convince all reasonable people. An argument is successful if it gives the audience pause, or makes those who disagree with the conclusion a little less confident, or expands intellectual empathy by demonstrating how a position could seem attractive to those who embrace it. Every time an argument has one of these effects, philosophical progress has been made.

We each think that we've come away from this exchange with a better appreciation of the difficulty and depth of the problem we set out to investigate—is morality real?—and the relationship between that question and other philosophical questions. Although neither of us was able to give an argument so compelling that it made the other's head explode, both of our minds have expanded. We hope the same is true for you.

Further Reading

Realism

Beginner: Midgely's "On Trying Out One's New Sword" (2005) is a great way to motivate thinking about moral relativism. Shafer-Landau's "Eleven Arguments against Moral Objectivity" in his *The Fundamentals of Ethics* offers brief rebuttals to common anti-realist arguments.

Intermediate: Michael Huemer's *Ethical Intuitionism* (2005), and Russ Shafer-Landau's *Moral Realism: A Defence* (2003) are both clearly written and rigorously argued. Sharon Rawlette's overlooked book, *The Feeling of Value* (2020) offers an outstanding defense of analytic descriptivism. Terence Cuneo's defense of the epistemic companions-in-innocence argument in *The Normative Web* (2007) is also quite accessible. Nicholas Sturgeon has many excellent papers on naturalistic realism including his famous response to Harman, "Moral Explanations" (1988). His "What Difference Does it Make Whether Moral Realism is True?" (1986) and "Doubts about the Supervenience of the Evaluative" (2009) are also well worth your time.

Advanced: David Enoch's *Taking Morality Seriously* (2011) and T. M. Scanlon's *Being Realistic About Reasons* (2014) are essential contemporary defenses of non-naturalist realism. Richard Boyd's "How to be a Moral Realist" (1988) is a sophisticated and comprehensive defense of synthetic naturalism. The truly brave will take on Frank Jackson's defense of analytic naturalism in *From Metaphysics to Ethics* (1998). All are quite dense, but well worth the time and effort.

Anti-realism and Skepticism

Beginner: Mackie's *Ethics: Inventing Right and Wrong* (1977) is a touchstone of contemporary writing on error theory and is frequently used in introductory ethics classes. Gilbert Harman's seminal defense of the explanation argument for moral skepticism in chapter 1 of *The Nature of Morality* (1977) is also beginner-friendly, and the rest of the book presents an accessible defense of relativism. Schroeder's *Non-Cognitivism in Ethics* (2010) is a shockingly accessible introduction to a very difficult topic. Finally, the Ring of Gyges thought experiment in Plato's *Republic*, Book 2 is a good way to motivate discussions of moral anti-realism.

Intermediate: Richard Joyce's *The Myth of Morality* (2001) is a more up-to-date version of Mackie's "queerness" argument. Schroeder's *Slaves of the Passions* (2007) presents the definitive defense of the Humean theory of reasons (although Schroeder is a realist). Jonas Olson's *Moral Error Theory* (2014) gives a definitive overview of the history of error theory. Christine Korsgaard's *The Sources of Normativity* (1996) is an ambitious defense of Kantian constructivism.

Advanced: Sharon Street's "A Darwinian Dilemma for Realist Theories of Value" (2006) and Richard Joyce's *The Evolution of Morality* (2007) are the most important and influential developments of evolutionary debunking arguments. Allan Gibbard's *Thinking How to Live* (2003) is the seminal contemporary work of quasi-realist expressivism.

Glossary

Analytic naturalism (analytic descriptivism): The view that moral terms can be defined in natural (descriptive) terms. For example, according to one version, "good" means "pleasure."

Anti-realism (moral): The denial of one or more of the three planks of moral realism. (See *realism, moral*).

Categorical normativity: Normativity that doesn't depend on the agent's desires or aims. Many have thought that moral duties are paradigmatically categorical.

Categorical normativity argument: The objection to realism according to which categorical normativity is metaphysically extravagant.

Causal theory of reference: The semantic theory according to which fundamental terms refer to whatever properties causally regulate their use within a community of language users.

Causal relativism problem (or the "moral twin Earth" objection): A standard objection to the causal theory of reference. In short, it's intuitively possible to live in a society whose tendencies to call things "good" are systematically unreliable. It's hard to see how the causal theory of reference could accommodate that intuition.

Cognitivism, moral: The idea that moral language serves to attribute moral properties to agents, actions, or states of affairs. This is in contrast to exclamations like "Boo!" and "Hooray!" and with imperatives "Be quiet!" which serve a different linguistic role.

Companions-in-innocence defense: A strategy of holding one kind of skepticism or anti-realism suspect because the arguments that support it (or similar arguments) supposedly support stronger and less plausible views. One metaethical

DOI: 10.4324/9781003183174-17

companions-in-innocence defense is that arguments for moral skepticism support epistemic skepticism (see *Cuneo's objection*).

Compositionality: The feature of language whereby sentences get their meanings from the meanings of the words that make up those sentences, and complex sentences (i.e., sentences that are made up out of simple sentences) get their meanings from the meanings of the simple sentences from which they're made.

Constructivism: The view that moral facts exist but are stance-dependent.

Cuneo's objection: A companions-in-innocence objection to Humeanism and Humean error theory that identifies epistemic normativity as the innocent companion. Epistemic normativity is categorical, and it's incoherent to doubt the existence of epistemic normativity, so it's incoherent to deny the existence of categorical normativity. (See *companions-in-innocence defense*; *Humeanism*; *categorical normativity*.)

Descriptive morality: The moral practices and beliefs of a group of people, as an anthropologist might document them.

Divine voluntarism (or "divine command theory"):   The view that God's commandments explain the most basic normative moral facts, e.g., murder is wrong *because* God forbids it.

ECP story: The complex, naturalistic explanation of our moral beliefs in terms of evolutionary, cultural, and individual psychological factors.

Empiricism: The view that all substantive knowledge ultimately derives from sensory observation alone.

Epistemological queerness argument: The objection to non-skeptical moral realism according to which moral knowledge would have to come from a weird source, such as a mysterious faculty of intuition.

Error theory, moral (or moral nihilism):   The conjunction of cognitivism and non-negotiable error. Moral language purports to describe reality, but always fails to describe it truthfully due to some non-negotiable feature of moral thought and language. It's also sometimes called "nihilism," though some error theorists eschew this label. (See *cognitivism*; *non-negotiable error*.)

Euthyphro dilemma: A standard objection to divine voluntarism that asks whether God's goodness or God's commandments have explanatory priority. Neither answer seems acceptable. The name is a reference to Plato's dialogue *Euthyphro*, in which Socrates presses a version of this problem. (See *divine voluntarism*.)

Evolutionary debunking argument (EDA):   A popular (although controversial) kind of argument for moral skepticism. EDAs begin from the premise that evolutionary factors explain our dispositions to form moral beliefs and conclude that this fact undermines those beliefs. (See *undermining defeater*.)

Explanationism: A cluster of views which analyze critical epistemic notions—knowledge, justification, non-accidentality, evidence—in terms of the concept of explanation. One popular explanationist view is that all (non-deductive) inference is "inference to the best explanation": a belief is justified if and only if it's part of the best explanation of some evidence.

Explanatory map: A subject's beliefs about the way the world is and the way the world works. Explanatory maps are structured by beliefs in general explanatory relations and generate predictions about the future course of events.

Expressivism: The view that moral assertions express the speaker's (non-cognitive) attitudes rather than report those attitudes or describe the world.

Finlay's objection: A prominent objection to error theory which argues that the supposed error in moral concepts isn't a part of our moral concepts at all, or at least not a "non-negotiable" part. So recognizing this error should make us revise our moral concepts, at most; not abandon morality.

Frege–Geach problem: A well-known objection to expressivism and other forms of non-cognitivism named after Gottlob Frege and Peter Geach. According to the objection, non-cognitivist theories can't explain the compositionality of moral language. (See *compositionality*.)

Hampton's objection: A prominent objection to Humeanism due to Jean Hampton. The requirement that one satisfy one's own desires is a categorical imperative; therefore, hypothetical normativity presupposes categorical normativity and so not all normativity is hypothetical.

Humean error theory: The version of error theory which accepts Humeanism and identifies categorical normativity as a non-negotiable error in our concept of morality. (See *Humean theory of normativity*; *categorical normativity argument*.)

Humean theory of normativity ("Humeanism"):   The view that all normativity is hypothetical and so no normativity is categorical. (See *hypothetical normativity*; *categorical normativity*.)

Hybrid expressivism: The view that moral statements have both an expressive component and a cognitive one. Thus, for example, a hybrid expressivist might say that "Stealing is wrong!" both reports the fact that stealing has the property of being wrong *and* expresses the speaker's disapproval of stealing.

Hypothetical normativity: Normativity that depends upon an agent's aims or attitudes. For instance, if Bob wants to see a movie in the theater, he has a reason to go see the movie. If he decides that he doesn't want to see the movie after all, then he no longer has a reason to go.

Instrumental value: The kind of value things have when they promote some further end which is intrinsically valuable. Something can be both intrinsically and instrumentally valuable.

Intrinsic value: Whatever is worth achieving or promoting for its own sake, whether or not it leads to something else.

Kantian constructivism: Constructivist views, derived from the work of Immanuel Kant, which hold that moral facts are universal because moral facts depend on stances that are constitutive of rational agency.

Korsgaard's objection: A prominent objection to Humeanism due to Christine Korsgaard. Because our reasons motivate us to act, the Humean will say that we have strongest reason to do what we're most strongly motivated to do, and thus irrational action is impossible.

Moorean argument: An argument that rejects a philosophical position or argument on the grounds that it's inconsistent with common sense without identifying where the target position goes wrong. Named for the philosopher G. E. Moore.

Moral overridingness: The idea that moral obligations trump all competing considerations about what to do.

Motivation argument: An argument against moral realism, one version of the "queerness" argument (see that entry), that proceeds from the thought that moral properties, if real, would be mysteriously motivating.

Naturalism: The idea that all properties we can know about are natural properties. Natural properties are commonly described as the kinds of properties that can be investigated by scientific, empirical methods.

Naturalism, moral: The view that moral facts are natural facts. (See *naturalism*.)

Non-cognitivism, moral: The view that moral judgments have some function other than representation. (See *expressivism*.)

Non-naturalist moral realism: The view that moral facts exist, and are mind-independent, but aren't natural facts. It's also known as moral "non-naturalism" and "robust realism."

Normative morality: The subject matter of ethics.

Normativity: "Guidingness." The sort of quality we refer to with words like 'good,' 'bad,' 'right,' 'wrong,' 'should,' 'ought,' 'reasonable,' 'virtuous,' etc. Notoriously hard to define, and hard to fill out that "etc." But most philosophers think they know it when they see it.

"Now what" problem: The problem for error theorists of giving a consistent, compelling account of how they should live their lives after accepting error theory.

One-term naturalism: The view that moral properties are natural properties but only one term (a moral term) refers to those properties.

Open-question argument: G. E. Moore's argument against analytic naturalism, which he believed, wrongly in the eyes of most contemporaries, generalized to all forms of moral naturalism. The idea is that because all questions of the form "X is N, but is X M?" (where N is a natural term and M a moral term) are "open," there is no analytic relation between the natural and the moral.

Overridingness, moral: The idea that if an action is morally wrong—in other words, if there's a moral duty not to do it—then that trumps all competing considerations in favor of the action: if it's wrong, then you shouldn't do it, no matter what.

Proportionalism: A widely accepted view according to which the normative weights of our hypothetical reasons are determined by the strengths of the desire we have to realize our various ends and the degree to which the action in question will promote that end.

Quasi-realism: A research program where moral anti-realists "earn the right" to say everything that realists say by various maneuvers in the philosophy of language.

Queerness argument: A family of arguments against moral realism which maintain that moral facts or properties, or the mental faculties by which we know them, would be unacceptably weird, and metaphysically unlike anything else we know about.

Rationalism: The view that we have some substantive knowledge that goes beyond what we learn by our senses.

Realism, moral: The view that (1) moral judgments represent the world as containing moral facts or properties, (2) there are moral facts, and (3) those moral facts are stance-independent. Some philosophers add that some of these moral facts are knowable.

Realism, robust: An ambitious form of non-naturalist moral realism that avoids quietism. Robust realists seek an account of the nature of moral facts that can productively answer the various metaphysical and epistemological objections to non-naturalism. (See *non-naturalist moral realism*).

Relativism, moral: The version of constructivism that says that the truth of moral claims is "relative" to the moral attitudes of some salient group or individual.

Relativity argument: The argument against moral realism that proceeds from the observation that moral practices differ between cultures and epochs. Those pressing the argument claim that the absence of stance-independent moral facts best explains this variation.

Skepticism, moral: The epistemological thesis that moral knowledge is impossible.

Stance-independence: Independence of the beliefs or attitudes of any agent or group of agents.

Supervenience challenge: Another variation of the queerness objection to realism (see above). In brief, the realist is challenged to explain why it seems impossible to have two things whose moral properties are different but which are otherwise identical.

Synthetic naturalism: The view that moral naturalism is true and at least some moral terms are fundamental and unanalyzable in descriptive terms. So a synthetic naturalist might agree that pleasure is good, but he would deny that pleasure is what the word 'good' *means*.

Tiefensee's objection: Sometimes known as the formal objection to the error theory, this is the view that there is no coherent formulation of error theory. Has both a simple form (which targets the claim that all moral judgments are false) and a sophisticated form (which relies on the theorem of deontic logic that everything is either forbidden or permissible).

Undermining defeaters (or undercutting defeaters): In epistemology, these are considerations which reduce the extent to which beliefs are justified, or prevent them from counting as knowledge, by casting doubt upon the evidence that supports them, or the reliability of how they were formed. For example, if a defense attorney exposes his client's accuser as an unreliable witness, that's an undermining defeater with respect to the evidence of his testimony.

Bibliography

Adams, Robert Merrihew. 1999. *Finite and Infinite Goods: A Framework for Ethics*. New York: Oxford University Press.

Al-Attar, Miriam. 2010. *Islamic Ethics: Divine Command Theory in Arabo-Islamic Thought*. New York: Routledge.

Alston, William. 1990. "Some Suggestions for Divine Command Theorists" in Michael D. Beaty (ed.), *Christian Theism and the Problems of Philosophy*. Notre Dame, IN: Notre Dame University Press.

Aristotle. 1984. *Metaphysics*. Trans. by W. D. Ross, in *The Complete Works of Aristotle: The Revised Oxford Translation*, Volume 2. Jonathan Barnes (ed.). Princeton, NJ: Princeton University Press.

Arvan, Marcus. 2019. "The Dark Side of Morality: Group Polarization and Moral Epistemology," *Philosophical Forum* 50(1): 87–115.

Associated Press. 2008. "Handicapped Bombers Kill Dozens in Iraq," retrieved from www.nbcnews.com/id/wbna22945797.

Ayer, A. J. 1936. *Language Truth and Logic*. London: Victor Gollancz, Ltd.

Baker, Alan. 2005. "Are There Genuine Mathematical Explanations of Physical Phenomena?" *Mind* 144(454): 223–238.

Baker, Derek Clayton. 2018. "Skepticism about Ought Simpliciter" in Russ Shafer-Landau (ed.), *Oxford Studies in Metaethics*. Volume 13. Oxford: Oxford University Press: 230–252.

Ballantyne, Nathan. 2019. *Knowing Our Limits*. Oxford: Oxford University Press.

Beardsley, Tobias. 2022. "Can Pascal's Wager Save Morality from Occam's Razor?" *Philosophia*, 50: 405–424.

Bedke, Matt. 2010. "Might All Normativity Be Queer?" *Australasian Journal of Philosophy* 88(1): 41–58.

Benatar, David. 2008. *Better Never to Have Been: The Harm of Coming Into Existence*. Oxford: Oxford University Press.

Benedict, Ruth. 2001. "Anthropology and Abnormality," in Paul K. Moser and Thomas L. Carson (eds.), *Moral Relativism*. Oxford: Oxford University Press: 90–89.

Bengson, John. 2015a. "Grasping the Third Realm," in Tamar Szabó Gendler and John Hawthorne (eds.), *Oxford Studies In Epistemology* Volume 5: 1–38.

———. 2015b. "The Intellectual Given," *Mind* 124(495): 707–760.

Blackburn, Simon. 1993. *Essays in Quasi-Realism*. Oxford: Oxford University Press.

———. 1988. "How to Be an Ethical Anti-Realist," *Midwest Studies in Philosophy* 12(1): 361–375.

———. 1984. *Spreading the Word*. Oxford: Oxford University Press.

Blanchard, Joshua. 2020. "Moral Realism and Philosophical Angst," in Russ Shafer-Landau (ed.), *Oxford Studies in Metaethics*, Volume 15: 118–139.

Björnsson, Gunnar, Caj Strandberg, Ragnar Francén Olinder, John Eriksson, and Fredrik Björklund (eds.). 2015. *Motivational Internalism*. Oxford: Oxford University Press.

Boghossian, Paul and Williamson, Timothy. 2020. *Debating the A Priori*. Oxford: Oxford University Press.

Boyd, Richard. 1988. "How to be a Moral Realist," in Geoffrey Sayre-McCord (ed.), *Essays on Moral Realism*. Ithaca, NY: Cornell University Press: Chapter 10.

Brambraugh, Renford. 1969. "A Proof of the Objectivity of Morals," *The American Journal of Jurisprudence* 14(1): 37–53.

Brandt, Richard B. 1954. *Hopi Ethics: A Theoretical Analysis*. Chicago, IL: University of Chicago Press.

Brink, David. 1989. *Moral Realism and the Foundations of Ethics*. Cambridge: Cambridge University Press.

Brown, Donald E. 1991. *Human Universals*. Philadelphia: Temple University Press.

Capra, Frank (director). 1946. *It's A Wonderful Life*. Liberty Films.

Card, Orson Scott. 1991. *Ender's Game*. New York: Tor.

Case, Spencer. 2020. "The Normative Error Theorist Cannot Avoid Self-Defeat," *Australasian Journal of Philosophy*, 98(1): 92–104.

———. 2019. "From Epistemic to Moral Realism," *Journal of Moral Philosophy*, 16(5): 541–562.

———. 2016. "Normative Pluralism Worthy of the Name is False," *Journal of Ethics and Social Philosophy*, 11(1): 1–19.

Chisholm, Roderick. 1973. *The Problem of the Criterion*, Milwaukee, WI: Marquette University Press.

Chomsky, Noam. 1988. *Language and the Problems of Knowledge: The Managua Lectures*. Cambridge, MA: MIT Press.

Christakis, Nicholas A. 2019. *Blueprint: The Evolutionary Origins of a Good Society*. London: Hachette.

Churchland, Paul S. and Patricia M. 1998. *On The Contrary: Critical Essays 1987–1997*. Cambridge, MA: MIT Press.

Cicero, Marcus Tullius. 2014. *De Officiis.* Trans. by Walter Miller. New York: The MacMillan Co.

Clarke-Doane, Justin. 2020. "The Ethics-Mathematics Analogy," *Philosophy Compass* 15(1): online.

———. 2012. "Morality and Mathematics: The Evolutionary Challenge," *Ethics* 122(2): 313–340.

Clifford, W. K. 1878/1999. "The Ethics of Belief," in Timothy J. Madigan (ed.), *The Ethics of Belief and Other Essays.* Amherst, Mass.: Prometheus: 70–96.

Cline, Brendan. 2018. "The Tale of a Moderate Normative Skeptic," *Philosophical Studies* 175(1): 141–161.

———. 2016. "Against Indispensability as a Guide to What There Is," *Philosophical Studies* 173(12): 3235–3254.

Clipsham, Patrick. 2019. "What's Left for the Companions in Guilt Argument?" *Ethical Theory and Moral Practice* 22(1): 137–151.

Copp, David. 2017. "Are There Substantive Moral Conceptual Truths?" in Diego E. Machuca (ed.), *Moral Skepticism: New Essays.* New York: Routledge: 91–114.

———. 2009. "Toward a Pluralist and Teleological Theory of Normativity," *Philosophical Issues* 19(1): 21–37.

———. 1995. *Morality, Normativity, and Society.* Oxford: Oxford University Press.

Cowie, Christopher. 2019. *Morality and Epistemic Judgement: The Argument From Analogy,* Oxford: Oxford University Press.

———. 2014. "In Defence of Instrumentalism About Epistemic Normativity," *Synthese* 191: 4003–4017.

Craig, William Lane. 2011. "Can We Be Good Without God?" retrieved from www.reasonablefaith.org/videos/lectures/can-we-be-good-without-god-london/.

Cuneo, Terence. 2014. *Speech and Morality: On the Metaethical Implications of Speaking.* Oxford: Oxford University Press.

———. 2007. *The Normative Web: An Argument for Moral Realism.* Oxford: Oxford University Press.

Cuneo, Terence, and Spencer Case. 2020. Review of *Morality and Epistemic Judgement: The Argument From Analogy* by Christopher Cowie, *Notre Dame Philosophical Reviews,* retrieved from https://ndpr.nd.edu/reviews/morality-and-epistemic-judgement-the-argument-from-analogy/.

Cuneo, Terence, and Russ Shafer-Landau. 2014. "The Moral Fixed Points: New Directions for Moral Nonnaturalism," *Philosophical Studies* 171(3): 399–443.

Davis, Gordon F. 2013. "Moral Realism and Anti-Realism Outside the West: A Metaethical Turn in Buddhist Ethics," *Comparative Philosophy* 4(2): 24–53.

DeLapp, Kevin. 2020. "The Metaethics of Maat," in Colin Marshall (ed.), *Comparative Metaethics: Neglected Perspectives on the Foundations of Morality*. New York: Routledge: 19–39.

Descartes, René. 1641/2017. *Meditations on First Philosophy*. Jonathan Bennett (trans.). Retrieved from www.earlymoderntexts.com/assets/pdfs/descartes1641.pdf.

Dockstader, Jason. 2022. "Tiantai Metaethics," *Australasian Journal of Philosophy*, 100(2): 215–229.

——. 2018. "Daoist Metaethics," *Journal of Value Enquiry*, 53(2): 309–324.

Dreier, James. 2004. "Meta-ethics and the Problem of Creeping Minimalism," *Philosophical Perspectives* 18(1): 23–44.

Edgerton, Robert. 1992. *Sick Societies: Challenging the Myth of Primitive Harmony*. New York: The Free Press.

Enoch, David. 2017. "Moral non-Naturalism," in Tristram McPherson and David Plunkett (eds.), *The Routledge Handbook of Metaethics*. New York: Routledge.

——. 2011. *Taking Morality Seriously: A Defense of Robust Realism*. Oxford: Oxford University Press.

——. 2006. "Agency, Shmagency: Why Normativity Won't Come from What Is Constitutive of Action" *Philosophical Review* 115 (2): 169–198.

Enoch, David and Tristram McPherson. 2017. "What Do You Mean 'This Isn't the Question?'" *Canadian Journal of Philosophy* 47(6): 820–840.

Faraci, David. 2019. *Groundwork for an Explanationist Account of Epistemic Coincidence*. Ann Arbor, MI: Michigan Publishing, University of Michigan Library.

Feldman, Richard. 2004. "Having Evidence," in Earl Conee and Richard Feldman (eds.), *Evidentialism: Essays in Epistemology*. Oxford: Oxford University Press: 83–108.

Finlay, Stephen. (2008). The error in the error theory. *Australasian Journal of Philosophy*, 86(3), 347–369.

——. 2009. "Against All Reason? Scepticism About the Instrumental Norm" in Charles R. Pigden (ed.), *Hume on Motivation and Virtue*. Basingstoke: Palgrave-Macmillan: Chapter 7.

——. 2014. *A Confusion of Tongues: A Theory of Normative Language*. Oxford: Oxford University Press.

Fletcher, Guy. 2018. "Pain for the Error Theory? A New Companions in Guilt Argument," Australasian Journal of Philosophy 96(3): 474–482.

Foot, Philippa. 2001. *Natural Goodness*. Oxford: Oxford University Press.

——. 1972. "Morality as a System of Hypothetical Imperatives," *The Philosophical Review* 81(3): 305–316.

Frankfurt, Harry G. 1988. "Freedom of the Will and the Concept of a Person," in Michael F. Goodman (ed.), *What is a Person?* Clifton, NJ: Humana Press: 127–144.

Frederick, Jim. 2010. *Black Hearts: One Platoon's Descent into Madness in Iraq's Triangle of Death*. New York: Random House.

Fuqua, Jonathan. 2021. "Metaethical Mooreanism," *Synthese* 199(3–4): 6943–6965.

Geach, Peter. 1956. "Good and Evil," *Analysis* 17(2): 33–42.

Gensler, Harry. 2013. *Ethics and the Golden Rule*. Hoboken: Taylor and Francis.

Gibbard, Allan. 2017. "Ethics and Science: Is Plausibility in the Eye of the Beholder?" *Ethical Theory and Moral Practice* 20(4): 737–749.

———. 2003. *Thinking How to Live*. Cambridge, MA: Harvard University Press.

———. 1990. *Wise Choices, Apt Feelings: A Theory of Normative Judgment*. Cambridge, MA: Harvard University Press.

Gilligan, Vince (writer) and Bernstein, Adam (director). 2008, February 10. "… And the Bag's in the River" (Season 1, Episode 3) [TV Series Episode]. Vince Gilligan, Mark Johnson, Michelle Maclaren (executive producers). *Breaking Bad*. High Bridge Entertainment; Gran Via Productions; Sony Pictures Television.

Goldman, Alvin. 1979. "What Is Justified Belief?" in G. Pappas (ed.) *Justification and Knowledge*. Dordrecht: D. Reidel: 1–23.

Greco, John. 2007. *Putting Skeptics in Their Place: The Nature of Skeptical Arguments and their Role in Philosophical Inquiry*. Digital edition. New York: Cambridge University Press.

Haidt, Jonathan. 2001. "The Emotional Dog and Its Rational Tail: A Social Intuitionist Approach to Moral Judgment," *Psychological Review*, 108(4): 814.

Hampton, Jean. 1998. *The Authority of Reason*. Cambridge: Cambridge University Press.

Hare, R.M. 1952. *The Language of Morals*. Oxford: Oxford University Press.

Harman, Gilbert. 1977. *The Nature of Morality: An Introduction to Ethics*. Oxford: Oxford University Press.

———. 1975. "Moral Relativism Defended," *Philosophical Review*, 84(1): 3–22.

———. 1965. "The Inference to the Best Explanation," *The Philosophical Review*, 74(1): 88–95.

1988. "Ethics and Observation," in Geoffrey Sayre-McCord (ed.), Essays on Moral Realism. Ithaca, NY: Cornell University Press: Chapter 6.

Herodotus. 1998. *The Histories*. Trans. Robin Waterfield. Oxford: Oxford University Press.

Hobbes, Thomas. 2017/1651. *Leviathan*. Jonathan Bennett (trans.). Retrieved from www.earlymoderntexts.com/authors/hobbes

Horgan, Terence, and Timmons, Mark. 2017. "The Phenomenology of Moral Authority" in *Moral Skepticism*. New York: Routledge: 115–140.

——. 1992. "Troubles on Moral Twin Earth: Moral Queerness Revived," *Synthese* 92(2): 221–260.

Huemer, Michael. 2000. "Naturalism and the Problem of Moral Knowledge," *Southern Journal of Philosophy* 38(4): 575–597.

——. 2001. *Skepticism and the Veil of Perception*. Lanham, MD: Rowman and Littlefield.

——. 2005. *Ethical Intuitionism*. New York: Palgrave Macmillan.

Hume, David. 1751/1998. *An Enquiry Concerning the Principles of Morals*. Tom L. Beauchamp (ed.), Oxford: Oxford University Press.

——. 1748/1999. *An Enquiry Concerning Human Understanding*. Tom L. Beauchamp (ed.). Oxford: Oxford University Press.

——. 1739–40/2000. *Treatise of Human Nature*. David Fate Norton and Mary J. Norton (eds.), Oxford: Oxford University Press.

Husi, Stan. 2011. "Why Reasons Skepticism is Not Self-Defeating," *European Journal of Philosophy* 21(3): 424–449.

Jackson, Frank. 1998. *From Metaphysics to Ethics: A Defense of Conceptual Analysis*. Oxford: Oxford University Press.

Joyce, Richard. 2019. "Moral and Epistemic Normativity: The Guilty and the Innocent," in Christopher Cowie and Richard Rowland (eds.), *Companions in Guilt Arguments in Metaethics*. New York: Routledge: 53–72.

——. 2006. *The Evolution of Morality*. Cambridge, MA: MIT Press.

——. 2001. *The Myth of Morality*. Cambridge: Cambridge University Press.

Kalf, Wouter Floris. 2018. *Moral Error Theory*. Cham: Palgrave Macmillan.

Kant, Immanuel. 1785/2018. "Groundwork for the Metaphysics of Morals" edited and translated by Allen W. Wood. New Haven; London: Yale University Press.

——. 1783/2004. *Prolegomena to Any Future Metaphysics*. Trans. and ed. by Gary Hatfield. New York: Cambridge University Press.

Kelly, Thomas. 2011. "Following the Argument Where It Leads," *Philosophical Studies* 154(1): 105–124.

——. 2008. "Common Sense as Evidence: Against revisionary Ontology and Skepticism," *Midwest Studies in Philosophy* 32(1): 53–78.

——. 2005. "Moorean Facts and Belief Revision, or Can the Skeptic Win?" *Philosophical Perspectives* 19(1): 179–209.

——. 2003. "Epistemic Rationality as Instrumental Rationality: A Critique" *Philosophy and Phenomenological Research* 66(3): 612–640.

Kim, Brian. 2017. Pragmatic Encroachment in Epistemology," *Philosophy Compass* 12: 1–14.

King, Peter. 2006. "Ockham's Ethical Theory," in *The Cambridge Companion to Ockham*, Paul Vincent Spade (ed.), Cambridge: Cambridge University Press: Chapter 10.

Kjellberg, Paul and Philip J. Ivanhoe. 1996. *Essays on Skepticism, Relativism, and Ethics in the Zhuangzi*. Albany, NY: State University of New York Press.

Koons, Jeremy Randel. 2000. "Do Normative Facts Need to Explain?" *Pacific Philosophical Quarterly* 81(3): 246–272.

Korman, Daniel Z., and Dustin Locke. 2023. "An Explanationist Account of Genealogical Defeat," *Philosophy and Phenomenological Research* 106(1): 176–195.

Korsgaard, Christine. 2009. *Self-Constitution: Agency, Identity, Integrity.* Oxford: Oxford University Press.

——. 1996. *The Sources of Normativity.* Cambridge: Cambridge University Press.

Kovach, Steve. 2014. "Harrison Ford Explained the Story Behind The Best Scene In 'Indiana Jones'" *Business Insider.* Retrieved from www.businessinsider.com/harrison-ford-reddit-ama-2014-4

Kremm, Douglas and Karl Schafer. 2017. "Metaethical Quietism," (pp. 643–658) in Tristram McPherson and David Plunkett (eds.), *The Routledge Handbook of Metaethics.* New York: Routledge.

Kurtz, Paul and William Lane Craig. 2009. "The Kurtz/Craig Debate: Is Goodness without God Enough?" in Robert K. Garcia and Nathan L. King (eds.), *Is Goodness without God Enough? A Debate On Faith, Secularism, and Ethics.* Lanham, MD: Rowman and Littlefield.

Leary, Stephanie. 2017. "Non-Naturalism and Normative Necessities" (pp. 77–105) in Russ Shafer-Landau (ed.), *Oxford Studies in Metaethics* Volume 12. Oxford: Oxford University Press:

Lewis, David. 1996. "Elusive Knowledge," *Australasian Journal of Philosophy* 74(4): 549–67.

Lewis, Peter J. Undated. "Interpretations of Quantum Mechanics," *Internet Encyclopedia of Philosophy*, retrieved from https://iep.utm.edu/int-qm.

Linnebo, Øystein. 2018. "Platonism in the Philosophy of Mathematics," in Edward N. Zalta (ed.), *The Stanford Encyclopedia of Philosophy*, retrieved from https://plato.stanford.edu/archives/spr2018/entries/platonism-mathematics/.

Lipton, Peter. 2004. *Inference to the Best Explanation*, 2nd ed. New York: Routledge.

Liu, Jeeloo. 2007. "Confucian Moral Realism," *Asian Philosophy*, 17(2): 167–184.

Lutz, Matt. 2021. "The Moral Closure Argument," *Journal of Ethics and Social Philosophy*, 19(1): 80–109.

2020. "The Reliability Challenge in Moral Epistemology," in Russ Shafer-Landau (ed.), *Oxford Studies in Metaethics* Volume 15. Oxford: Oxford University Press: 284–308.

——. 2018. "What Makes Evolution a Defeater?" *Erkenntnis* 83(6): 1105–26.

——. 2014a. "The 'Now What' Problem for Error Theory," *Philosophical Studies* 171(2): 351–371.

———. 2014b. "The Pragmatics of Pragmatic Encroachment," *Synthese* 191(8): 1717–1740.

Lutz, Matt and James Lenman. 2018. "Moral Naturalism," in Edward N. Zalta (ed.), *The Stanford Encyclopedia of Philosophy*, retrieved from https://plato.stanford.edu/archives/spr2021/entries/naturalism-moral/.

Mackie, J. L. 1977. *Ethics: Inventing Right and Wrong*. London: Penguin.

Magnus, P. D. 2008. "Reid's Defense of Common Sense," *Philosophers' Imprint* 8(3): 1–14.

Majors, Brad. 2007. "Moral Explanation," *Philosophy Compass* 2(1): 1–15.

McAllister, Blake. 2016. "Re-evaluating Reid's Response to Skepticism," *Journal of Scottish Philosophy* 14(3): 317–339.

McCain, Kevin. 2014. *Evidentialism and Epistemic Justification*. New York: Routledge.

McHugh, Conor, and Jonathan Way. 2016. "Fittingness first," *Ethics* 126(3): 575–606.

McKhail, John. 2007. "Universal Moral Grammar: Theory, Evidence and the Future," *Trends Cognitive Science* 11(4): 143–152.

Midgely, Mary. 2017. *Why Can't We Make Moral Judgments?* London: Bloomsbury.

———. 2005. "On Trying out One's New Sword on a Chance Wayfarer," in *The Essential Mary Midgely*, New York: Routledge: 218–224.

Miller, Christian. 2018. *The Character Gap: How Good Are We?* New York: Oxford University Press.

Moody-Adams, Michele. 1998. *Fieldwork in Familiar Places: Morality, Culture, and Philosophy*, Cambridge, MA: Harvard University Press.

Moore, G.E. 1903. *Principia Ethica*. Cambridge: Cambridge University Press.

———. 1993. *G. E. Moore: Selected Writings*, edited by Thomas Baldwin. New York: Routledge.

Morriston, Wes. 2012. "God and the Ontological Foundations of Morality," *Religious Studies* 48(4): 15–34.

———. 2009. "What if God Commanded Something Terrible? A Worry for Divine-Command Meta-ethics," *Religious Studies* 45(3): 249–267.

Nozick, Robert. 1981. *Philosophical Explanations*. Cambridge, MA: Harvard University Press.

Oddie, Graham. 2005. *Value, Reality, and Desire*. New York: Oxford University Press.

———. 1982. "Armstrong on the Eleatic Principle and Abstract Entities," *Philosophical Studies* 41(2): 285–295.

Olson, Jonas. 2014. *Moral Error Theory: History, Critique, Defense*. New York: Oxford University Press.

Orwell, George. 1981. "Politics and the English Language" in *A Collection of Essays*. New York: Harvest Books: 156–170.

Papineau, David. 2020. "Naturalism," in Edward N. Zalta (ed.), *The Stanford Encyclopedia of Philosophy*, retrieved from https://plato.stanford.edu/archives/sum2021/entries/naturalism/.

Parfit, Derek. 2011. *On What Matters* Volume 2. Oxford: Oxford University Press.

Pascal, Blaise. 1670/1958. *Pensées*. Introduction by T. S. Eliot. New York: E. P. Dutton & Co.

Pigden, C. R. 2007. "Nihilism, Nietzsche and the Doppelganger Problem," *Ethical Theory and Moral Practice*, 10(5): 441–456.

Pinker, Steven. 2002. *The Blank Slate: The Modern Denial of Human Nature*. New York: Penguin Books.

Plantinga, Alvin. 2000. *Warranted Christian Belief*. Oxford: Oxford University Press.

Plato. 1997. *Euthyphro*, G. M. A. Grube (trans.) in John M. Cooper and D. S. Hutchinson (eds.), *Plato: Complete Works*. Indianapolis, IN: Hackett Publishing.

Polanyi, Michael. 1966. "The Message of the American Revolution," *The American Scholar* 35(4): 661–676.

Priest, Graham, Francesco Berto, and Zach Weber, "Dialetheism," The Stanford Encyclopedia of Philosophy (Summer 2023 Edition), Edward N. Zalta & Uri Nodelman (eds.), forthcoming URL = <https://plato.stanford.edu/archives/sum2023/entries/dialetheism/>.

Prinzing, Michael. 2017. "The Revisionist's Rubric: Conceptual Engineering and the Discontinuity Objection," *Inquiry*, 2017: 1–27.

Pust, Joel. 2001. "Against Explanationist Skepticism Regarding Philosophical Intuitions," *Philosophical Studies* 106(3): 227–258.

Quine, W. V. O. 1981. "On the Nature of Moral Values," in his *Theories and Things*. Cambridge, MA: Belknap Press of Harvard University Press: Chapter 6.

Quine, W.V.O. and Ulian, J.S. 1970. *The Web of Belief*. New York: Random House.

Railton, Peter. 2017. "Moral Naturalism," in Tristram McPherson and David Plunkett (eds.), *The Routledge Handbook of Metaethics*. New York: Routledge.

———. 1986. "Moral Realism," *The Philosophical Review* 95(2): 163–207.

Rawlette, Sharon. 2020. *The Feeling of Value: Moral Realism Grounded in Phenomenal Consciousness*, First Ebook Edition. (self-published).

Rawls, John. 1971. *A Theory of Justice*. Cambridge, MA: Harvard University Press.

Reid, Thomas. 1764/2017. *An Inquiry Into the Human Mind*, translated into modern English by Jonathan Bennett. Retrieved from www.earlymoderntexts.com/assets/pdfs/reid1764.pdf.

Richeson, David S. 2008. *Euler's Gem*. Princeton, NJ: Princeton University Press.

Rieder, Travis N. 2016. "Why I'm Still a Proportionalist," *Philosophical Studies* 173(1): 251–270.

Rinard, Susanna. 2018. "Reasoning One's Way Out of Skepticism" in Kevin McCain and Ted Poston (eds.), *The Mystery of Skepticism: New Explorations*. Boston: Brill 2018: Chapter 14.

———. 2013. "Why Philosophy Can Overturn Common Sense," in Tamar Szabo Gendler & John Hawthorne (eds.), *Oxford Studies in Epistemology*, Volume 4. Oxford: Oxford University Press.

Rosen, Gideon. 2020. "What is Normative Necessity?" in Mircea Dumitru (ed.), *Metaphysics, Meaning, and Modality: Themes from Kit Fine*: 205–233.

———. 2010. "Metaphysical Dependence: Grounding and Reduction," in Bob Hale and Aviv Hoffmann (eds.), *Modality: Metaphysics, Logic, and Epistemology*. Oxford: Oxford University Press: 109–136.

Rosenberg, Alex. 2011. *The Atheist's Guide to Reality: Enjoying Life Without Illusions*, digital edition. New York: W.W. Norton and Company, Inc.

Ross W.D. 1939. *The Foundations of Morality*. Oxford: Oxford University Press.

Rowe, William. 1979. "The Problem of Evil and Some Varieties of Atheism," *American Philosophical Quarterly*, 16(4): 335–341.

Russell, Bertrand. 1944. "Reply to Criticisms," in P. A. Schilpp (ed.), *The Philosophy of Bertrand Russell*. Evanston, IL: Northwestern University.

Sabbir, Mir. 2019. "Nusrat Jahan Rafi: Burned to Death for Reporting Sexual Harassment," retrieved from www.bbc.com/news/world-asia-47947117/.

Sampson, Eric. 2023. "Moorean Arguments Against the Error Theory: A Defense," in Russ Shafer-Landau (ed.), *Oxford Studies in Meta-ethics*, Volume 18. Oxford: Oxford University Press: 191–217.

Scanlon, T. M. 2017. "Normative Realism and Ontology: Reply to Clarke-Doane, Rosen, and Enoch and McPherson," *Canadian Journal of Philosophy* 47(6): 877–97.

———. 2014. *Being Realistic about Reasons*. Oxford: Oxford University Press.

———. 1998. *What We Owe to Each Other*. Cambridge, MA: Belknap Press of Harvard University Press.

Schama, Simon. 2007. *Rough Crossings: The Slaves, The British, and the American Revolution*. New York: HarperCollins.

Schroeder, Mark. 2010. *Non-Cognitivism in Ethics*. New York: Routledge.

———. 2009. "Hybrid Expressivism: Virtues and Vices," *Ethics*, 119(2): 257–309.

———. 2007. *Slaves of the Passions*. Oxford: Oxford University Press.

———. 2008. *Being For: Evaluating the Semantic Program of Expressivism*. Oxford: Oxford University Press.

———. 2005. "Realism and Reduction: The Quest for Robustness," *Philosophers' Imprint* 5: 1–18.

Sepielli, Andrew. 2020. "Quietism and Counter-Normativity," *Ergo.* (doi:10.3998/ergo.1114).

Setiya, Kieran. 2012. *Knowing Right From Wrong.* Oxford: Oxford University Press.

Shafer-Landau, Russ. 2020. *The Fundamentals of Ethics*, 5th edition. Oxford: Oxford University Press.

——. 2007. "Moral and Theological Realism: The Explanatory Argument," *Journal of Moral Philosophy* 4(3): 311–329.

——. 2003. *Moral Realism: A Defense.* Oxford: Oxford University Press.

Sidgwick, Henry. 1981/1907. *The Methods of Ethics*, 7th edition. Indianapolis, IN: Hackett Publishing Company.

Simmons, Scott. 2020. *Nihilism and Argumentation: a Weakly Pragmatic Defense of Authoritatively Normative Reasons.* Bowling Green State University: Dissertation.

Singer, Peter. 1972. "Famine, Affluence, and Morality," *Philosophy and Public Affairs* 1(3): 229–243.

Sinhababu, Neil. 2019. "One-Person Moral Twin Earth Cases," *Thought: A Journal of Philosophy* 8(1): 16–22.

Sinnott-Armstrong, Walter (ed.). 2008a. *Moral Psychology, Volume 1: The Evolution of Morality: Adaptations and Innateness.* Cambridge, MA: MIT Press.

——. 2008b *Moral Psychology, Volume 2: The Cognitive Science of Morality: Intuition and Diversity.* Cambridge, MA: MIT Press.

——. 2008c. *Moral Psychology, Volume 3: The Neuroscience of Morality: Emotion, Brain Disorders, and Development.* Cambridge, MA: MIT Press.

——. 2006. *Moral Skepticisms.* Oxford: Oxford University Press.

Smith, Michael. 1994. *The Moral Problem.* Malden, MA: Blackwell Publishing.

Spielberg, Steven (director). 1981. *Raiders of the Lost Ark.* Lucasfilm.

Stein, Joseph. 1964. *Fiddler on the Roof.* New York: Music Theater International.

Stevenson, C.L. 1944. *Ethics and Language.* New Haven: Yale University Press.

Stojanovic, Isidora. 2017. "Moral Relativism" in Tristram McPherson and David Plunkett (eds.), *The Routledge Handbook of Metaethics.* New York: Routledge.

Street, Sharon. 2017. "Nothing 'Really' Matters, but That's Not What Matters," in Peter Singer (ed.), *Does Anything Really Matter? Essays on Parfit and Objectivity.* Oxford: Oxford University Press. 121–48.

——. 2009. "In Defense of Future Tuesday Indifference: Ideally Coherent Eccentrics and the Contingency of What Matters," *Philosophical Issues* 19: 273–298.

——. 2006. "A Darwinian Dilemma for Realist Theories of Value," *Philosophical Studies*, 127(1): 109–166.

Streumer, Bart. 2017. *Unbelievable Errors: An Error Theory about All Normative Judgements.* Oxford: Oxford University Press.

———. 2013. "Can We Believe the Error Theory?" *Journal of Philosophy* 110(4): 194–212.

Stroud, Sarah. 1998. "Moral Overridingness and Moral Theory," *Pacific Philosophical Quarterly* 79(2): 170–189.

Sturgeon, Nicholas. 2009. "Doubts about the Supervenience of the Evaluative", in Russ Shafer-Landau (ed.), *Oxford Studies in Metaethics*. pp. 53–92.

———. 1988. "Moral Explanations" in Geoffrey Sayre-McCord (ed.), *Essays on Moral Realism*. Ithaca, NY: Cornell University Press.

———. 1986. "What Difference Does It Make Whether Moral Realism is True?" *Southern Journal of Philosophy*, 21(S1) (Special Issue on Moral Realism): 115–141.

Thomson, Judith Jarvis. 2008. *Normativity*. Peru, Illinois: Open Court Publishing Company.

Tiefensee, Christine. 2020. ""Ought" and Error." *Journal of Philosophy*, 117(2): 96–114.

Tiefensee, Christine and Gregory Wheeler. 2022. "Why Formal Objections to the Error Theory are Sound," *Analysis*. Online.

Unwin, Nicholas. 1999. "Quasi-Realism, Negation and the Frege-Geach Problem," *The Philosophical Quarterly* 49(196): 337–352.

Vanrie, Wim. 2021. "What We All Know: Community in Moore's "A Defence of Common Sense" *Journal of the History of Philosophy*, 59(4): 629–651.

Van Roojen, Mark. 1996. "Expressivism and Irrationality," *Philosophical Review* 105(3): 311–335.

Van Norden, Bryan. 2008. *Mengzi: With Selections from Traditional Commentaries*, Indianapolis, IN: Hackett Publishing.

Väyrynen, Pekka 2021a. Normative Naturalism on Its Own Terms. *Organon F*, 28(3): 505–530.

2021b "Thick Ethical Concepts," *The Stanford Encyclopedia of Philosophy* (Spring 2021 Edition), Edward N. Zalta (ed.), URL = <https://plato.stanford.edu/archives/spr2021/entries/thick-ethical-concepts/>.

Veber, Michael. 2021. "The Epistemology of No-Platforming: Defending the Defense of Stupid Ideas on University Campuses," *Journal of Controversial Ideas* 1(1): 1–20.

———. 2019. "Why Not Persuade the Skeptic? A Critique of Unambitious Epistemology," *International Journal for the Study of Skepticism* 9(4): 314–338

Watson, Gary. 1996. "Two Faces of Responsibility," *Philosophical Topics* 24(2): 227–248.

Westermark, Edward. 1932. *Ethical Relativity*. London: Kegan Paul, Trench, Trubner & Co.

Wielenberg, Erik J. 2014. *Robust Ethics: The Metaphysics and Epistemology of Godless Normative Realism*. Oxford: Oxford University Press.

Williams, Bernard. 2008. "Internal and External Reasons," in Jonathan E. Adler and Lance J. Rips (eds.), *Reasoning: Studies of Human Inference and its Foundations*. Cambridge Cambridge University Press: 60–66.

——. 1993. *Ethics and the Limits of Philosophy*. New York: Routledge.

Wittgenstein, Ludwig. 1969. *On Certainty*. Elizabeth Anscombe (ed. and trans). New York: Basil Blackwell.

——. 1965. "I: A Lecture on Ethics," *The Philosophical Review* 74(1): 3–12.

Wodak, Daniel. 2017. "Why Realists Must Reject Normative Quietism," *Philosophical Studies*, 174(11): 2795–2817.

Wolterstorff, Nicholas. 2004. "Reid on Common Sense," in *The Cambridge Companion to Thomas Reid*, Cuneo, Terence and René van Woudenberg (eds.), New York: Cambridge University Press: 77–100.

Wong, David B. 1995. "Pluralistic Relativism," *Midwest Studies in Philosophy*, 20(1): 378–399.

Wright, Crispin. 1992. *Truth and Objectivity*. Cambridge, MA: Harvard University Press.

Yablo, Stephen. 1992. "Mental Causation," *The Philosophical Review* 101(2): 245–280.

Zagzebski, Linda Trinkaus. 2015. *Epistemic Authority: A Theory of Trust, Authority, and Autonomy in Belief*. Oxford: Oxford University Press.

Zhao, Xinkan 2021. "On the Dialectical Disadvantage of the Error Theorist: A Reply to Clipsham," *Philosophia* 49(2): 861–871.

Zhong, Lei. 2019. "The Hard Problem for Soft Moral Realism," *Journal of Philosophy* 116(10): 555–576.

Zimmerman, Aaron. 2017. "Veneer Theory," in Diego E. Machuca (ed.), *Moral Skepticism: New Essays*. New York: Routledge: 199–243.

Index

240 Index